Theology on the Menu

Food – what we eat, how much we eat, how it is produced and prepared, and its cultural and ecological significance – is an increasingly significant topic not only for scholars but for all of us. *Theology on the Menu* is the first systematic and historical assessment of Christian attitudes to food and its role in shaping Christian identity. David Grumett and Rachel Muers unfold a fascinating history of feasting and fasting, food regulations and resistance to regulation, the symbolism attached to particular foods, the relationship between diet and doctrine, and how food has shaped inter-religious encounters. Everyone interested in Christian approaches to food and diet or seeking to understand how theology can engage fruitfully with everyday life will find this book a stimulus and an inspiration.

David Grumett is a Research Fellow in Theology at the University of Exeter. He is author of *Teilhard de Chardin: Theology, Humanity and Cosmos* (2005), *De Lubac: A Guide for the Perplexed* (2007) and of articles and book chapters on theology and food, modern French Catholic thought, science and religion and biblical interpretation.

Rachel Muers is Lecturer in Christian Studies at the University of Leeds. She is the author of *Keeping God's Silence: Towards a Theological Ethics of Communication* (2004), *Living for the Future: Theological Ethics for Future Generations* (2008) and of articles and book chapters on theological ethics and feminist theology.

Rachel Muers and David Grumett are joint editors of *Eating and Believing: Interdisciplinary Perspectives on Vegetarianism and Theology* (2008).

A new generation of British theologians is taking the debate over diet to the highest levels of scholarly and moral reflection, and Grumett and Muers are leading the way. Rather than trying to score points or pick fights, they demonstrate how food lies at the intersection of the spiritual and the material, and they offer their readers the tools, including the historical context, to make eating one of the primary tasks of thinking. This is now the book to read in seminary and college courses in moral theology, or simply to deepen your own practice of thoughtful eating.

Stephen Webb, Wabash College, USA

In this outstanding book David Grumett and Rachel Muers offer us something quite original. Despite their own different moral positions on relevant issues, the authors have produced a seamless common text that is invariably informative about the complexities of Christian attitudes over the centuries, sometimes amusing but always challenging. Without doubt they have succeeded in putting food on the menu of important unresolved theological issues that merit further consideration.

David Brown, University of St Andrews, UK

In this sweeping study of the practice and interpretation of Christian dietary choice from antiquity to the contemporary period, Grumett and Muers illuminate the web of common impulses and deep ambiguities surrounding food abstinence, especially vegetarianism. The choice not to eat animal flesh, while associated in Christain tradition with snctuty, discipline, spiritual purity, and liturgical rhythms, also incites suspicion of heresy, pagan and Jewish sympathies, and non-communal elitism. The authors demonstrate through analysis of scripture, ritual, historical food practices and controversies, that the Christian menu signifies understandings of creation, animals and humans as created beings, sacrifice, and the place of the body in religious identity.

Teresa Shaw, author of *The Burden of the Flesh: Fasting and Sexuality in Early Christianity*

Theology on the Menu is a rich exploration of the diversity and complexity of Christian attitudes toward meat, fasting, and broader dietary issues. Drawing on an eclectic range of historical and scriptural sources, Grumett and Muers have used food as a fruitful entry point for the study of lived religion. Theologians, historians, and anyone interested in religious foodways will find their work valuable and thought-provoking.

Peter Harle, University of Minnesota, USA

Theology on the Menu

Asceticism, meat and Christian diet

David Grumett and Rachel Muers

Routledge
Taylor & Francis Group

LONDON AND NEW YORK

First edition published 2010
by Routledge
2 Park Square, Milton Park, Abingdon, Oxon OX14 4RN

Simultaneously published in the USA and Canada by Routledge
270 Madison Ave, New York, NY 10016

Routledge is an imprint of the Taylor & Francis Group, an informa business

Typeset in Sabon by
Taylor and Francis Books
Printed and bound in Great Britain by
CPI Antony Rowe, Chippenham, Wiltshire

British Library Cataloguing in Publication Data
A catalogue record for this book is available from the British Library

Library of Congress Cataloging in Publication Data
Grumett, David.
    Theology on the menu : asceticism, meat, and Christian diet / David
Grumett and Rachel Muers.
        p. cm.
    Includes bibliographical references and index.
    1. Food–Religious aspects–Christianity. 2. Nutrition–Religious aspects–
Christianity. I. Muers, Rachel. II. Title.
    BR115.N87G78 2010
    220.8'6132–dc22
                        2009032028

ISBN10: 0-415-49682-9 (hbk)
ISBN10: 0-415-49683-7 (pbk)
ISBN10: 0-203-86349-6 (ebk)

ISBN13: 978-0-415-49682-7 (hbk)
ISBN13: 978-0-415-49683-4 (pbk)
ISBN13: 978-0-203-86349-7 (ebk)

Contents

Acknowledgments

This book was made possible by a grant from the Arts and Humanities Research Council. Our research project, titled 'Vegetarianism as Spiritual Choice in Historical and Contemporary Theology', ran from 2006 to 2009 and was based at the Universities of Exeter and Leeds. We acknowledge with gratitude the AHRC's support, including practical advice offered by staff members during the grant period. Christopher Southgate was a research associate on the project during its first year, and his intellectual contribution and companionship have been invaluable throughout. Mark Wynn, as co-investigator in the project's final year, has been a much valued conversation partner. The Department of Theology at the University of Exeter and the Department of Theology and Religious Studies at the University of Leeds have provided stimulating intellectual environments for our research, and we are grateful to colleagues for this.

As part of the project, we convened an interdisciplinary colloquium and a seminar series at the University of Exeter. The papers from these events have already appeared in *Eating and Believing: Interdisciplinary Perspectives on Vegetarianism and Theology*, eds Rachel Muers and David Grumett (New York and London: T&T Clark, 2008). We are most grateful to all participants, both those who presented papers and those who contributed to the discussions, who have helped to advance our thinking in ways too numerous to list. We especially thank David Clough for sustained interest and support, and John Wilkins for helping us to forge interdisciplinary connections. David Brown offered extensive, careful and insightful comments on a draft manuscript, and it has been a pleasure to work with Amy Grant and Lesley Riddle at Routledge.

Preface

At the opening of the second book in his classic course in Christian ethics, *The Instructor*, Clement of Alexandria stridently condemns the consumer society of late antiquity. Denouncing elaborate menus, he protests that some people 'dare to call by the name of food their dabbling in luxuries, which glides into mischievous pleasures'. Such persons, 'surrounded with the sound of hissing frying-pans, and wearing their whole life away at the pestle and mortar', are 'all jaw, and nothing else', partaking of 'luxurious dishes, which a little after go to the dunghill'.[1] Among the skills of cookery, Clement singles out for special criticism the 'useless art of making pastry' which, he contends, vitiates the tastebuds and imperils moral discretion. To justify his protestations, Clement offers many examples of foodstuffs responsible for luxurious immorality: lampreys from the Sicilian Straits, eels of the Maeander and kids found in Melos; mullet from Sciathus, mussels of Pelorus and oysters of Abydos; sprats of Lipara and the Mantinican turnip; the beetroot of the Ascraeans, cockles of Methymna, turbot from Attica and thrushes of Daphnis; dried figs of Greece, Egyptian snipes and Median peafowl. Worse still is that gluttons, not content with such exotic fare, 'alter these by means of condiments' and 'gape for sauces'.

That such an eminent theologian, known better for his Christian Platonist apologetics, should spend time and energy targeting practical matters of diet might seem strange. Why does he do so? Partly due to pastoral concern for the moral and physical health of his Christian flock. Clement states firmly that Christians must, when choosing food, eschew all culinary temptations. They should 'reject different varieties, which engender various mischiefs, such as a depraved habit of body and disorders of the stomach'. His attack also seems to be motivated by other concerns, such as the construction of a distinctive Christian identity, and a belief in moderation shared with classical ethicists. Furthermore, he objects to the time, energy and travel required by quests to extend menus and recipe books.

From the perspective of everyday material life, Clement's concern with the foods people eat is reasonable and even commendable. They contribute much to human pleasure, memory, labour and sociability. With this in mind, it is perhaps modern theologians and Christian ethicists who need to justify their failure to take proper account of the theological importance of everyday eating. More attention is given to issues that few Christians have to address regularly, such as abortion, war, nuclear weaponry and euthanasia, than to a topic which might help them live more faithful daily lives and witness such lives to others.[2]

The importance of food to human beings is memorably encapsulated in Ludwig Feuerbach's aphorism that people are what they eat. But its attribution serves to expose some of the potential pitfalls it presents for Christians. The idea could be accepted as part of a speculative immanentism according to which humankind's conception of God is also no more than a projection of needs and desires, whether material or spiritual. But when first presenting his thesis in the course of reviewing a book on nutrition by the physiologist Jacob Moleschott, Feuerbach appears to have been motivated by a desire for rational social and political reform, showing the absurdity of organizing society according to abstract principles that ignore the basic fact that humans need food to live. As a result of this oversight, a high proportion of the population had been consigned to poverty.[3] The idea also features in a later essay on sacrifice. In this discussion, Feuerbach presents sacrifice as human feeding of the gods with human food, thus helping to establish the reciprocity of the relationship between representations of humanity and divinity, in which humans, by selecting foods to sacrifice, offer up their own self-image to God, who is therefore a reified image of humanity composed of the foods that humans eat.[4] For Feuerbach, human life is characterized by the unending appropriation of objective reality into the subjective body, which suggests that humanity, while always dependent on matter, can never fully assimilate that matter nor be reduced to it.[5]

As we complete this project, we are also aware that food, although gaining its importance from its status as a basic ongoing material human need, is implicated in a range of social and political issues. We hear frequently about the harmful effects of intensive farming and global trade injustice, and in the West about rising levels of obesity, cancer, heart disease and anorexia. Discussion of these is punctuated by news of another health scare resulting from infected farm animals or contaminated food, and protests about the domination of local farmers, food suppliers and consumers by supermarkets and agribusiness. Furthermore, there is increasing awareness that current global patterns of food production and consumption, especially of meat, are ecologically unsustainable. Livestock farming is responsible for about 9 per cent of total carbon dioxide emissions, but 37 per cent of methane and 65 per cent of nitrous oxide, as well as 68 per cent of all ammonia emissions. Citing these figures, a United Nations report by leading scientists has stated that, worldwide, livestock are a bigger cause of climate change than road transport.[6]

These are all good reasons for theologians to be concerned about food and to consider what distinctive contributions they might offer to debates about food. Because of this wider social and intellectual context, a significant part of our project will be interdisciplinary. But Christian theologians also have much to learn from their own tradition. A common impression is that food practices, abstentions, rules and taboos are features of other religions, but in historical perspective the idea that they are absent from Christianity is completely untrue. A key aim of this study will therefore be to recover and rearticulate distinctively

Christian dietary practices and to consider how these unsettle the current terms of dietary debates. Notwithstanding Clement's accusations, there is much in the history of Christian food practices which affirms the goodness of eating and the activities surrounding it, such as the requirement in the Rule of Benedict that the cellarer look on all the monastery's cooking utensils 'as upon the sacred vessels of the altar'.[7]

But even a fairly straightforward text like Benedict's Rule opens to the attentive reader a strange food world. Its key prohibition of the flesh of quadrupeds does not map conveniently onto classic modern vegetarian categories, and reminds us that there is no Christian tradition of abstention from fish. Yet vegetarianism is now becoming a looser and more diverse commitment with multiple definitions coexisting.[8] In this context, Christians have an opportunity to contribute their own understandings of the concept.

The term 'vegetarianism' is, nevertheless, conspicuously absent from our title. This is partly because it is, for want of a better expression, a bit of a mouthful. But there are more substantive reasons for avoiding the term. It was developed only in the mid nineteenth century and is therefore of limited usefulness for understanding a tradition stretching back at least two millennia and for speaking out of that tradition. Instead, we would identify the key loci continuing through our study as asceticism and meat: the call to dietary moderation set against a background of discomfort with extreme self-denial, and a persistent awareness of the problematic nature of meat.

This study is about practices and reasons for practices. In the course of the research, various little-known facts and histories have been unearthed and analyzed. Moreover, well-known figures and ideas have been viewed from nonstandard perspectives. We began work well aware of the range of explanations advanced by previous scholars for the food rules of the Hebrew Bible and continued concern in the New Testament with issues surrounding food and eating. Assessing the relative importance of these explanations has been part of our work, but we have also seen the continuing impact on dietary practices of discourses about heresy and orthodoxy, both within Christianity and in Christian polemics with Judaism and Islam. Drawing on a wide range of material, we do not seek to present a single normative view of 'Christian diet'. We do, however, unfold a history which we invite Christians and others to inhabit, based on the conviction that food and eating are much neglected topics in Christian theology and cannot remain so.

So this book is not intended to promote any particular set of dietary rules. As it happens, although both its authors generally avoid meat, neither is strictly vegetarian. We do, however, wish to show that when Christians have engaged with food issues, including vegetarianism and its antecedents, they have been concerned with a far wider range of issues than simply animal welfare. We wish to return these issues to the theological agenda as well as to situate meat abstention and meat eating in historical context. Although some past attitudes are now little more than relics, even a practice such as animal sacrifice can offer valuable insights for the present day, because some of its founding assumptions remain relevant. Indeed, for vegetarians it is not necessarily a concession to accept that historic reasons for meat abstention sometimes had little to do with animal welfare. Rather, by acknowledging the variety of motives for meat abstention, present-day vegetarians can find in past practice principles which challenge all modern views of food consumption, and so draw meat eaters into a debate that, even if not leading them immediately to vegetarianism, will engender more reflective food practices. Food issues are not just about healthy eating, but about how humans live under God.

1 Eating in the wilderness

In this opening chapter, we shall situate abstinence from meat within the historic Christian tradition of asceticism. In late ancient society and through much of the medieval era, Christians promoted practices similar to those of modern vegetarians. These practices were by no means universal, and the specific foods permitted and excluded do not correspond conveniently with modern vegetarian categories. A recurring Christian norm of abstention from red meat is nevertheless identifiable, both within religious orders and among lay people. Indeed, meat abstention can be seen, at least historically, as a foundational element of Christian identity and discipline. Our task in this chapter will be to begin to trace the origins and development of practices of meat abstention, and to understand their changing significance within Christianity.

Voices in the wilderness

Our quest for the origins of Christian dietary asceticism begins in the deserts of Egypt, Palestine and Syria. By the third century, large numbers of Christians in these regions were withdrawing from urban society into the desert in search of a simple, solitary existence devoted to prayer and meditation. They became known as anchorites, and their flights were motivated by several different factors. Sporadic imperial persecution, which began with Claudius and Nero not long after the death of Jesus, continued well beyond the conversion of Constantine in 313. In Egypt, Christian hermits followed an already established path of retreat from the city to escape the civil and religious obligations increasingly imposed on citizens by an expansionist state, including compulsory works of public service. Refuge in the desert was also sought by farmers wishing to avoid the burden of taxation, and local officials were paid a reward for each fugitive apprehended and resettled.[1] There existed, finally, the constant threat of military conscription, with attempts made to enlist even some anchorites into the army.[2]

Yet withdrawal into the desert was motivated by more than purely pragmatic concerns. Desert life opened new possibilities for intensified prayer and penitence. The ambitious missions of the apostle Paul and his associates had transposed the message of Jesus the Galilean from its rural lakeside setting into major urban centres like Ephesus, Corinth and Rome. Retreat back to the margins of society enabled religious men, and some women, to continue to lead a strict Christian life away from the distractions, temptations and compromises of urban living, and thus to re-encounter the Gospel message in its full force and seriousness. Desert life became part of a structural development of Christian identity in which the countercultural dimension of Christianity was witnessed anew in a harsh and alien environment that imposed tight natural constraints on diet.

By their flight into the desert, anchorites reaffirmed a long biblical tradition linking retreat, fasting and abstinence. Particularly eloquent genealogies of these disciplines are offered by Tertullian and Jerome, two of their greatest admirers.[3] By abstaining from the fruit of the tree of the knowledge of good and evil, Adam remained in paradise.[4] By preserving unclean animals on board the ark during the flood and then absolutely prohibiting their consumption, God established a dietary ethic of general restraint extending to all foods.[5] The people of Israel fasted on manna in the wilderness while longing for the fleshpots of Egypt.[6] They thirsted at Rephidim before defeating the Amalekites in battle.[7] Moses fasted twice on the mountain where he received the two sets of commandments, each time for forty days.[8] Hannah fasted repeatedly, the Lord opened her womb and she gave birth to Samuel.[9] The people of Israel under Samuel fasted at Mizpah before subduing the Philistines.[10] Israel's army fasted at the command of Saul after routing the Philistines.[11] David hid in the desert when fleeing Saul, with words of Psalm 63 attributed to him there: 'My soul thirsts for you, my body longs for you, in a dry and weary land where there is no water.'[12] Following Ahab's accession to the throne of Israel, Elijah withdrew to a desert ravine where ravens brought him food and he drank water from a brook.[13] Even Ahab fasted, despite his impiety, and thus postponed the Lord's judgement on his house.[14] King Hezekiah vested in sackcloth, a sign of fasting, after which the Lord struck down the enemy army of Assyria.[15] Daniel and his companions subsisted on vegetables and water while residing in the court of King Nebuchadnezzar of Babylon, with the result that they 'looked healthier and better nourished than any of the young men who ate the royal food' and were rewarded with knowledge and prophetic insight.[16]

Jesus himself, according to the gospels of Matthew and Luke, inaugurated his ministry by undergoing forty days of testing by Satan in the desert, then resisted the temptation to turn stones into bread. Had he succumbed to this temptation, he would have demonstrated his divine Sonship as well as assuaged his desperate hunger.[17] Anna fasted in the Temple, where she encountered the child Jesus and prophesied about his role in Jerusalem's redemption.[18] John the Baptist inhabited the wilderness and ate simple foods, usually identified as locusts and wild honey.[19] Paul endured several fasts for the sake of the Gospel.[20]

A similar biblical narrative of dietary indiscipline and its consequences was unfolded by Tertullian and later by Gregory the Great.[21] Adam and Eve were expelled from paradise because they disobeyed God's command not to eat from the tree of the knowledge of good and evil.[22] Esau sold his birthright to Jacob his twin in exchange for red lentil stew and bread after returning from the country famished.[23] The inhabitants of Sodom ate excessively and were later destroyed by God.[24] The sons of Eli were killed and the ark of God captured after they consumed raw fatty meat from the sacrifices without first boiling it.[25] Jonathan feasted on honey after the Israelite army routed the Philistines in battle and thereby broke the fast declared by his father Saul, after which God did not speak to Saul until his son's sin had been publicly identified.[26] The man of God from Judah was killed and eaten by a lion after disobeying God's command not to dine in the house of the prophet from Bethel.[27] John the Baptist was killed during a banquet and his head displayed on a serving dish.[28]

Despite the multiple possible role models just presented, the hero of many desert fathers was John the Baptist. John's identity as a strict ascetic is established clearly in Matthew's gospel, where *akrides* and *meli* are presented as the only foods he ate, rather than as some items among others on his menu.[29] A voice crying in the wilderness announcing the coming of the Messiah, John offered in his ascetic life, dress and diet the most detailed scriptural role model of an anchorite. Understandably, given his central significance in the anchoretic life, the question of precisely what foods John ate was hotly contested. The obscure term *akrides* was often translated as 'locusts', but this rendering appeared to challenge the ascetic ideal of abstinence from the flesh of all living beings. The *akrides* were therefore variously regarded as the inside of a plant, the seeds of the cotton plant, the tips of branches of plants, herbs, or plant roots in the shape of locusts.[30] The *meli* was also problematic. It was most easily interpreted as 'honey', but Epiphanius of Salamis and other commentators were quick to identify the bitterness of this particular honey, again out of fear that John's ascetic credentials be undermined.[31]

By framing their abstinence within biblical narratives, ascetics identified it as Christian rather than pagan.[32] Dietary abstinence was thus promoted by appeals to a scriptural tradition as well as being a response to the changing social context of Christian discipleship. There has been a tendency to understate the likely influence of scripture on this developing ascetic identity, due in part to a failure to recognize the importance of fasting and asceticism generally in scripture. It has also been assumed that anchorites lacked education, based on the supposition that no educated person would embrace such a lifestyle. In fact, many were by no means unlettered. Anchorites were familiar with scriptural texts through both their own reading and oral tradition, and consciously formed their identity around them. Samuel Rubenson defends the general levels of education and literacy in the Egyptian countryside during this period, and argues that Greek philosophy and Origenist theology were disseminated fairly widely among the Christian desert dwellers including Anthony of Egypt.[33] Their relative invisibility in retrospective accounts is a result, he argues, of the 399 and 400 condemnations by Theophilus of Alexandria and Pope Anastasius of teachings attributed to Origen.[34] The accounts of the anchorites' lives reflect the issues that the chattering classes of Constantinople and elsewhere would have been interested in: food and sex, not abstract doctrine.

It cannot be assumed, moreover, that anchorites were typically ignorant of Christian theology. In several accounts of their lives, the acquisition, copying or memorization of scripture and other texts feature.[35] Furthermore, recent revisionist studies of Gnosticism in Egypt have questioned the view that its intense spiritual intellectualism was restricted to discrete communities that were defined by clear boundaries separating them from a supposed Christian orthodoxy.[36] This is evidenced most obviously by the case of Evagrius of Pontus, compiler of the abstruse *Kephalaia Gnostika* but who also features in the *Sayings* and the *Lausiac History* as a frugal eater who for sixteen years restricted himself to bread and a little oil, completely avoiding fruit and grapes as well as meat and other cooked food.[37] The general picture is one of a confluence of dietary discipline and the intellectual apperception of faith.

It is also important to understand Christian fasting as a gradual transformation of Jewish fasting. The narratives of faithful and unfaithful eating already presented suggest that the Hebrew Bible was at least as important a source of inspiration for Christian fasting practices as New Testament texts. Four annual fasts, observed during the fourth, fifth, seventh and tenth months, were instituted following the destruction of the first Temple to mark respectively the breaching of the walls of Jerusalem by the Babylonians, the city's fall, the death of Gedaliah (governor of Judah) after the fall, and the beginning of the siege.[38] But especially pertinent is the increased practice of fasting by Jews following the destruction of the second Temple, which coincided with the time when Christian identity was being forged.[39] In Rabbinic discourse from this era, meat eating was debated in response questions about whether flesh could be eaten now that the altar to which it was brought was in abeyance.[40] One objection raised to this line of argument, somewhat mischievously, was that if meat were excluded from the diet on these grounds, all foods should be avoided because they too would on occasions have been offered at the Temple. What goes unchallenged, however, is the suggestion that some small part of a meal should be omitted in memory of Jerusalem.

One Jewish group noted for their asceticism were the Therapeutae, whom Samuel Rubenson describes as the 'first Christian monks'.[41] Their dining is described by Philo: 'The table … is kept clear of animal flesh, but on it are loaves of bread for nourishment, with salt as a seasoning, to which hyssop is sometimes added as a relish to satisfy the fastidious.'[42] Sumptuous cuisine, by which Philo primarily means meat, is avoided because it 'arouses that most insatiable of animals, desire'. He defends abstention from meat by likening consumption of animal flesh to the savagery of wild beasts.[43] This insight is more likely to have been drawn from classical or even Buddhist traditions than from Jewish ascetic theology, showing the range of religious influences on diet in this period.[44]

The anchorite's diet and the anchorite's body

Christian anchorites thus adopted their ascetic lifestyle for a range of political, social, spiritual and biblical reasons. But what form did this lifestyle take?

Which specific foods and types of food did they eat, and from which did they abstain? A selection of dietary practices is portrayed in the *Lives of the Desert Fathers*, including extreme austerities. Some anchorites avoided cooked foods. Macarius of Alexandria, for instance, ate for seven years nothing but raw vegetables and rehydrated pulses. During the following three years, he confined himself to a small bread loaf each day with just enough water to allow digestion, adding one flask of oil per year and milk suckled from the teat of an antelope calf while on a journey. On another occasion, he endured a Lenten fast moderated solely by a weekly Sunday helping of cabbage.[45] Dorotheos of Thebes survived on dry bread accompanied by a small bundle of green herbs and a little water.[46] Abba Hellarios ate just bread and salt.[47] In old age, Abba Elias consumed a small morsel of bread and three olives every evening, although when younger took food only once a week.[48] Some ascetics, such as John the Hermit, are reported to have subsisted exclusively on the Eucharistic host.[49] One of them, Hero of Diospolis, complemented the host with just one meal every three months as well as any wild herbs he found. Other ascetics confined themselves exclusively to raw vegetables. Abba Or ate only pickled vegetables, typically just once a week.[50] Abba Theon consumed only raw vegetables and shared his meagre water supply with wild animals.[51] Abba Pityrion took a little cornmeal soup twice a week.[52] Amoun of Nitria confined his diet to a small quantity of wheat every two months.[53] In Palestine and Syria, where especially rigorous practices existed, there was a tradition of 'shepherds' or 'grazers' who ate only grass, often alongside wild animals – a practice analogous to that of the *turytta* class of Indian ascetics, who perform *govrata* or 'cow-vow'.[54] Plants collected in Palestine might have included mannouthia (a type of thistle), melagria (a root plant), maloah (also known as salt bush or mallow) and the seeds of capers.[55]

Comparison of the foods mentioned in these *Lives* with the standard fare of the wider populace suggests that anchorites chose from much the same selection of foods as those generally available.[56] The distinctiveness of their diet derived not from the strangeness of the foods eaten but from the small quantities apparently consumed and the reliance of particular hermits on particular foods. In other words, the diet of ascetics was a standard diet reduced by refusals and abstentions, even though the degree of reduction was sometimes overstated by chroniclers keen to present highly rigorous dietary standards to potential followers and a fascinated wider public.

Meat was one of the first and most obvious components of a standard diet to be excluded. From the perspective of modern vegetarianism, it would be easy to associate the anchorites' abstinence from animal flesh with a sense of kinship with animals resulting from a life spent close to nature. Abstinence could alternatively be seen as deriving from a belief that animals and their flesh were in some sense unclean. The first alternative is more plausible: many stories certainly exist of these Christian hermits living in fellowship with animals and, as in the case of the 'grazers' previously described, eating with animals. This contact would not have occurred if animals had been viewed as unclean. Nonetheless, the primary concern shaping ascetic practices was not animal welfare. For instance, various anchorites are reported to have worn furs and other animal skins to guard against the cold. There are even occasional stories of anchorites killing animals, such as the crocodile slaughtered by Abba Helenus as punishment for having eaten many people, after it had ferried him across a river on its back following an expedition to find a priest to say mass.[57] In the desert, meat abstinence needs to be understood as part of a wider discipline of which the central principle was the spiritual government and transformation of the ascetic's body.

Although accounts of anchorites' lives abound with great feats of abstinence, conflicting images emerge of the effects of fasting on the body. In particular, no consensus is identifiable about whether fasting is good for the body or bad for the body. Indeed, a key thematic tension is evident in the presentation of the relationship between dietary discipline and physical health. This might seem surprising, since the extreme seriousness with which abstinence was undertaken cannot be doubted. The hermit Eustathius, for example, is described as being so thin that sunlight was visible between his ribs.[58] Some accounts present the hero or heroine as benefiting from their asceticism. Anthony of Egypt, for instance, is reputed to have lived on bread, salt and water, remaining healthy and dying aged 105.[59] Palladius states of Abba Isidore that, although he had inhabited a mountain cell, 'his slender frame was so well-knit by grace that all who did not know his manner of life expected that he lived in luxury'.[60]

Other *Lives* portray a body brought close to death by infirmity and illness. John of Lycopolis is recorded as being so exhausted by his endeavours that his beard ceased to grow. He ate just fruit, and even this only after sunset.[61] Palladius describes his own illnesses of spleen and stomach following three years in the desert.[62] In other cases, ascetics are presented as enjoying reasonable bodily health until old age, when degeneration occurs rapidly. Blessed Benjamin, for example, developed a 'body so greatly swollen that another man's fingers could not get round one finger of his hand', yet continued to heal visitors from the relative comfort of a specially constructed chair.[63] On his death, the lintels and doorposts of his hut had to be dismantled before his body could be carried out for burial. The cancerous ulcer afflicting Stephen the Libyan had to be 'cut away like hair', yet the hermit is reported as 'behaving just as if another man were being cut', talking with visitors and weaving palm branches while the operation was carried out.[64]

This lack of consistent presentation of the likely effects of fasting on the body seems peculiar from a modern biological perspective. Yet the primary object of the *Lives* is not to give an account of the impact of diet on bodily health. Although fasting would evidently have affected hermits' bodies in different ways, the opposing extreme effects described in the *Lives* point to deeper authorial motivations of a theological kind. Whether the ascetic retains youthful radiance or dies a slow and painful death, he or she is presented as blessed by God for faithful discipline. The effects of this divine blessing are perceived in the body, with the ascetic being blessed either with superior bodily health or with the determination to persevere to the end, despite the debilitating physical consequences of their fasting.

As part of this emphasis on the blessings experienced by the ascetic, the desert was regarded as a place of spiritual provision and sustenance, with the imagery of food and eating gaining symbolic significance in sharp contrast with actual fasting. Such imagery was developed with especial eloquence by the monastic founder Eucherius of Lyons, who in his fifth-century paean 'In Praise of the Desert', echoing Isaiah and the Psalmist, portrays the desert as a place of fertility. He avers of this 'temple of our God without walls' and 'paradise of the spirit':

> I am convinced that God, in foreknowledge of the future, prepared the desert for the saints to come. I believe he wanted some parts of the world to be rich in the fruits of agriculture and other parts, with drier climate, to abound with holy men. In this way the desert would bear fruit. When he 'watered the hills from the heights above', the valleys were filled with plentiful crops. And he planned to endow the sterile deserts with inhabitants, lest any land go to waste.[65]

The desert is thus presented as a space providentially reserved by God for special purposes in which spiritual fruit grows and is harvested. Extending this metaphor, Eucherius proclaims:

> No field however fertile can compare with the desert. Is some country known for its fine grain? In the desert thrives the wheat that satisfies the hungry with its richness. Is some country joyful over its heavy grapevines? The desert yields an abundance of wine that 'rejoices the human heart'. Is some country famous for its lush pastures? The desert is the place where those sheep contentedly graze of whom Scripture says, 'Feed my sheep'.[66]

The desert is thus presented, by means of sensuous food imagery and scriptural allusion, as a paradise in which the human need for physical food is transposed into the spiritual realm and there satisfied by divine providence.

Although the ascetics whom Eucherius so admires withdrew from society and its obligations, they did not cease to exert social influence. This reveals a key difference between Christian anchorites and the pagan Greek ascetics such as the Pythagoreans. The vegetarianism of the Pythagorean elite, who inhabited groves of trees outside the city, had limited consequences for ordinary citizens.[67] Admittedly, the theurgic late Neoplatonist Iamblichus presents them as engaged in mission, conversion and the founding of ascetic communities.[68] But these communities did not seek to transform society: their members withdrew from urban life and did not expect wider society to observe their practices.[69] Christian ascetics, by contrast, participated selectively and to limited degrees in social, economic and publicity networks as best served their own needs. For example, palm mats could be woven in the cell and exchanged for food. Mats would also be exchanged for more palm branches, from which further mats could be made. The celebrity status which the anchorites acquired, and the cult of mystery consequently surrounding them, depended on their inaccessibility being relative but not total. It was *partial* withdrawal from the centres of social space to its liminal regions that made figures like Anthony of Egypt the focus of such intense public interest.[70] Their heroic exploits, including feats of dietary abstinence, were invoked and recreated for the edification and curiosity of admirers unable to visit the desert to seek out these spiritual athletes in person.[71] Pagan ascetics, in comparison, embraced less rigorous dietary regimes than Christian anchorites.[72] The stricter desert discipline of Christians could, therefore, be interpreted in comparative context as demonstrating their spiritual superiority over pagans.[73]

Although the ascetic culture of anchorites was a product of the desert space itself, levels of abstention exceeded those imposed by the physical constraints of even that harsh environment. Voluntary denial of almost all bodily sustenance became the principal characteristic feature of their life. This seems to have been due partly to the increasingly harmonious relations existing between Christians and state authorities in the Constantinian era, with accounts of these food-related feats replacing descriptions of martyrdom as the primary narratives of spiritual endurance.[74] By means of hagiography, the desert also became a virtual place in which religious practices were taught and promoted among people who did not themselves inhabit that place.[75] Accounts of the lives of anchorites founded a new didactic place in which spiritual discipline and practices, especially those centred on dietary abstinence, could be presented and learned. The ultimate hope of hagiographers was that the desert would spread into the city as fascinated readers themselves voluntarily adopted these practices.

From gluttony to lust

Modern accounts of early Christian asceticism frequently fail to acknowledge its origins in political theology and biblical theology, presenting dietary abstinence in particular as part of a systematic and frequently obsessive quest to expunge from the human body every trace of sexual desire. On this basis, interpreters argue that the primary and final purpose of fasting was to regulate lust and ultimately to eliminate it. At the very least, fasting becomes a symptom of a more general denigration of the body that is centred on the denigration of sexual activity. Viewed in this context, dietary abstinence can easily appear as little more than a pathological denial of desires that are fundamental to human flourishing. Sigmund Freud, for instance, saw asceticism as a function of psycho-sexual neurosis based on the repression of lust and aggression.[76] The privileging of a sexual hermeneutic in interpretations of asceticism can be traced back at least to Ernst Troeltsch, who in 1912 quaintly attributed the growth of asceticism in early Catholicism to the 'neuropathic weakening of vitality, due to a certain weariness and slackness of the sex instinct, caused by ignorance of the laws of sex'.[77]

This reduction of questions about food practices to questions about sexuality is problematic, not least because it ignores the wider social and political context of such practices sketched at the beginning of this chapter. Yet in early

Christians' accounts of their food practices, the association of the avoidance of lust with the avoidance of gluttony does feature prominently. Anchorites knew that their food choices affected their sexual desire. More specifically, they believed that reducing their overall food intake and avoiding some foods altogether would reduce this desire. They might well have learnt about the severe adverse effects of extreme fasting on the reproductive system from contemporary famines, seeking to endure them voluntarily for spiritual ends.[78]

The key principle that was presumed to govern this causal relationship between diet and sexuality was that foods and human bodies both exhibited the four properties of heating, cooling, drying and moistening. Anchorites confined themselves to very small quantities of foods classified as 'cold' and 'dry'. 'Hot' and 'moist' foods were excluded from the diet, being considered to fan the flames of sexual passion.[79] Meat was viewed as the paradigmatic 'hot' food, with many puns linking the sexual pleasures of human flesh with the dietary temptations of animal flesh and the carnality of *carne*. Water was often allowed only for the sole purpose of aiding digestion, although even this was sometimes rejected in favour of xerophagy, the restriction of liquid intake.[80] Tertullian, for instance, commended this practice at times of pressure, persecution and other difficulty.[81] In extreme cases, the notion that some foods possessed warming and moistening properties transmuted into the idea that all foods possessed such properties. Anthony of Egypt is reported as describing sexual passion as a movement 'which comes from the nourishment and warming of the body by eating and drinking' which 'causes the heat of the blood to stir up the body to work'.[82]

The existence of a relationship between fasting and a decline in sexual function has been demonstrated empirically.[83] It cannot be assumed, however, that this provided the anchorites' sole or principal motivation for fasting. There was certainly an ongoing preoccupation with eliminating nocturnal seminal emissions, with monastic superiors like Dioscorus voicing a belief, undoubtedly correct, that seminal fluid was depleted by fasting.[84] Yet an exclusive focus on the sexual motives for fasting can be assimilated too easily into a critique of Christianity's alleged denigration of the physical body in general and of sexuality in particular. Even though fasting suppressed lust, escaping the body and sexuality was not its ultimate purpose.

The suppression of lust in order to liberate the person to pursue alternative spiritual ends is better seen in the wider social context of the rise of desert monasticism previously outlined. One reason lust is portrayed as problematic is that it implicates the individual in social networks of consumption that would impede spiritual contemplation. As Peter Brown states, sexual temptation was recognized as a drive 'toward fateful conscription, through marriage, into the structures of the settled land'.[85] In one episode, an unnamed brother tormented by thoughts of fornication leaves the monastery declaring that even ten wives could not satisfy his burning desire. Some time later, Abba Paphnutius, the superior of the monastery, meets the deserter while on a journey in Egypt. The man is carrying baskets of shellfish, which in the ancient world were considered peasant food. Recognising his superior, he introduces himself with shame, explaining that although he has taken only one wife, he has a 'great deal of trouble satisfying her with food'.[86] The lapsed brother then repents and returns to the monastery, becoming a full monk as a result of this chastening experience of the economics of family life. Another account, of Abba Olympios, describes him similarly as being tempted to fornication and marriage. In response, the abba moulds a statue of a woman out of mud and makes himself work in order to feed her. The next day he makes another statue, this time of a girl, and forces himself to labour even harder in order to feed his wife and clothe this imaginary child. He ends up exhausted by these labours, and resolves that he does not, after all, desire a wife, and thus attains a state of inner peace.[87] These stories encourage the male reader to call to mind the work that supporting a wife and family would be likely to require, with immersion in worldly cares heralding the end of contemplative life.

The motif of lust exercised a performative function in narratives such as these in consequence of the social ties it would be likely to bring. The notion that sexual preoccupations provided the central organizing idea for monastic life depends, however, on the imposition of postmodern Western signifiers of self and identity onto a very different context. The prominence and quantity of detail about the paucity of foods eaten suggests, instead, that the bodily temptation uppermost in the minds of many desert fathers was not lust but gluttony. In the words of Peter Brown once again, 'food and the unending battle with the ache of fasting always counted for more than did the sexual drive'.[88]

As medieval theology developed, much discussion of the relative priority of gluttony and lust occurred in order to determine which was the primordial sin from which the six other cardinal sins originated.[89] In this early period of Christian moral theorizing it was frequently argued that gluttony gave birth to lust rather than that lust engendered gluttony. The eating by Adam and Eve of the fruit of the tree of the knowledge of good and evil planted in the middle of the Garden of Eden was itself seen as the origin of humanity's fall.[90] The couple's loss of sexual innocence was regarded as the consequence of this dietary transgression, not its cause. Evagrius of Pontus thus placed gluttony first in his list of vices in his late-fourth-century treatise to Eulogios, followed by fornication, describing gluttony by means of a profusion of stark imagery as

> the mother of fornication, nourishing the thoughts with words, the relaxation of fasting, the muzzling of ascesis, terror over one's moral purpose, imagining of foods, picturer of condiments, a dissolute fawn, unbridled madness, a receptacle of disease, envy of health, an obstruction of the throat, a groaning of the innards, the extremity of insults, a fellow initiate in fornication, pollution of the intellect, weakness of the body, wearisome sleep, gloomy death.[91]

It is important to realise that Evagrius is addressing highly disciplined ascetics who, as Teresa Shaw writes pithily, 'would like a few vegetables with their rock-hard piece of bread'. Why does he attack the natural desire for food so fiercely? Not because of the sinfulness of the act of eating itself, but because of the wider nexus of desires and social commitments which that act signifies: variety, satiety, security, fellowship and health. Gluttony thus 'represents much more than just the desire for food; it is the desire for the former lifestyle and community that have been renounced by those in the desert'.[92]

The priority of gluttony over the other vices was accepted by John Cassian in his *Institutes*, a founding text of monasticism in southern France.[93] Gregory the Great also saw moral purification commencing with the 'fight against gluttony',[94] regarding it as 'plain to all that lust springs from gluttony, when in the very distribution of the members, the genitals appear placed beneath the belly. And hence when the one is inordinately pampered, the other is doubtless excited to wantonness'.[95] The implication of this hierarchy of sins for the spiritual life is well stated by Owen Chadwick: 'Because gluttony acquires its capital place in the list as the root instigator of the corrupting series, fasting and abstinence must become the first and most valuable element in all ascetic practices.'[96]

If gluttony constituted the primary sin and was the reason for Adam and Eve's expulsion from paradise, fasting could be viewed as the means of expiating that sin and regaining paradise, or even attaining an angelic state.[97] Through fasting, humans could become like Adam and Eve prior to the fall, who fasted not in penitence but as a result of simple innocence and detachment from bodily concerns. The angelic state, moreover, while not necessarily physically disembodied, suggested the gaining of a new spiritual body unencumbered by those concerns.

One pathway out of the desert and its ascetic rigours leads, therefore, through the denigration of the body towards heroic efforts by the individual to become, in effect, disembodied, disengaging from physical concerns. Yet this is not the only pathway along which the anchorites may lead us. As we have already seen, the anchorite's fasting body was, even in the desert, not independent of its social and economic contexts: the desert, as it were, 'fed into' and transformed the city. As asceticism became more explicitly a practice of communities, its capacity to reshape social and economic contexts, including patterns of food production and consumption, became a more obvious topic for theological reflection.

Cities in the sand

In accounts of the lives of anchorites the desert is presented as a school for the cultivation of virtue, especially temperance, by means of food practices. For this reason, the desert became an increasingly desirable spiritual destination. In his *Life of Anthony*, Athanasius of Alexandria describes an explosion in asceticism as ever increasing numbers retreated into the wilderness: 'Cells arose even in the mountains, and the desert was colonised by monks, who came forth from their own people, and enrolled themselves for the citizenship in the heavens.'[98] This, he continues, led Satan to complain to Anthony, with deceitful modesty: 'I have no longer a place, a weapon, a city. The Christians are spread everywhere, and at length even the desert is filled with monks. Let them take heed to themselves, and let them not curse me unreservedly.'[99]

Emergent monasticism thus gave rise, in the words of Samuel Rubenson, to an 'urbanisation of the desert'.[100] This can be understood, first of all, as a colonization of desert space by monks. Yet scholars have recently begun to recognize a second colonizing process in existing urban areas, with growing numbers of people, both single and living in communities, embracing monastic practices.[101] The spiritual discipline and withdrawal which the hermit life offered appealed to many, but did not need to be pursued in an actual desert space far removed from civilization. In either case, this urbanization was characterized not simply by an expansion in the numbers of hermits but by transformations in the structure of their life. The desert vocation opened the possibility of a spiritually and physically disciplined life pursued in separation from the cares which a family would bring and the temptations of urban living. Yet hermits inhabiting the desert in isolation were at constant risk from attack or robbery, and lacked a support network in times of illness or spiritual crisis. Solitary living also seems to have precipitated psychological delusions in many hermits in the form of diabolic visions.[102] In the case of city-dwellers – known as *remnuoth* by Jerome and *sarabaites* by Cassian and Benedict – temptations were very close to hand, and critics regarded these figures as generally ill-disciplined in diet and other behaviour.

In reality, both the desert and urban forms of the solitary life seem to have promoted and rewarded obsessive behaviour. This engendered jealousy, with ascetics competing to establish who among them was capable of the greatest feats of abstinence. One writer stated of the hermits that

> all of them everywhere by trying to outdo each other demonstrate their wonderful ascetic discipline. Those in the remotest places make strenuous efforts for fear anyone else should surpass them in ascetic practices. Those living near towns or villages make equal efforts, though evil troubles them on every side, in case they should be considered inferior to their remoter brethren.[103]

For these reasons, solitary desert-dwellers began to band together in communities under the leadership of an elder who imposed a common rule on all. The size of these communities is striking, even if exaggerated in contemporary reports. The community of Pachomius was reported by Palladius to number 1,400, while that of Ammon, derived from Pachomius, comprised 3,000 monks.[104] Sarapion was purported to be superior of an 'enormous community numbering about ten thousand monks'.[105]

The consequences of this development for eating patterns and food avoidances were considerable. The rules of the new communities promoted not the extreme abstinence witnessed among many solitary anchorites, but a moderated asceticism which enabled members to participate in the common life and manual labour necessary to sustain the community.[106] This shift is exemplified in the

earliest extant monastic rule, produced by Pachomius around 320, which privi-
leges moderate ascesis in cenobitic life over excessive ascesis in solitary life.[107] In
some later monastic rules, including the strict Carthusian Rule, the option to
pursue a higher level of abstention is also expressly forbidden.[108] Because, in
Charterhouses, food is brought to monks in their cell rather than being consumed together, this rule functions differently, with the solitary monk not permitted to refuse the portion of food brought to him.

In the Pachomian community, the staple foods were charlock, herbs, preserved olives, bread loaves, cheese made from cow's milk, and for the sick and
aged, a little pork.[109] Pork was probably chosen primarily because, in Roman
Egypt, it was the most common meat.[110] Nevertheless, Palladius relates that the
pigs were kept partly as a convenient means for disposing of chaff and left-over
food scraps. The possibility that in the Pachomian community there might be
uneaten food requiring disposal is striking. Other items appear to have been
eaten too, including vegetables, dates and fruits.[111] Just as pertinent as the range
of permitted items were the rules governing their consumption. Monks were
strictly forbidden to harvest, take or collect foods on their own initiative. This
prohibition applied especially to those responsible for harvesting and cooking.
Even fallen fruit was not to be picked up and eaten by the monk who discovered
it, but placed at the foot of a tree for later collection and distribution.[112] Moreover, those monks working in the fields had to carry with them vegetables
preserved with salt and vinegar, and not undertake any alfresco cooking.

Why were dietary rules formulated in such detail and applied with such
rigour? They evidently promoted obedience and discouraged divisive ascetic
competitions between members of the community. Moreover, lack of dietary
discipline was one of the reasons the city-dwelling monks were presented by
their detractors as hypocritical, detestable and wretched.[113] An even more
important factor motivated these strictures, however. It would be easy to presume that early monastic communities consisted of people who affirmed basic
Christian doctrines and expressed their Christian identity through such doctrines. Yet during the era of monastic development which we have been considering, the idea of Christian orthodoxy was still being forged and the content
of that orthodoxy formulated. Scholars now place increasing emphasis on the
doctrinal plurality of early monastic communities, which, as already seen,
probably included people with Gnostic interests as well as Manichean sym-
pathisers.[114] In this context of an absence of agreed detailed doctrinal formulations around which community identity could be constructed, the role of
common dietary rules in fostering such identity was vital.

Within the dietary framework applicable to all, provision was sometimes
made for monks who wished to follow a stricter dietary regime. They were
given small loaves to be eaten in their cells accompanied only by salt. This more
ascetic diet was not actively promoted, however, as suggested by the requirement that it be taken by a monk in his cell rather than in public. In another
Pachomian community, discreet fasting seems to have been possible for monks
taking meals in the refectory owing to the generously proportioned hoods of

their sheepskin cloaks. These hoods had to be worn during meals, with the diners seated at table with heads bowed so that no-one could see his neighbour. This made it impossible to see who was eating the full range of foods available and who was fasting. One author explains: 'Each one practises his own asceticism in secret: it is only for the sake of appearance that they sit at table, so as to seem to eat.'[115]

Notwithstanding this discretion and freedom to choose whether or not to fast, conflicts seem to have occurred in other places when fasting monks came into contact with monks who were not fasting. In one account, some Egyptian brothers are welcomed into a monastery and express shock at the ravenous eating of its members, who have been fasting all week, at the Saturday meal. The visitors are then exhorted by the priest to fast for a week, eating only raw food and this only once every two days, while the resident monks fast completely for the entire week. The visitors, unaccustomed to such rigorous practice, quickly become tired, and when the Saturday meal finally arrives, eat voraciously.[116] As a result of this imposed abstention they experience the discipline of fasting, and their hosts forgive their earlier hasty judgement. The perseverance of these guests is greater than that of another group of visiting monks, who when faced with a similar situation escape secretly from the monastery in which they are staying rather than endure its meagre fare of bread, salt and vinegar.[117]

The dietary practices of large numbers of monks gathered together in one place could evidently make a significant impact on the regional economy. A large community could potentially have obtained exotic foods or foods of a higher quality from further afield than individual families, and could stockpile food for its members during a famine. In this early period of monastic history, however, it seems likely that, as a result of their strict discipline, monks living in community enjoyed a dietary standard no more than equal to that of the surrounding populace. They lived in a condition of practice-based solidarity with their locality and region, grounded in a greater degree of abstention than that imposed by their material conditions as a large community. This is echoed by Basil of Caesarea, who in his rule compiled around 350 promotes not the denial of bodily sustenance but simplicity of diet. He relates this simplicity to the place where the community is located, stating:

> We ought to choose for our own use whatever is more easily and cheaply obtained in each locality and available for common use and bring in from a distance only those things which are more necessary for life, such as oil and the like or if something is appropriate for the necessary relief of the sick – yet even this only if it can be obtained without fuss and disturbance and distraction.[118]

Basil does not really appear to be conducting a « lutte contre la gourmandise », as one commentator has claimed.[119] The prescription just quoted suggests that his community followed a moderate diet rather than observing continual rigorous abstention. In any case, of more interest for our purposes is how Basil explicitly situates the eating practices of particular communities. What constitutes a moderate diet is not prescribed once and for all – on the basis of, say, biological arguments or a scripturally-derived authoritative model of the ascetic – but is discerned in each location in a way that acknowledges the reciprocal relationship between the ascetic community and its wider social, economic and geographical context.

In the rules of early monastic communities, dietary regulation was used as a means of influencing temperament and bodily dispositions in order to promote internal order and harmony between body, mind and spirit. Monks were expected to foster a body from which every desire for sensory or sexual gratification had been expelled.[120] Philip Sheldrake has explored how the fasting that was key to this enterprise transformed social life within the walls of the monastery.[121] This is well described in the *Life of Brendan of Clonfert* by the holy man Barinthus, who describes a journey undertaken with Brendan to visit a similar group of monks, the Community of Mernoc, who inhabited an island. Barinthus recalls:

> When we reached the island, the brethren came to us out of their cells, like a swarm of bees; and though their dwellings were divided from one another, there was no division in their converse, or counsel, or affection. And their only victuals were apples and nuts, and roots of such kinds of herbs as they found.[122]

In this description, the unity of the community is associated explicitly with the simplicity of its foodstuffs and their easy availability.

Yet as a result of the solidarity between monastery and surrounding society, fasting brought about a wider social transformation. Just as the renown of the desert ascetics extended beyond the boundaries of their barren environment, the more concrete effects of the choices made by monastic communities spread through their wider community. Basil emphasises the transformative power of monastic asceticism; in fasting, he says, 'the whole city generally, and all its people, are brought together in well-ordered harmony: raucous voices put to rest, strife banished, insults hushed'.[123] He proceeds to describe the transformation that fasting brings about not only of individual persons but of the whole city. By means of the solidarity deriving from Christian practice, social space itself is redeemed. Fasting, Basil states, preserves health, keeps husbands faithful, sustains marriages, prevents bloodshed, quietens cooks and servants, limits debt and reduces crime.

Basil thus argues that fasting effects the harmonious ordering of human society. It would be simplistic to read his text as comprising empirical claims about the biological effects of moderate diet, or as a theologically determined representation of the monastery as the guarantor of earthly harmony. Yet the food practices of monastic communities materially affected their social and economic contexts. The sweeping transformations through changes in food practices to which Basil and others refer therefore reflect not only a theological vision of the monastery-in-society but also aspects of historical experience.

In some of these accounts, the transformation of society through dietary practice is even depicted as extending to animals. Animals are presented as adopting ascetic disciplines, and as accepting obedience similar to that which would be expected of humans entering monastic life, especially by abstaining from meat.[124] This theme appears already in the accounts of the lives of the desert ascetics. In one episode, Abba Macarius is brought a sheepskin by a hyena that has just killed the sheep. The hermit refuses to accept the skin until the hyena has promised that she will not again kill any living animal, assuring her that whenever she is unable to obtain food by other means, she may come to him and he will feed her with his own bread. The hyena agrees to this arrangement and Macarius accepts the sheepskin, which he sleeps on until his death, and praises God for giving the hyena wisdom.[125] Another account describes Abba Gerasimos encountering a lion with a thorn in its paw. The hermit removes the thorn and bandages the wound, but the lion refuses to leave and becomes part of the monastic community, receiving the name Jordanes and eventually being given responsibility for care of the ass that the community uses to carry water. The ass later disappears, and the lion is suspected of having killed and eaten it – a charge which he bears stoically. But it later emerges that the ass had been stolen by camel-drivers, and it is returned joyously to the monastery by the lion, whose innocence is finally established.[126]

Such stories point to a distinctive motivation for promoting meat abstention by animals. The theological status of animal abstention is different from that of humans, because whereas after the Flood humans received permission to eat meat, animals were never granted this dispensation.[127] Animals that eschewed meat in a specifically Christian context were therefore regarded not as pursuing supererogatory asceticism but as reverting to the diet which God had always intended for them through a combination of their own spiritual obedience and guidance by a holy person, who adopts the animal as a disciple. The return of animals to the dietary regime deemed natural for them is thereby achieved partly as a result of human agency via a spiritual taming process.

In accounts of early monastic practices, meat abstinence transforms the whole natural order, reconfiguring the relationships existing between humans and animals, and among animals themselves. Nonetheless, in seeking to understand the importance of this tradition for theological reflection on food, excessive focus on the status of animals detracts from more significant issues. These include the ancient tradition of Christian reflection on the meanings of food, in which biological and social considerations are interrelated and both are understood theologically. The physical body of the individual ascetic and the social body of the monastery become sites of blessing for a wider community. Food practices, especially abstention from meat, both enact and convey this shared blessing.

2 Food in the ordered city

In the desert, anchorites controlled their own fasting. Yet as organized religious communities became established and spread into southern Europe, food practices became strictly codified. An associated development was the transposition of these practices into the weekly, seasonal and annual cycles of wider society. This transformed social, political and economic relationships. But patterns of abstinence would not have taken such deep root in society if they had not been founded on an acceptance of existing cycles and relationships as constituting the reality into which they were incarnated.

Max Weber famously argued that, during early modernity, practices previously located in the monastery were transposed into the private Reformation hearth, and that these practices inadvertently provided an ethic that promoted the development of the capitalist economy. In *The Protestant Ethic and the Spirit of Capitalism*, he dramatically asserted that, at the Reformation, Christian asceticism 'strode into the market-place of life and slammed the door of the monastery behind it, and undertook to penetrate just that daily routine of life with its methodicalness, to fashion it into a life in the world, but neither of nor for this world'.[1]

The process which Weber identified of the spread of a monastic ethos from monasteries into wider society is significant given that, in the earlier middle ages, monasteries were bastions of abstinence from red meat. Furthermore, from the perspective of dietary discipline generally, his thesis merits attention because it associates asceticism with empowerment rather than with a morbid denial of human embodiment. Weber also draws attention to the need to situate dietary practices, whether abstinent or gluttonous, in their social, political and economic contexts. In our first chapter, we have already called into question modern assumptions that food practices had no impact on these contexts. In this chapter, we shall explore in greater detail how Christians embraced asceticism precisely because of the social, political and economic transformations it effected.

These relationships show that not much can be said about 'asceticism' or 'dietary restriction' in general. Any explanation which treats asceticism as a single entity, and then seeks to explain it in terms of something else, is likely to obscure the complexities of actual ascetic practice. In this chapter, as we trace the movement of asceticism from the desert into the city, and from the monastery into the world, we shall observe the multiple effects of dietary restriction and how these interact with theological reflection. We shall begin, however, by examining in greater detail a prior phase in the development of Christian dietary practice: the process by which the extreme individual asceticism of the anchorites was transformed into rules of moderation.

Monastic moderation

A key marker of Christian monastic identity was abstinence from red meat. This was enshrined in the Rule of Benedict, compiled in the mid sixth century, which became the standard in communities in the Christian West. It instructed unequivocally: 'Except the sick who are very weak, let all abstain entirely from the flesh of four-footed animals.'[2] Benedict of Nursia established a principle of moderation in monastic diet quite different from the extreme asceticism of most anchorites. Clear continuities can be identified between this principle and Classical traditions of dietary advice.[3] In the same key chapter of his Rule, Benedict envisaged a single daily meal at which 'every table should have two cooked dishes, on account of individual infirmities, so that he who perchance cannot eat of one, may make his meal of the other'. A third dish of fruit or vegetables could be included, if available, adding to the minimum of two choices normally available. The daily bread ration remained the same if supper was taken at a later hour, with the cellarer instructed to reserve one third of the ration for this later distribution. Flexibility was still possible, however. The abbot was given discretion to augment these rations if the person was performing heavier manual work than usual. Two chapters previously, Benedict had specified that the elderly and children should not be subject to the full rigours of the rule with respect to food or the hours at which it is taken.[4]

Several aspects of these rules merit comment. First, they promote a principle of choice within boundaries, with diners able to opt for one of two principal dishes. Second, community members were expected to engage in manual work, with an increased bread ration available at the abbot's discretion to support this. Thus is recognized a correspondence between the amount of work performed and the quantity of food required. Such pragmatism is absent from the *Lives* of the anchorites. Third, flexibility is possible, in consequence both of the abbot's discretionary powers and the element of personal choice just identified. Fourth, red meat is crucially regarded as inessential to the diet of a normal healthy adult. It is a sign of weakness, reserved for children and the sick, not a sign of strength. Fifth, in the special provisions for the elderly and the young, a degree of rigour is recognized in the standard rule that not everybody would be able to observe.

Some Christian writers advocating moderation drew on Galen, and it is likely that Benedict was influenced by him. This second-century Greek physician and philosopher is not typically seen as an ally of Christians, but is reported as praising Christians for their 'self-discipline and self-control in matters of food and drink' by which they have 'attained a pitch not inferior to that of genuine philosophers'.[5] An Arabic legend even existed that Galen was a Christian and the uncle of Paul, dependent on a highly unrealistic early dating of his corpus. In any case, his ideas helped form the milieu in which Benedict developed his Rule. Basil of Ancyra, writing in the mid fourth century, discusses how the balancing of the bodily humours (heat, cold, dryness and moisture) may be promoted by consuming foods containing properties that will reduce specific bodily humours and increase others. His methodology is far more nuanced than that evident in the earlier accounts of anchorites, recognizing that different diets will be suited for different people due both to varying natural bodily constitutions and to diverse lifestyles.[6] Whether Basil applies these principles to men and women consistently seems unclear in places: although the wise virgin is instructed not to weaken her body if it is already cold and dried up as a result of sickness or old-age, the regime he in fact promotes for virgins seems sufficiently severe to be likely to promote precisely these effects.[7] Nevertheless, he presents a methodology which could at least potentially be used to identify and address the effects on the body of an excessively harsh dietary regime, as well as to diminish the negative effects of insufficient restraint. The abbot of a small monastery would be well placed to perform the role of the physician administering his disciples' diet, observing each person's devotion, health and manual labour and employing appropriate discretion and sensitivity to prescribe a suitable regime.

Aided by Benedict, developing Christian tradition shifted away from extreme asceticism towards this more pragmatic ideal of dietary discipline. Fasting came increasingly to be seen as providing a path to distinct spiritual ends whose fulfilment depended on a basic level of physical flourishing. This focus is apparent in the *Conferences* of John Cassian, who spent the first part of his life in Egypt and Palestine before travelling to Marseilles where in 415 he founded two monasteries, one for men and another for women. This document comprises summaries of interviews that Cassian and his companions conducted with Egyptian and Palestinian monks, and was an important catalyst for the transposition of monasticism into Europe. In one of the *Conferences*, Abba Moses insists that fasting is not in itself perfection, but aids perfection by creating conditions in which contemplation and virtue may be fostered.[8] He tells several stories of monks who have compromised their vocation through excessive dietary austerities. These include brother Heron, who refused to join the rest of his community even for the Easter feast. While the celebrations were happening he was accosted by a demon whom he mistook for an angel, and cast himself down a well in order to prove the great merit of his abstinence. He was pulled out, died three days later, and was buried as a suicide.[9] Moses censures immoderate fasts and vigils on the notable grounds that 'excessive abstinence is still more injurious to us than careless satiety: for from this latter the intervention of a healthy compunction will raise us to the right measure of strictness, and not from the former'.[10] In other words, it is easier to moderate indulgence than extreme asceticism. Moses then recommends to Cassian and his companions a newly established regime by which all brothers eat small quantities of the same food regularly. Diverse practices had previously existed, with some brothers eating only beans and others just fruit and vegetables. A uniform ration was therefore determined of two bread loaves daily.[11]

Moses' advice is notable in prescribing unwavering uniformity even on Sundays and days when guests visit.[12] Monks maintaining this pattern would need no additional food on Sundays or other special days. If additional food were taken on these days, a smaller ration would be required during the rest of the week, or quite possibly nothing at all, as a result of the additional sustenance previously received. Why not opt, therefore, for this latter option, frequently practised and previously described, of complete abstinence through the week with a feast on Sunday? Cassian rejects this option on the grounds that it would establish a cycle of excessive abstinence followed by indulgence that would, over time, be likely to promote gluttony. This is illustrated by the example of brother Benjamin, who on alternate days ate none of his bread ration in order to enjoy a feast of four loaves once every two days, so that he might 'give way to his appetite by means of a double portion'. Abba Moses continues: 'Through the two days of fasting he was able to acquire his four rolls, thereby getting the chance both to satisfy his longings and to enjoy a full stomach.'[13] Benjamin ultimately forsakes monastic life, returning 'back to the empty philosophy of this world and to the vanity of the day' because he 'obstinately chose his own decisions in preference to what had been handed down by the fathers'.

The standard daily ration should be maintained, Moses explains, even when guests visit, by reservation of one of the two loaves for the day. If a brother comes to visit during the afternoon, the loaf can be eaten then, or consumed in the evening if no guest has appeared.[14] An adjustment to this regime is permitted during Eastertide, however. In his account of the interview with Abba Theonas, Cassian allows for an adjustment of normal practice during this fifty days' celebration which lasted until Pentecost. The adjustment is modest, however, permitting the food that would normally be taken at the mid-afternoon main meal ('the ninth hour') to be enjoyed at midday ('the sixth hour'). It is stated explicitly that no adjustment of the type or quantity of food consumed is to be made, 'for fear lest the purity of body and uprightness of soul which has been gained by the abstinence of Lent be lost by the relaxation of Eastertide'.[15]

Cassian also discusses dietary discipline in his fifth book of *Institutes*, in which he presents the common goal of spiritual abstinence as best served by varying levels of abstinence for different people. In so far as an objective measure of degrees of abstinence is possible, some community members will be suited to a stricter degree than others owing to differences in mental steadfastness, bodily health, age and gender.[16] Indeed, when specific foods are discussed, this is often in order to show the difficulty of forming general prescriptions: moistened beans do not agree with everybody, for example, and fresh vegetables or dry bread will suit some people but not others. In defining gluttony, Cassian does not therefore focus solely on the specific types of food eaten, but adopts a broader perspective which takes account of their simplicity and ease of preparation. He advises:

> Food should be chosen not only to soothe the burnings pangs of lust, still less to inflame them, but which is easy to prepare and which is readily

available for a moderate price, and it should be held in common for the brothers' use. Now there are three types of gluttony: one is a compulsion to anticipate the regular time of eating; another is wanting to fill the stomach with excessive amounts of any sort of food; the third is delighting in the more delicate and rare dishes. A monk therefore must take threefold care against these: firstly he must wait for the proper time of meals; then he must not yield to overeating; thirdly he should be happy with any sort of common food.[17]

Cassian's comments in the *Institutes* also reflect interest in the importance of location in forming dietary disciplines, and in the issues which emerge when practices are transposed from one place into another. He compiled the *Institutes* at the request of Bishop Castor of Aptia Julia in order to acquaint readers with Egyptian and Palestinian monastic practice. He states of Egyptian monastic diet that 'in our country neither the climate nor our own weakness could tolerate' such discipline.[18] It is clear that he does not intend to restrict his own two communities in southern Gaul to bread.

Cassian's teacher at Constantinople had been John Chrysostom. Although he does not lay down guidelines for monastic formation in the same systematic way, Chrysostom promotes a similar spirit of moderation, which appears to have had an effect on his pupil. He writes:

Fasting is a medicine; but a medicine, though it be never so profitable, becomes frequently useless owing to the unskilfulness of him who employs it. For it is necessary to know, moreover, the time when it should be applied, and the requisite quantity of it; and the temperament of body that admits it; and the nature of the country, and the season of the year; and the corresponding diet; as well as various other particulars; any of which, if one overlooks, he will mar all the rest that have been named.[19]

By characterizing fasting as a medicine, Chrysostom makes clear that it exists to remedy human weakness. It would not, by implication, be required in a state of original or final perfection, if either could be supposed to exist. Chrysostom's audience consisted primarily of lay people, for whom dietary advice would have been informed by ideas about human health and even social respectability.[20] This tempered yet serious lay asceticism found its way, through Cassian, into monastic tradition in the form of Benedictine moderation, and thus back again into lay practice in ways which will now be examined.

Beyond the monastery: the social fast

How did dietary restriction contribute to the ordering of communities beyond the monastery walls? Aline Rousselle sheds light on a much earlier movement from monastery to society than that discussed by Weber, impressively defending the role of monasticism in constructing Christian identity in the Constantinian era. A notable feature of Rousselle's analysis is her situating of monastic asceticism in Foucauldian mode within the wider classical tradition of the formation, regulation and disciplining of human bodies. These processes shaped ideas about sexual morality, adultery and marriage, promoting sexual continence but by no means sexual abstinence. By using harsh dietary regimens to eliminate physical sexual activity and even the desire for such activity, Rousselle argues, desert asceticism constituted a radical intensification of this pre-Christian tradition.

These early monastic perceptions of the body, based on the critical appropriation and transformation of classical themes, were transposed, she suggests, back into emergent Christian society in moderated form as a result of the spread of institutional Christianity, which appealed to existing secular perceptions of the body and gender relations. She concludes:

> What might have been simply a short-lived phenomenon in an exploited Egypt came into contact both with male repugnance for marriage in Greek countries and with the aversion of the women of the Roman world to the legal and social conditions of marriage.[21]

The consequent transposition of elements of the monastic ethos into the family was crucial, Rousselle suggests, in perpetuating this ethos through future generations and in fostering new monastic vocations.

Christian dietary disciplines thereby became gradually assimilated into structured public observance.[22] Fasting became a common enterprise which was related theologically to the church calendar and the seasonal cycle. Dietary disciplines, especially abstention from meat, thus contributed to the ordering of human society through liturgy and relationships with the natural world.

A general overview of the pattern of fasts in the West can be given, even though details of practice varied according to time and place. The principal and most ancient season of abstinence was Lent, lasting more than six weeks. No red meat or dairy products could be eaten during this entire period, although fish was permitted. Moreover, only one meal per day was allowed. Much debate surrounded the time at which this meal should be taken, with sunset identified as the ancient practice. By about the ninth century, the meal was commonly scheduled in the mid afternoon, with this time being defended in the tenth-century Anglo-Saxon poem *Seasons for Fasting*.[23] By the fourteenth century, however, a midday meal was being promoted by scholastic theologians. In consequence, a second lighter evening meal, known as a collation, became increasingly common. The other area of gradual Lenten relaxation was the consumption of dairy products (excluding eggs), which was accepted in Germany and Scandinavia from about the ninth century although resisted for much longer in France and England.

The second fasting season was Advent, the period leading up to Christmas. The word Advent meant 'coming', and fasting during the season heightened the sense of waiting and expectation that would be realized in the Christmas celebration of Christ's birth at Bethlehem. The earliest Advent fasts seem to have been modelled on Lent and lasted about the same time. In sixth-century France, Gregory of Tours promoted an observance commencing on Saint Martin's Day (11 November), with fasting required on the Mondays, Wednesdays and Fridays of each week.[24] The Advent fast was therefore of equal length to the Lenten fast but less intense. By the time of Charlemagne, a full daily fast was universally required although for a reduced period starting at the beginning of December. Advent thus came to be distinguished from Lent by its shorter duration.

Also notable were the ember days, which comprised the Wednesdays, Fridays and Saturdays following the feast of Saint Lucy (13 December), the first Sunday in Lent, the feast of Pentecost, and Holy Cross Day (13 September). These were anciently linked with the seasonal cycle and had both Jewish and pagan precedents, but also corresponded with the church calendar.[25] The days following Pentecost commemorated the fasting which, according to all three Synoptic Gospels, Christ stated his disciples would undertake after he was taken from them.[26] Two other sets of days fell in Advent and Lent. The final trio, occurring in September, were not biblically connected but conveniently marked the end of summer, falling just before the autumnal equinox. Similarly, the Advent ember days heralded the winter solstice and the conclusion of autumn, as well as occurring during a Christian fast. In an ingenious exposition, Jacobus de Voragine associated these quarterly observances with the bodily humours predominant at different times of the year. He reasons:

> Spring is warm and humid, summer hot and dry, autumn cool and dry, winter cold and wet. Therefore we fast in the spring to control the harmful fluid of voluptuousness in us; in summer, to allay the noxious heat of avarice; in autumn, to temper the aridity of pride; in winter, to overcome the coldness of malice and lack of faith.[27]

Several alternative formulations are offered, but most adopt a similar methodology of associating the season connected with each set of days with a particular imbalance of bodily humours in need of correction. Yet the correction seems to be primarily spiritual and lacks the biological consistency of Basil of Ancyra's previously discussed. In particular, it is unclear how fasting in autumn, classified as a cool and dry season, would rebalance the body physically. But in principle, this scheme is quite possibly developed as a response to the problem which Galen identified of the 'disharmonic mixing' of humours and seasons, with the foods naturally available during a particular season not those best suited to redressing the humoural imbalances induced by that season.[28] Very obviously, meat – a warming food – was available most easily during the warmer seasons. Albert Magnus gave this balancing scheme greater biological rigour by examining the varying humours of different humans and animals and showing in great detail how, by preferring the meat of one animal over another, humans may balance their own humours with an appropriate complementary mixture.[29]

Abstinence from red meat was also required on every Wednesday (identified as the day when Judas Iscariot agreed to betray Jesus), every Friday (the day of the crucifixion of Jesus), and every Saturday (the day when Jesus lay in the tomb), unless a feast fell on one of these days.[30] Fasting was also prescribed for the eves of various feasts and festivals. As late as the 1662 Book of Common Prayer, these are listed as the vigils of Christmas, the Purification of Mary, the Annunciation, Easter Day, Ascension Day, Pentecost, Saint Matthias, Saint John the Baptist, Saint Peter and Saint Paul, Saint James, Saint Bartholomew, Saint Matthew, Saints Simon and Jude, Saint Andrew, Saint Thomas and All Saints. Thus, even allowing for some double counting, well over half the days of the year were classed as fasts, and meat could not be eaten on any of those days.

Why did this complex pattern of fasts develop and persist for so long? Explanations relating to the natural order are supported by liturgical and theological justifications. The theme that fasting provided 'medicine' which contributed to bodily health was combined with an interest in the seasons, promoting the health of the individual and social bodies by keeping them in harmony with changes in the natural world on which they depended. This is most apparent in the case of the Lenten fast. In the desert, the year-round fast of Christian hermits and communities reflected the continual barrenness of the space they inhabited. Yet as Christianity spread, fasting practices were transplanted into regions with obvious seasonal cycles of abundance and scarcity where hunger stalked rich and poor alike.[31] Lenten observance could conveniently be integrated into those natural cycles, such that abstinence from red meat, poultry and dairy products became a function of practical reality sanctified by the Church. Lent could thus be viewed as little more than the formal and structured recognition by both Church and society of a period of scarcity that would naturally occur in Europe during late winter and early spring. C.J. Bond hence argues that Lent 'made a virtue of necessity by requiring a six-week abstinence from meat at the end of the winter, when most domestic livestock other than animals kept for breeding had already been slaughtered'.[32] Slaughter of the last remaining animals would have depleted future stocks as well as animals used for ploughing, transportation and dairy production. Fasting can thus be regarded as the sanctified acceptance by humans of the natural rhythms of the earth and of the wisdom of nature.[33]

The idea that nature exhibits an order built around the seasons, places and animal life is beautifully unfolded in *Piers Plowman*, in which the dreamer perceives 'how closely Reason followed all the beasts, in their eating and drinking and engendering of their kinds'.[34] He laments shortly after that 'Reason ruled and cared for all the beasts, except only for man and his mate; for many a time they wandered ungoverned by reason'.[35] Langland's vision of sun and sea, sandy shores, the mating places of birds and beasts, nesting spots and woodlands carpeted with flowers presents an ordered world from which humans can learn, even though the human mind will be unable to fathom the intricacies of its working. The best, it seems, for which humans can hope is a level of understanding sufficient to conform their life to the patterning of the life of nature such that they may enter into its harmony and share its fruits. Dietary practices conforming to natural cycles are intrinsic to this patterning, which Langland sees particularly in animals' 'eating and drinking'.

A variety of theological justifications for the Lenten fast have been given, few of which refer explicitly to its seasonal appropriateness. John Cassian identifies the fast's origins in the biblical requirement that the people of Israel tithe one tenth of their possessions and firstfruits.[36] Viewed from this perspective, Lent amounts to the offering of 'tithes of our life and ordinary employments and actions, which is clearly arranged for in the calculation of Lent'.[37] By counting the six weeks of Lent, excluding Sundays, and adding the half day of the Easter Eve fast when the Saturday fast, which would usually end at sunset, is prolonged until the dawn of Easter morning, a final figure of thirty-six-and-a-half days is calculated, which equals precisely one-tenth of the year. According to this interpretation, observance of the Lenten fast enabled lay Christians to fulfil in their bodies the biblical requirement of tithing.

The idea that Lent lasts forty days because it commemorates the fast of this duration undertaken by Christ in the wilderness provides, of course, the better-known basis for its origin and length. Patristic writers did not always make this connexion, however. Athanasius, for instance, makes no such association, referring instead to various Old Testament figures who fasted for periods of often unspecified duration.[38] Moreover, if the fast had been entirely conceived as an imitation of the fasting of Christ, it would have made greater sense for it to have been located in its pre-Niceaen position in the calendar beginning on 7 January immediately following Epiphany, the date on which Christ's baptism was commemorated. As Mark states of Christ at the conclusion of his otherwise brief Gospel account of this event: '*At once* the Spirit sent him out into the desert.'[39] Yet founding the Lenten fast on the greatest source of theological authority possible, the example of Christ himself, was key to promoting its continued observance and entrenching it publicly. In the West, it eventually became seen as necessary to begin the Lenten fast midweek so that, subtracting Sundays, it lasted precisely forty days. This was required in the Rule of the Master and also promoted by Pope Gregory the Great by means of various supporting number symbolism such as the multiplication of the number of elements (four) by the number of commandments in the Decalogue (ten).[40] The first day of Lent became known as Ash Wednesday because this was the day on which public penances commenced. The association of Lent with Christ's fasting in the wilderness has been particularly popular in modern times.[41]

Lenten obligations intensified the natural seasonal lurches between frugality and feasting. This is illustrated by the excesses of Shrovetide or Mardi Gras, when pancakes and other foods such as doughnuts were cooked in order to exhaust the perishable dairy products which the following day would be banned. The importance of food in this folk feast, which in Britain encompassed Shrove Sunday, Collop Monday and Shrove Tuesday, is well illustrated by the naming of its second day, when 'collops' or cuts of fried or roasted meat were traditionally eaten.[42] Also widespread around this time was what Ronald Hutton calls the 'ritualized mistreatment of poultry', with which cockfighting seems to have been linked.[43] The Lenten ban on egg consumption rendered hens effectively unproductive, and 'cock throwing', in which a tethered bird was killed by having objects thrown at it from a distance, became in the eighteenth century a popular pastime and subsequently the first blood sport in Britain to be outlawed.

The stark opposition of feasting and fasting in popular culture is illustrated by the late-medieval literary and artistic motif of the 'debate' between Lent and Carnival, the latter meaning literally a time of bidding meat farewell. This discourse escalated into a 'full fledged, deadly combat on the battlefield' between the severe Lord Lent and the overbearing, hedonistic Lord Carnival.[44] Each potentate is, of course, successively deposed by the other. Just as, on Ash Wednesday, Carnival is banished and Lent installed, so Easter heralds the restoration of Carnival. In Scotland and northern England, 'pace' (i.e. paschal) eggs were exchanged in celebration in order to use up the glut developed during Lent, perhaps including hard-boiled specimens for reasons of preservation, and a tithe was sometimes required at this time of year.[45] The connection of Easter with renewed feasting is especially clear in the Hungarian and Estonian languages, in which the words describing the feast, respectively *Húsvét* and *Lihavõtted*, mean literally 'meat-taking' or 'meat-buying'. The victory of Lord Carnival could, of course, never be more than temporary, as the depredations of Lent would undoubtedly return at their appointed time. Yet Carnival was an opportunity to celebrate. Moreover, in post-Reformation Europe full participation in the festivities was a means of affirming Catholic loyalties and snubbing Protestant criticisms of the Church's historic calendar.[46]

In the understanding and practice of Lenten fasting, we see a season of natural frugality incorporated into theological reflection and made part of Christians' re-performance of the narratives of salvation history and situating of themselves within those narratives. Specific aspects of practice, and interpretations of scripture and doctrine, informed and shaped each other. Importantly, these included explicit reflection on the natural appropriateness of the fast. Lent might have made a Christian virtue out of a seasonal necessity, but seasonal necessity could itself be understood as an aspect of a wider divine order.

In interpretations of Christian dietary discipline, the capacity of fasting to bring human life into conformity with natural provisions and seasons has been given insufficient attention. In particular, later-medieval fasting has too often been presented as no more than submission to arbitrary ecclesiastical dictates, just as fasting in the earlier middle ages continues to be attributed to sexual neuroses. Yet a conception of fasting as engendering social and ecological harmony is, in isolation, itself in danger of neglecting the practical, ideological and spiritual mechanisms by which fasting was actually sustained.

It is clear that fasting was in practice not straightforwardly a leveller of rank nor even a means of unifying society around a shared commitment to abstinence. Wealth and social station made a considerable difference to people's experiences of fasting. In order to alleviate the severities of Lent, persons of sufficient means could obtain freshwater fish from rivers and fishponds. This is why turbot became known as the 'king of Lent'. Moreover, people inhabiting coastal areas might well enjoy access to sea fish. Yet dried cod, known as 'stockfish', was the best option available to most people. This fish was pre-served by drying and beating with hammers for at least an hour, and rehydrated for a minimum of two hours. It was finally boiled and eaten with butter or mustard.[47] Such fare, it can easily be imagined, did little to satisfy appetites, and was a source of continual resentment during what were, at the best of times, naturally bleak months.

Bridget Henisch describes in splendid detail the hatred felt by many ordinary people towards the Lenten fast, and the devices that evolved to reduce its rigours. Herring and shellfish took the place of red meat, and oil replaced animal fat for frying.[48] The simnel cake associated with Mid-Lent Sunday (also Mothering Sunday or Simnel Sunday) demonstrated the ingenuity of cooks and food suppliers in negotiating the Lenten strictures. For people of sufficient means, Lent was a popular time for buying imported dried fruits and nuts, which were then not in season in northern Europe.[49] An especially useful substitute for dairy products, which were prohibited during this season, were almonds, which continue to fea-ture in modern cookery as the base ingredient of marzipan. These could either be made into a milk by blanching, grinding and steeping in water, and used as a binding ingredient instead of eggs, or puréed by heating and draining.[50] With the addition of yeast to aid rising and saffron for yellow colouring, a cake could be prepared which, even if it resembled a sweet bread more closely than its modern successor, provided a welcome tasty treat to cheer the gloomy Lenten season.[51]

Testing Weber's thesis that the 'Protestant ethic' was a product of secularized monasticism against the key example of dietary practice demonstrates some of its shortcomings. The thesis is unconvincing to the extent that it presents practice as an 'ethic' abstracted from wider political and social life, which is simply transposed from the monastic sphere into secular society. Ludo Milis, in his history of monasticism, develops a more useful focus on tangible material practices, including dietary disciplines. He suggests that it was the secular clergy and mendicant friars, not the monastic orders, who were responsible for the diffusion of spiritual practices through wider medieval society as a result of their greater dependence on that society.[52] Yet even Milis' analysis neglects the wider social, ecological and political dynamics underlying the preservation of practices in particular places. One extremely important dimension was the role of civil governments in promulgating and enforcing sumptuary legislation. This extended to other aspects of cultural and social life too, such as clothing. The power of fasting lay not simply in the power of the individual against the gov-erning authorities, nor in the power to maintain social harmony and harmony with the natural world. It was also a civic power to build and maintain a state.

The public fast

It might be expected that jettisoning all dietary regulations would have been one way for newly Protestant states to demonstrate that they had extirpated some of the most deeply engrained medieval Catholic practices. In so doing, they would have followed the path set by Lollardy, which is frequently regarded as a precursor of Protestant Reformation movements two centuries later. In Lollard heresy trials, issues surrounding the breaking of fasts arose commonly, and penances involving food, such as fasting on bread and water every Friday for a year, were commonly handed down.[53] At the English Reformation, however, fasting was not abolished but continued to be imposed by the state according to the traditional pattern. This was part of a long tradition of sumptuary legislation that dated back to the Anglo-Saxon period.[54]

In 1536, two years after the Suppression Act which inaugurated monastic dissolution, King Henry VIII promulgated an injunction instructing that 'no person shall from henceforth alter or change the order and manner of any fasting-day that is commanded and indicted by the Church ... until such time as the same shall be so ordered and transposed by the King's Highness' authority'.[55] The serious consequences of breaking a fast were stated in Edward VI's first 'Proclamation for the abstaining from flesh in the Lent time' of 16 January 1547, which warned: 'Whosoever shall, upon any day heretofore wont to be fasted from flesh ... eat flesh contrary to this proclamation, shall incur the king's high indignation, and shall suffer imprisonment and be otherwise grievously punished at his majesty's will and pleasure.'[56] The following year, Saturday was added as a second meatless day by Act of Parliament on the grounds of historic – that is, pre-Reformation – precedent.[57] Three years later, on 9 March 1551, the penalties for infringing the new fast day were more precisely defined: a fine of ten shillings for the first offence, along with ten days in prison.[58] The fasting days, by this time known often as 'fish days', were preserved by Elizabeth I and indeed multiplied, with Wednesday added to Friday and Saturday in 1563 as a third legally enforceable meat-free day.[59]

More than two decades earlier, in 1538, Henry VIII had repealed the Lenten ban on the consumption of dairy products, including milk, butter, eggs and cheese, in order to relieve pressure on fish stocks during the season and probably also to appease the populace by making the fast a little easier.[60] This measure created the conditions in which hot cross buns made with dairy products could become associated with Good Friday. They would later, under Elizabeth I, be seen as problematic due to their Catholic symbolism, especially the pastry cross on top and associations with the reserved Eucharistic host, with the result that in 1592 their sale was restricted to Good Friday, Christmas and funerals.[61]

Yet although the range of foods from which abstention was required was reduced, the strictness of the remaining proscriptions was undiminished. The political importance of maintaining and even strengthening the Lenten abstention from red meat is articulated in an important passage from the 'Homily of fasting' from the *Second Book of Homilies* produced in the early 1560s and issued in final form in 1571.[62] These homilies were legally appointed to be read in rotation in churches, with their official status as Church of England teaching defined in the thirty-fifth Article of Religion. Several points are worth noting. First, the homily calls the people to 'obedience, which by the Law of God we owe to the Magistrate, as to God's minister', and thus refuses any simple dichotomy between sacred and secular authorities and practices. This is not a cynical justification of the use of religious practices for political ends, but a call made on Christian conscience by the state, which exercises legitimate authority in areas of public policy. Because dietary practices affect social and economic relations, they have implications for such policy. Second, the homily particularly encourages meat abstinence by the well supplied and wealthy, on the grounds that it leaves more food from the land's 'fair pastures' for others at cheaper prices, in order that the 'increase of victuals upon the land may the better be spared and cherished, to the sooner reducing of victuals to a more moderate price, to the better sustenance of the poor'. Wealthy people would clearly experience the most restrictions during a fast because under normal circumstances they would enjoy easier access to the foods prohibited. Third, a striking argument is made linking the preservation of fish days with civil defence and the avoidance of war. Fasting is associated not with weakness, but with strength, virility, and territorial integrity in the face of aggression by hostile foreign powers. In the Elizabethan context of a scepter'd isle 'environed with the sea', fish days supported fishermen who could form the basis of a navy and well as maintain coastal ports, 'that the old ancient glory should return to the Realm, wherein it hath with great commendations excelled before our days, in the furniture of the Navy of the same'.

Despite these various public benefits, a breakdown in fasting disciplines during the following decades contributed to food shortages among the poor. Archbishop Whitgift's admonition for preachers of 1596 urged that

> housekeepers being of wealth would be content in their own diet to avoid excess, and to use fewer dishes of meat in this time of dearth, and to forebear to have suppers in their houses on Wednesdays, Fridays and fasting days, whereby much might be spared, that would be better bestowed a great deal on the relief of the poor.[63]

Whitgift here seeks to restrict food consumption by employing spiritual exhortation. This suggests that civil legislation was not seen as the sole means of dietary control, and that the function of preaching was not simply to justify such legislation. Spiritual considerations continued to play an important independent role.

The Anglican divine Richard Hooker gives a key exposition of the importance of fasting in the context of the Elizabethan settlement. He complains in his *Laws of Ecclesiastical Polity* that 'much hurt hath grown to the Church of God through a false imagination that Fasting standeth men in no stead for any spiritual respect, but only to take down the frankness of nature, and to tame the wildness of flesh'.[64] Hooker was obviously well aware of the Elizabethan civil context of fasting being useful 'for the maintenance of seafaring men and preservation of cattle', but sees this as evidence that fasting has a place in the divinely ordained natural order. He defends set times for fasting such as Lent because these 'have their ground in the Law of Nature, are allowable in God's sight, were in all ages heretofore, and may till the world's end be observed, not without singular use and benefit'.

Hooker makes explicit the interweaving of scriptural, traditional and natural justifications for fasting, which were earlier apparent in justifications for the Lenten fast. He traces its roots to Israelite observance, as well as drawing on Jerome, Augustine and Calvin to develop an understanding of Christian dietary tradition, which forms a normative standard against which current practices and attitudes to fasting may be measured. He recognizes Christian traditions of voluntary fasting by individuals and common abstinence at set times, implying that both are useful in so far as they promote the spiritual health of the personal and collective bodies. Fasting thus becomes a means of empowerment, and Hooker extends this analogy in characteristic Elizabethan fashion to a military context. Such Christian discipline 'teacheth men, in practice of ghostly warfare against themselves, those things that afterwards may help them, justly assaulting or standing in lawful defence of themselves against others'.[65]

Hooker situates his defence of fasting historically, censuring the extreme Montanist fasting associated with Tertullian but equally criticizing the blanket opposition to fasting by Arius.[66] Drawing on the writings of Ignatius of Antioch and Irenaeus of Lyons to develop his analysis, Hooker identifies both extreme abstinence and complete dietary liberty with heresy. He thus develops the classic Elizabethan defence of fasting on the grounds that it is enjoined by both tradition and nature, is spiritually useful and fosters the common good.

The traditional pattern of fasts was found to be advantageous for the maintenance of political order even after the Reformation. Hooker's work shows how this political function of fasting could be related to the consonance of the seasonal fasts with a divinely ordained natural order. Another aspect of public fasting in the Reformation, however, was the development of occasional fasts. Periodic fasts called for primarily political reasons had ancient precedents. Fasting across his empire was, for example, a major element of Charlemagne's public policy.[67] A fast was called in the spring of 793 after a revolt by Pippin the Hunchback, and in 805 a three-day fast occurred following bad weather, crop failure and famine.[68]

At the Reformation, however, public fasts called in response to specific situations developed alongside new opposition to the traditional pattern of seasonal fasts by some other theologians. In his *Institutes*, Calvin locates the origins of the occasional public fast in the Old Testament. In his words:

> when pestilence begins to stalk abroad, or famine or war, or when any other disaster seems to impend over a province and people, then also it is the duty of pastors to exhort the Church to fasting, that she might suppliantly deprecate the Lord's anger.[69]

A fast, Calvin argues, should be measured by duration, quality of food, and quantity. On no account should the 'encroachment of superstition' be permitted: indeed, no fasting at all would be preferable to that. Calvin singles out Lent for special criticism, arguing that, contrary to widespread supposition, this fast was not divinely inaugurated. Christ fasted not to set an example to others, he contends, but to 'prove that his doctrine was not of men, but had come from heaven'.[70] Moreover, Christ did not fast repeatedly or annually but 'once only, when preparing for the promulgation of the Gospel'. Calvin asserts: 'It was therefore merely false zeal, replete with superstition, which set up a fast under the title and pretext of imitating Christ.'[71] To this was added 'rudeness and ignorance in the bishops, lust of power, and tyrannical rigour, with abundant exquisite delicacies replacing the excluded flesh'.

The political implications of occasional fasts become evident in England in 1642, when the Long Parliament abolished the complex pattern of fasts which had evolved in the medieval period, instigating in their place a single fast on the final Wednesday of each month.[72] This system was instituted at the time of the Irish Rebellion. The sense of public emergency which this event precipitated was maintained, Hugh Trevor-Roper argues, in the context of a permanent state of 'public emergency' in the struggle between Parliament and King. A rupture in the political order was achieved partly through a rupture in the pattern of fasts.

The monthly fast instituted by the Long Parliament was abolished in April 1649 on grounds of neglect.[73] It had possibly outlived its political usefulness. More importantly, however, the old pattern of Christian fasts, organically evolved and linked with the seasonal cycle and popular Christian devotion, had through long usage captured the sympathies of society more readily than a system designed to serve the political interests of the time. At the Restoration, this historic pattern of fasts was reinstituted but with only limited success. The final proclamation of fasting in England was made by King Charles II in 1664, and the last prosecutions for infringements also occurred in this decade.[74] The statute for fish days was eventually repealed in 1856 on grounds of disuse.[75] Although various 'national days of fasting and humiliation' were proclaimed during the nineteenth century, such as for deliverance from cholera in 1832, these were optional.[76] They served primarily as an opportunity for political exhortation, whereas the nationally observed Lenten fast had constituted a serious extended time of collective self-denial.

Tudor monarchs had had often viewed demands for non-seasonal public fasts with suspicion.[77] Fasting which broke with the seasonal order drew attention to a possible collapse of public order which could be viewed as a state of emergency. An example is the optional public fasts called during the Victorian era, such as in 1857 for the Sepoys' Revolt, termed more popularly the Indian Mutiny. These were also disliked by political radicals, who regarded them as superstitious, and by religious dissenters of various shades, who saw them as unwarranted government interference in religion.[78] Additional, excessive or transgressive fasting could exercise disruptive power in situations such as these, where an existing set of social relationships was reinforced by shared or prescribed patterns of dietary practice.

The power of ascetic resistance

In classical antiquity, fasting was also seen as disruptive by virtue of being prophetic.[79] Christian fasting has, in certain contexts, also functioned prophetically, as recognized by Michel Foucault. He acknowledges that in emerging Christian monasticism, dietary regulation was not motivated by primarily sexual concerns, recognizing that its purpose was the discipline and empowerment of the whole body. In fact, he suggests, an increasing preoccupation with sex came to displace this holistic vision only much later in *secular* social ethics.[80] Foucault's picture of Christian dietary asceticism is closer to his better-known view of *classical* austerity – a practice of personal empowerment which both unifies the self and contributes to shaping the wider social world,[81] as suggested by the translation of 'ascesis' as athletic training or exercise. Moreover, Foucault considers how, in the later medieval period, asceticism functioned as a lay style of spirituality in opposition to the burgeoning pastoral power structures of the church. He classifies asceticism as the first element of 'anti-pastoral' conduct or 'pastoral counter-conduct'. Asceticism comprises, in Foucault's words, an 'exercise of self on self; it is a sort of close combat of the individual with himself in which the authority, presence, and gaze of someone else is, if not impossible, at least unnecessary'.[82] The effects of the superfluity of external regulation to the ascetic are intensified by the reflective nature of the ascetic project, in which the internal suffering of the self becomes the central focus of an individual's spirituality via immediate and direct experience. The competitive challenge to other ascetics which feats of dietary abstinence presented are in tension, moreover, with the unifying dynamic of hierarchical pastoral authority. Finally, in the state of *apatheia* which the ascetic attains, her body is directly identified with the body of Christ, thus sidelining classic institutional systems of mediation such as the ordained priesthood and the Eucharist.

Asceticism is thus characterized by a 'specific excess that denies access to an external power'. Foucault states

> Insofar as the pastorate characterizes its structures of power, Christianity is fundamentally anti-ascetic, and asceticism is rather a sort of tactical element of reversal by which certain themes of Christian theology or religious experience are utilized against those structures of power.[83]

Particularly interesting in this context is the use of fasting by Christian individuals or groups to stake specific political claims. This tradition is prominent in Ireland, extending from Saint Patrick to the 1980s hunger strikes in the Maze Prison in Belfast, in which ten paramilitary prisoners died.[84] In Irish history, fasting has been recognized as a means of 'distraint' by which one person may exact a claim from another of greater status and power, such as a debt from an employer or landlord. The plaintiff might, for instance, fast every day outside the house of the person against whom he wished to make the claim until it was settled. In previous ages, this procedure had a quasi-legal status and would also have provided a means of exerting strong moral and social pressure on powerful people to fulfil their social and political responsibilities.[85] Fasting was seen as having quasi-mystical power, such that it was a 'procedure in some way dangerous to resist'.[86]

The pre-Christian origins of this practice are clear.[87] It nevertheless became a central strand in the prophetic witness of Irish saints such that in the late twentieth century it could be viewed as a distinctively native and Catholic symbolic act. Many centuries earlier, holy men undertook fasting missions in order to achieve political ends such as the release of prisoners.[88] In the *Life of Saint Patrick*, however, the practice assumes a new dimension reminiscent of Jacob grappling with God at Peniel.[89] Patrick fasts not against a human opponent but against God. In the story, Patrick ascends Cruachan Aigle and is met by an angel, who informs him that God will not answer his demands because they are excessive, obstinate and numerous. Patrick refuses to leave the rock until either he is dead or all his requests have been granted. After forty days the mountain is filled with black birds tormenting Patrick, but then white birds replace them. The angel informs him that God will grant a whole series of requests, ranging from the release of twelve prisoners from the torments of Hell to the permanent expulsion of the Saxons from Ireland.[90] In the words of Fred Robinson, 'what appears to the modern Christian as a form of sacrifice and humiliation may once have been, in some of its aspects, a way of taking the kingdom of heaven as it were by violence'.[91]

Recent scholarship shows how Foucault's motif of 'tactical reversal' also explains the fasting practices of women at various points in Christian history, and why in the later medieval period so many extreme ascetics were women. These issues have puzzled scholars. As Veronika Grimm states in relation to late antique texts on women's fasting: 'Modern commentators are still at a loss in trying to explain ... Christian propaganda that so violently rejected the healthy human body with its basic biological needs.'[92] Several explanations have been advanced. Fasting discourses were, it has been argued, employed by celibate male clerics like Jerome as a spiritual means of exercising physical control over women's bodies. Grimm shows how the female body was seen as vulnerable to invasion by alien and unclean objects, and how in fasting discourses foods were frequently portrayed as precisely such objects.[93] She suggests that Jerome projected his sexual anxieties onto women, portraying them as sensuous, lewd, corrupt, drunk and deceitful, and that as a result he advocated more rigorous ascetic standards for women than for men.[94]

So was women's fasting an external imposition designed to maintain their inferior position in the natural and social orders? Certainly the majority of Jerome's letters on fasting are addressed to women, and enjoin them to fast as a means of maintaining the health and orderliness of their female bodies, which are by implication dangerous or endangered. Within these letters, advice not to eat meat is often implied as part of a general dietary abstinence, but occasionally it is explicit, as in Jerome's letter to the widow Furia.[95] Meat is not singled out for special censure, however; vegetables can be just as dangerous in inflaming passions and heating the body because of the flatulence they induce, so even they must therefore be eaten sparingly. Jerome cites Galen in his support, appealing to his theory of the balancing of hot and cold humours in the body. Jerome asserts that the bodies of boys, young men, fully-grown men and women glow with an interior heat and consequently that for persons of these ages all food is injurious which tends to promote this heat: while on the other hand it is highly conducive to health in eating and in drinking to take things cold and cooling.[96]

Galen would not, however, have accepted Jerome's premise that so many types of people suffer from a natural heat which needs to be subdued. Indeed, Galen suggests that, in adolescents, fasting and hunger produce yellow bile which increases sexual drive.[97] The premise is essential to Jerome in his use of Galen's theory, however, because it enables him to promote, contra Galen, a rigorous fasting regime for various categories of people, including women. Jerome also appeals to Paul's general advice given in Romans 14.21 not to eat meat or drink wine. By omitting the condition 'if it will cause your brother to fall', he turns a contingent principle applying to particular social circumstances into a norm of conduct, especially for women.

Teresa Shaw has also explored how, in late antiquity, fasting was regarded by many of its male proponents as an activity particularly suited to women, who were encouraged to fast more frequently or more rigorously than men. Women are possibly able to sustain severer fasting than men owing to the greater tendency of their bodies to make use of fat rather than lean tissue to compensate for lack of food.[98] Indeed, John Chrysostom argues that fasting can accentuate female beauty.[99] Yet prolonged fasting could in practice frequently result in women losing their physical female characteristics, shrivelling their breasts, growing body hair, ending menstrual periods and bringing infertility. The female fasting virgin, whether living with her family or in a religious community, became the ideal role model for widows and even married women. She was represented as the bride of Christ, with her sexual desires sublimated into a spiritual eroticism entirely shorn of any element of physical experience or expression.[100] This subjugated body, deemed worthy of praise partly because it appeared unattractive to men, is sometimes presented as cold, sculpted and stony, and sometimes as becoming masculine.

In the later middle ages, women's fasting was shaped by a different nexus of symbolic, biological and political factors. Evaluating contemporary accounts of fasting women, Caroline Walker Bynum argues that their dietary discipline was not simply a revival of the attitudes of anchorites but connected with the adoration of the flesh of Christ in the Eucharist.[101] Key to Bynum's position is her contention that food functioned, in later medieval times, as a 'basic image' for women but not for men. This is reflected, she persuasively argues, both in accounts of women's Eucharistic devotion and by the greater centrality of descriptions of fasting in hagiographies of women than in hagiographies of men. Through fasting, women entered into the bodily sufferings of Christ on the cross, with their suffering flesh assimilated to his suffering flesh. Food thereby became, in social terms, a resource which a woman could use to exert control over both herself and her world, releasing her family from the obligation of paying a dowry and avoiding teenage marriage to an older man, domestic drudgery and possible death in childbirth. Bynum argues that women's fasting practices frequently enabled them to determine the shape of their lives – to reject unwanted marriages, to substitute religious activities for more menial duties within the family, to redirect the use of fathers' or husbands' resources, to change or convert family members, to criticize powerful secular or religious authorities, and to claim for themselves teaching, counselling, and reforming roles for which the religious tradition provided, at best, ambivalent support.[102]

According to Bynum, women in the later medieval period used fasting to subvert the social and theological roles assigned to them, forging a new charismatic identity by refusing to align themselves with standard configurations of food and gender, and the material dependence on fathers, husbands and clergy which these entailed. This reaction against the moderation urged by church leaders amounted, Bynum concludes, to a rejection of an 'institution that made a tidy, moderate, decent, second-rate place for women and for the laity'.[103]

Veronika Grimm demonstrates the importance of understanding particular fasting practices in their social and theological contexts. She also calls into question the reading of extreme asceticism either as the simple 'subjugation' of dangerous bodies by external forces, or as the claiming by women of political and social power which they would otherwise have been denied. After all, the heroine's exceptional virtuoso abstinence needs to be seen in the context of conformity by most women to patterns of feasting and fasting. The virtuoso ascetic relied on a context of thought and practice within which diet was not a matter of indifference.

In concluding this chapter, let us recapitulate our key findings so far. Rigorous and clearly defined dietary abstinence, especially from red meat, has been a key Christian discipline from a very early stage in the forging of Christian identity. Such abstinence has been inspired by a rich stream of biblical narrative, in which foods and abstinence from particular foods feature prominently. The examples of particular holy persons and accounts of their lives became another important means by which dietary practices were distilled and transmitted. In the monastic communities which arose around various of these inspiring spiritual leaders, such practices were moderated but also consolidated, spreading well beyond the monastery walls to encompass wider Christian society and placing significant demands on lay Christians. Good eating was sometimes seen as in accordance with nature, as in the vision of Piers the Plowman, and elsewhere as requiring intervention to remedy its deficiencies, as by Albertus Magnus in his presentation of humoural theory. Yet the developments which occurred during the first millennium established a distinctive Christian dietary discipline, the key requirements of which were abstention from red meat and general moderation.

3   Secularizing diet

The process by which dietary discipline ceased to be a primary means of expressing Christian identity was long and complex. This progressive estrangement of diet from faith was due partly to specific identifiable shifts in the character of religious life and its regulation. More significant, however, was an instability latent in the rules for monastic living as they developed in the early Christian centuries. As has been seen, a key aim of these rules was to moderate excessive ascetic feats, which harmed the body and disrupted community life, rather than to promote higher degrees of asceticism or even to preserve an existing degree of asceticism. Nevertheless, their effects were markedly different in medieval Western societies, in which extreme asceticism was less highly respected. Moreover, as will be seen in this chapter, from the early thirteenth century a revised model of Christian dietary discipline was provided by the Franciscans and Dominicans. This marked in some respects a return to the simplicity and poverty of diet of the anchorites. It nevertheless also amounted to a relaxation of monastic discipline, which had originally been predicated on a stable and ordered dietary regime. For the first Franciscans and Dominicans, living among secular society and begging for alms as mendicants, a degree of dietary flexibility was essential.

Christian dietary discipline has so far been regarded principally in light of scripture and ascetic traditions. By the fourth century, however, a new project was gaining momentum: the definition of Christian doctrinal orthodoxy and the preservation and transmission of that orthodoxy. Patterns of Christian dietary discipline had previously been established by the fairly straightforward appropriations by Christians of models of dietary discipline drawn from scripture and other spiritual traditions with which they had contact. The increasingly prominent doctrinal context meant, however, that diet gradually became an important means by which communities and individuals with an increasingly clear and distinct sense of their Christian identity distinguished themselves from other groups and individuals of other religions.

This chapter will begin by returning to the Benedictine Rule and considering why the decline in abstention from red meat in monasteries occurred. We shall then examine the impact made by the new mendicant orders of the thirteenth century by focusing on Francis of Assisi, and finally consider the developing doctrinal and philosophical implications of these practices.

Spaces, times and bodies in Benedict's Rule

Benedict of Nursia had first-hand experience of the rigours of an ascetic life. In his cave at Subiaco, which he inhabited for three years, his food consisted of bread lowered on a rope by the monk Romanus, which was taken from his own portion. A bell was tied to the end of the rope to alert Benedict to the descent of his meagre fare.[1]

Despite his inaccessibility, Benedict received a request from a small community of monks to become their spiritual father, which he accepted, and this provided his introduction to communal monastic life. Benedict intended his Rule to be for just such small communities of about twelve people, emulating the people who gathered around Christ as apostles.[2] Although the communities which developed around some of the anchorites are alleged to have comprised hundreds or even thousands of members, the model that Benedict established during his own lifetime was a network of far smaller communities. Each existed independently under a superior but with a common rule of life and spiritual oversight from Benedict. This model of authority distributed in small local communities made local interpretation of the Rule necessary from the beginning. This emerged from complex interactions between theological reflection, the form and location of the monastic communities, and their changing relationships to wider theological and cultural contexts.

The physical configuration of monastic communities impacted on dietary practice. In the original, small communities, the number of rooms available for different activities was limited. All meals were taken in the refectory, as assumed in the Rule. Even while away from the monastery for the day on business, a brother was prohibited from eating without the abbot's permission.[3] Strict asceticism was maintained in these early communities, spreading at a very early date into Celtic monasteries where the principal fare consisted of bread and herbs seasoned with salt.[4] The larger monasteries developing by the tenth century were, by contrast, far larger and more complex institutions. The refectory remained the principal location for the main meal of the day, and in this large hall the dining practices of the original Rule were generally observed.

During the thirteenth century a second room known as the 'misericord' was added, however, in which meat could be eaten.[5] This term suggests the granting of mercy and compassion, and such rooms were therefore probably first created to cater for sick or aged monks unable to observe normal dietary standards. This relaxation of the normal rule was justified on the grounds that the prohibition of quadruped flesh applied only to meals taken in the refectory. But once this point had been conceded, it was only a matter of time before the misericord became more extensively used. On days that were not fasts, a rota was drawn up detailing which community members would dine in the refectory and which in the misericord. The aim of this rota was to ensure that a sufficiently high proportion of people were present for each meal in the refectory, usually one half or two thirds.[6] The issue of whether this proportion was taken from the total population of the house or from the total number of diners at an individual meal was a source of further relaxation and attempted regulation.

The misericord enabled many members of the community to eat irregular food on numerous days each year, but did not provide a space large enough to accommodate everybody on occasions when the meal itself was irregular. The most obvious example was the evening supper, taken during the cold winter months despite the fact that the rule made provision for such a meal only during Eastertide.[7] As a result, at Westminster Abbey during the fourteenth century a third dining room was brought into use and another rota established to determine which community members should dine there and which in the misericord. This room, known as the 'cawagium' (literally a stall), was simply a partitioned section of the refectory.[8] The construction of such a space would have left no significant mark on the fabric of the building, so it can reasonably be supposed that a third space was created in some other monasteries, even if not by exactly this method. That the designation of a third room for dining was deemed necessary shows the continuing importance of Benedict's Rule, and the significance of the spatial location of dining practices. These different dining rooms were not simply spaces in which food was eaten, but locations for obedient and regulated communal consumption, even if this strained interpretation of the rule to its limits.

Distinctions also developed between meaty dishes (*carnea*) and flesh-meat (*carnes*).[9] The former encompassed muscle tissue, offal and entrails, meaning that fritters – the inglorious forerunners of modern fast-food hamburgers – and other dishes made with these inferior types of meat could be eaten. The consumption of *carnea* in the refectory came to be regarded as permissible, provided they did not include any actual flesh-meat. The status of bacon was also raised, with Gerald of Wales complaining that some monks enjoyed it yet claimed to abstain from flesh-meat.[10] *Carnes*, in contrast, could only be consumed in the misericord or cawagium.

As early as 1082, the new Norman prior of Winchester discouraged his community from eating flesh by providing exquisitely prepared fish dishes.[11] Many different varieties of fish were available, as listed in the manuals of sign language used to communicate during meals, which normally had to be taken in silence. At Bury in the mid fourteenth century, the menu might have included herring, salmon, eels, lamprey, sturgeon and trout.[12] At Ely around 1500, there were no signs for red meat or poultry, whereas those for fish included lamprey, salmon, pike, trout, cuttlefish, and obviously eels.[13] Similar items were available at Fleury, with the addition of mullet, and in the late eleventh century at Cluny.[14] Interestingly, none of these lists includes shellfish, which were considered an insubstantial food fit only for the poor.[15]

Shifts in monastic diet cannot, however, be explained solely by changes in the physical shape and location of the communities. Local abbatial authority was enshrined in Benedict's Rule, and this was a further key factor that changed dietary practices. The relationship which enabled the ascetic practices of the desert to develop and be disseminated, continued by Benedict, was that of teacher and disciple. The didactic model in which the formation of new ascetics occurred was one in which the spiritual father, or abba, commanded absolute authority and respect, and demanded the unquestioning immediate obedience of his disciple. The disciple's will could thereby be subjected entirely to spiritual concerns.

The authority of the abba in the deserts of Egypt and Palestine was transposed into monastic rules and assigned to the abbot or other local superior. The extensive discretion fundamental to abbatial authority is suggested by the simple meaning of the Aramaic term 'abba' as 'father', and well expressed in the words of Jesus in Gethsemane: 'Abba, Father ... not my will but yours be done.'[16] Although the abbot's various roles were stated in Benedict's Rule, the specific ways in which he might exercise authority were not defined exhaustively. Moreover, the abbot was frequently exempt from the Rule as it applied to all other members of the community.

This is particularly evident in the case of hospitality. Guests were held in the highest honour, and responsibility for hosting them lay, therefore, with the abbot. The guest was considered to represent Christ, whose words to his disciples are cited in the Rule: 'I was a stranger and you took me in.'[17] John Cassian also likens the guest to Christ when describing the guest as the bridegroom to whom the community is espoused.[18] Benedict states the practical implications of this theology clearly: 'The superior shall break his fast for the sake of a guest, unless it be a special fast day which may not be violated; but the brethren shall observe the customary fasts.'[19] This chapter of the Rule also directs that a separate kitchen be provided for the abbot and guests so that the guests do not disturb the brethren. Basil of Caesarea even took his guests hunting.[20]

Cassian had experienced being welcomed as Christ during his grand tour of Egypt and Palestine undertaken to gather information about methods of community organization. His *Institutes* therefore offer a guest's perspective on monastic practice. In the following story, Cassian shows how the arrival of his own group as guests unsettled the normal practice of one community. He recalls:

> When we had come from the region of Syria and had sought the province of Egypt, in our desire to learn the rules of the Elders, we were astonished at the alacrity of heart with which we were there received so that no rule forbidding refreshment till the appointed hour of the fast was over was abolished, such as we had been brought up to observe in the monasteries of Palestine; but except in the case of the regular days, Wednesdays and Fridays, wherever we went the fast was broken: and when we asked why the daily fast was thus ignored by them without scruple one of the elders replied: 'The opportunity for fasting is always with me. But as I am going to conduct you on your way, I cannot always keep you with me. And a fast, although it is useful and advisable, is yet a free-will offering. But the exigencies of a command require the fulfilment of a work of charity. And so receiving Christ in you I ought to refresh Him but when I have sent you on your way I shall be able to balance the hospitality offered for His sake

by a stricter fast on my own account. For "the children of the bridegroom cannot fast while the bridegroom is with them": but when he has departed, then they will rightly fast.'[21]

Several aspects of this episode are noteworthy. When the travellers arrive at a monastery early in the day, before the normal hour for dining, food is eaten regardless. The two exceptions to this practice are Wednesdays and Fridays, which both mark events in the passion of Christ and so involve encounters with Christ in a different register. The fast's full duration is made up later, however – a practice justified with the biblical verse alluded to in the final phrase that would later be used in support of the Pentecost fast and its associated ember days, as discussed in Chapter Two.[22] Above all, however, the destabilization of normal custom that the guest causes is Christologically grounded and not merely lax practice.

Receiving guests was a major part of monastic life and is presented in Benedict's Rule as an obligation.[23] The presence of guests obviously impacted on food practices within the community, despite the attempts previously noted to limit disruption, and was recognized in rules and customaries. Even the austere Carthusian Rule of 1127–28 permitted the prior to suspend the charterhouse's fast if a bishop, abbot, or member of another religious order arrived. These guests were to be received at the prior's own table, whereas no others were to be received by the community at all.[24] It seems, however, that it was often precisely high-status guests who caused most disruption to the monastery's ordinary dietary patterns. This problem became sufficiently important to receive the attention of an ecumenical council. By the time of the Council of Vienne, convened in 1312, powerful visitors to Cistercian abbeys – which also possessed strict dietary regimes – appear to have been exploiting their privileged status. The Council recorded:

> We have heard with sorrow that prelates visiting the monasteries of the Cistercian order, although charitably received and courteously served with all that is needful, are nevertheless not content with the food prescribed by the monastic rule. Contrary to the privileges of the said order they demand meat [*carnes*], and if it is not served to them, they obtain it by force.[25]

The canon proceeds to accommodate these insistent demands by ordering that, in future, bishops wishing to be served meat be relocated away from the formal monastic area. It states that they

> may if they wish be served with meat [*carnium*], on days when it is permitted, in the houses of the monasteries if these are available, but outside the monastic precincts, notwithstanding any privilege to the contrary; if the houses are not available, they may be served within the monastic precincts but not inside the religious door, as it is called.

The welcome of guests seems, therefore, to have been another factor contributing to the progressive relaxation of dietary discipline and tolerance of meat eating.[26]

The abbot's role as provider of hospitality extended not only to guests visiting the monastery from other places, but also to members of his own community. Benedict states: 'Let the abbot always eat with the guests and pilgrims. But when there are no guests, let him have the power to invite whom he will of the brethren. Yet, for discipline's sake, let one or two seniors always be left with the brethren.'[27] In the small communities envisaged by Benedict this practice probably had little impact on diet, but in the larger monasteries that later developed, the abbot acquired his own accommodation and independent household. David Knowles emphasizes the importance and extensive usage of this entitlement, describing how abbots would send food, including meat, from their own table to other parts of the monastery for consumption.[28]

Care of sick monks was enjoined on the abbot and entire community, with a separate room and attendant assigned. This room became the infirmary of the larger later medieval monasteries, in which special dietary rules applied. The Rule stated: 'Let the use of fleshmeat be granted to the sick who are very weak, for the restoration of their strength; but, as soon as they are better, let all abstain from fleshmeat as usual.'[29] This chapter places special responsibility on the abbot for ensuring that the needs of sick community members are met, and the exemptions from normal dietary discipline granted to the sick are presented as part of his general authority to vary discipline – a feature of his role especially clear in the Rule of Saint Augustine.[30] In some houses, the infirmarian asked permission for exemptions on behalf of individual patients, and not even all sick persons ate meat.[31] It seems likely that the development of the misericord was a product of this practice of permitting sick persons an irregular diet, with the category of sickness gradually expanded beyond that of serious illness. As part of attempts to prevent abuses, refectory attendance could be monitored to ensure that monks who were not ill did not take meals in the misericord.[32] This was no innovation: from the eighth century, refectory attendance during Lent had been enforced in secular religious orders, whose members shared a common life but ministered in the community and did not always inhabit the same building.[33]

There is at least one example of the infirmary diet being regulated far more tightly. The Rule of the Templars, a non-monastic religious order, prohibited particular foods there – lentils, shelled broad beans, goat, mutton, veal, eels and cheese – as well as banning meat eating on Fridays and urging careful restrictions on the use of exceptions.[34] This, interestingly, was in a context where meat eating was permitted in the refectory on Sundays, Tuesdays and Thursdays, as well as at Christmas, All Saints, the Assumption, and apostles' feasts.[35] Despite this less stringent practice, the compiler of the Rule was evidently anxious to limit opportunities for abuse, which might have become a serious problem in this privileged order of military knights.

In these rules governing the infirmary, meat eating is understood as a sign of weakness. The people regarded as possessors of strength, both spiritual and physical, have no need of foods that impart strength. This is a different logic from that assumed through much of the modern period, when meat has been seen as representing strength and as a necessary foodstuff for people regarded as strong – typically, adult men engaged in manual labour. Benedict might have drawn on a previous iteration of this modern idea of eating founded on the principle of resemblance. In a homily on Numbers, Origen alludes to Paul's reference in Romans 14.2 to two people, one whose faith allows him to eat anything and another who is weak and so eats only vegetables, asserting:

> One person who is quite healthy and has a strong bodily constitution needs strong food and has the conviction and confidence he can eat everything, like the strongest of athletes. But if someone perceives he is weaker and feeble, he is pleased with vegetables and does not accept strong food because of the weakness of his body. And if someone is a child, although he cannot put what he wants into words, still he seeks no other nourishment than that of milk … Every rational nature needs to be nourished by foods of its own and suitable for it.[36]

Benedict, by contrast, assumes a dialectical conception of the relation between food and the body – that the weakened body requires stronger food in order to restore it to a state of equilibrium.

So far as children and the elderly are concerned, Benedict stipulates that 'on no account let the rigour of the Rule in regard to food be applied to them'.[37] He also allows young and elderly persons to take meals before the regular hours. Such a concession would have been most important during Lent, when fasting was prescribed until evening, with the daily meal thus scheduled about three hours later than the regular mid-afternoon meal 'at the ninth hour'.[38] These exemptions were made possible, at least in part, by gifts of food or of property or rights that would supply an income to provide additional food.[39]

The position of the abbot, particularly in his roles of host and provider for the sick, was therefore important in gradually changing dining expectations and practices. Also important, however, was the relationship of the monasteries to the calendar of feasts discussed in Chapter Two. Gregory the Great describes how Benedict, while living in his cave at Subiaco, was brought food on Easter Sunday by a priest living some distance away. Owing to his long separation from church and society, Benedict was unaware that it was Easter. The priest ventured to suggest to Benedict that he should not be fasting because it was the feast of the resurrection, and Benedict invited him to remain with him while they shared food and conversation.[40] Yet this change of menu is not reflected in Benedict's Rule. He made no provision for different foods to be eaten during celebratory periods in the church year. Even during Eastertide, the pre-eminent festal season, his sole concession was to move lunch forward to midday and allow supper in the evening. Indeed, Benedict stipulated that 'the life of a monk ought at all times to be Lenten in its character'.[41] But the medieval multiplication of feasts and commemorations fundamentally altered the simple and fairly uniform seasonal cycle that he had envisaged.[42] In particular, although the earlier medieval dietary calendar could be regarded as a product of the natural seasonal cycle and the realities of provision which it imposed, the dating of saints' days rarely had any seasonal foundation. They were more likely to be connected with specific historic events such as the translation of relics.

In order to endow the many feast days that occurred through the year, communities received gifts from lay people to supplement normal provision. These days included all the familiar major feasts, as well as many saints' days, Sundays and obits commemorating abbots and sometimes other past officers of the monastery.[43] This gift economy expanded, fuelled by popular piety and the penitential system, with particular gifts sometimes assigned to specific groups of people within the monastery such as children or the elderly. The additional dishes provided were known as 'pittances', and served either singly or shared by two people. The Carthusian Rule limited these to cheese, fish or eggs, and stated in addition that only one could be eaten at any meal.[44] Other orders, in contrast, permitted a far greater range and quantity of additional food. Even in Cistercian houses, pittances were so frequent and widespread that they became a normal part of provision indistinguishable from the basic fare.[45] This pattern of gift giving is an example of the permeability of the monastery's walls: although monastic practices shaped secular fasting and feasting, the monks' own food practices were shaped by what they received from wider society.

Regulating and critiquing monastic feasting

How were these shifts in monastic diet viewed by outsiders? Meat eating in monasteries was more common in Saxon England than on the continent, where somewhat stricter discipline was maintained. Following the Norman conquest of England, Norman abbots reimposed the more rigorous standards required by Benedict's Rule, and these seem to have been maintained until the early thirteenth century.[46] A large number of episcopal visitations to monasteries were conducted during the 1250s and 1260s to enquire into the reported breaking of fasts and eating of flesh. These visitations confirm that, by this time, considerable concern had developed about irregular dietary discipline. Notably, far fewer women's houses were found to be at fault than men's houses, in proportion with the numbers of each that were visited.[47]

Attempts to impose more stringent discipline continued to fail. In England, the 1336 constitution of Pope Benedict XII, *Summa Magistri*, accepted many of the lower standards that had become widespread, correcting only the worst abuses. Benedict had been a Cistercian abbot before becoming pope and was noted for his personal austerity and reforming zeal.[48] Many people resisted the tighter discipline he imposed, however, with the result that he was subject to visceral criticism, including for his own obesity.[49] This was unfair, not least because Benedict in fact accepted much of the relaxation that had become common. For example, Chapter 26 of his constitution permitted meat eating outside the refectory on Sundays, Mondays, Tuesdays and Thursdays. One half of the whole community had to be present in the refectory on these days, however, and meat eating was entirely prohibited during Advent and from Septuagesima until Easter.[50] These regulations need to be seen in the wider context of Benedict's attempt to place monasteries that had become virtually autonomous under the control of provincial chapters. Yet the strictness of the new regulations was resented by many communities, with abbatial discretion employed to bring their requirements into closer conformity with local custom.[51]

A similar dynamic of the reform of abuses accompanied by acceptance of many of the less rigorous practices, which had become widespread, is identifiable among the Premonstratensians. Unlike monks, these canons often worked in parishes and were therefore more closely integrated into wider society. Nevertheless, the order had been founded by Norbert of Xanten on a strictly ascetic basis which had included a perpetual ban on meat consumption. By the late sixteenth century this was being so widely ignored, through both formal dispensations and simple rule-breaking, that a reform led by Servais of Lairuelz re-established meat abstention, though only during Advent and Lent and on the ember days, Wednesdays, Fridays and Saturdays, as well as the eves of certain feasts.[52] This led to stricter practice in many houses, but the overall result was official endorsement of a far lower level of dietary discipline.

In medieval England, periodic attempts were made to limit the dining of the wider populace. These began in 1336, when the size of meals was restricted to two courses, or three on festivals. This was followed in 1363 by a regulation limiting grooms and servants to one dish of meat or fish per day.[53] In Reformation England, a collective attempt was made by the archbishops, bishops, deans and archdeacons to moderate the extravagance of their dining. Archbishops would not exceed six meat or fish dishes in a single sitting, bishops five, and deans and archdeacons four. These dishes would all have been placed on the table at once, this being the standard practice before the nineteenth century, when dishes began being served individually in a series of courses. Of 'second dishes' (desserts), archbishops might have four, bishops three, and deans and archdeacons two. The regulations for higher-class fish and game were particularly detailed, stating that

> of the greater fishes or fowls there should be but one in a dish, as crane, swan, turkeycock, haddock, pike, tench; and of less sorts but two, viz. capons two, pheasants two, conies two, woodcocks two: of less sorts, as of partridges, the archbishop three, the bishop, and other degrees under him, two; of blackbirds, the archbishop six, the bishop four, the other degrees three; of larks and snytes, and of that sort, but twelve.[54]

The constitution continued that 'whatsoever is spared by the cutting off the old superfluity, should yet be provided and spent in plain meats for the relieving of the poor'. Appended to the minute, however, is a note 'that this order was kept for two or three months, till, by the disusing of certain wilful persons, it came to the old excess'.

Criticisms of lax monastic dining feature prominently in other medieval texts. The clergyman and chronicler Gerald of Wales describes the lavish proceedings when dining with the monks of Christ Church, Canterbury in their refectory as follows:

sixteen very costly dishes or even more were placed upon the table in order, not to say contrary to all order. Finally, potherbs [vegetables] were brought to every table but were little tasted. For you might see so many kinds of fish, roast and boiled, stuffed and fried, so many dishes contrived with eggs and pepper by dexterous cooks, so many flavourings and condiments, compounded with like dexterity to tickle gluttony and awaken appetite.[55]

This critique addresses several points: the expense of the food provided, the number of dishes, the complexity of the recipes used, and the suggestion that they were designed to stimulate sinful lusts. Gerald then recounts an amusing story of the monks of Winchester, who along with their Prior

prostrated themselves in the mud before Henry II, and complained to him with tears and lamentations that Bishop Richard whom they had as their head in lieu of an Abbot, had deprived them of three dishes. And when the King inquired how many dishes were left them, they replied 'ten'. 'And I,' said the King, 'am content in my court with three. Perish your Bishop, if he does not reduce your dishes to the number of mine!'[56]

The polemical nature of the traveller's tales of a Celtic apologist in Plantagenet England of course needs to be taken into account when judging the likely truth of claims made. But it is at the very least clear that eating practices were being used to critique the spiritual and moral standards of monasteries, and that readers would understand and appreciate such a critique.

Similar themes appear in *Piers Plowman*. The dreamer is invited to dine at the castle within which Learning resides, where the honoured guest is a Master of Divinity who is a friar. Conscience is served by Scripture with 'many different dishes – dishes of Augustine and Ambrose and all the four Evangelists'. The friar, however, eats 'costlier foods, special puréees and ragouts', a choice attributed to his comfortable life funded by bequests from wealthy patrons. Hence his sauce tastes 'too tart' because it is 'pounded into an acrid mess in a mortar called *Post-mortem*'.[57] In other words, suggests Langland, the friar is dining off the wealth of the dead, paid to him in order that they might be saved from their sins. In fact, Langland implies, it is the friar himself who will taste torments after death, represented by the vomiting up of the torrents of food that he currently devours. Thus gluttony prefigures death, and is a commerce with death in which death is savoured in current earthly life. The dreamer recollects that the friar 'gobbled up countless different dishes – minced meat and puddings, tripes and galantine and eggs fried in butter', and wishes that the 'dishes and platters surrounding this great Doctor were molten lead in his guts' in order that he might experience the self-mortification about which he was preaching just four days previously before the Dean of St Paul's.[58]

In *The Canterbury Tales*, the figure of the monk is introduced memorably by his favourite meal: 'A fat swan loved he best of any rost.' The reader is told with mock sincerity how the monk governs his small community in a spirit of wisdom and sensitivity to changing times:

> Ther as this lord was keeper of the celle,
> The rule of Saint Maure or of Saint Beneit,
> By cause that it was old and somedeel strait –
> This ilke Monk let olde thinges pace
> And held after the newe world the space.[59]

The friar following behind is presented as 'an esy man to yive penaunce, there as he wist to have a good pitaunce'.[60] Exploitation of the pittance system by clergy is again alleged, with Chaucer suggesting that they allowed an easy confession when it was made worth their while. In the late-fourteenth century context of recurring famine, Chaucer's use of food imagery for the purposes of religious satire here and at many other points in his epic narrative is especially pointed.[61]

These critiques of clerical dining show that many late-medieval monasteries and friaries had little in common with the ascetic desert communities from which they originated. From an ascetic perspective, feasting was ambiguous, and when enjoyed to excess provided foundations for the wider late-medieval critique of monastic and clerical discipline that formed one part of the background to Protestant Reformations. Yet Bonnie Effros, in her study of much earlier Merovingian Gaul, points out that, even then, feasting rites had 'long represented one of the major components of gift exchange and thus fictive kinship', affirming that earlier medieval feasting was not evidence of laxity but a sign of divine generosity.[62] Moreover, as has been seen in this chapter, the giving of pittances provided a means by which laypeople could associate themselves with religious life through actively supporting that life. This prefigured a new development in that life, to which we shall now turn.

Mendicant flexibility

The preceding discussion suggests that, by 1500, the diet of many monastic houses had come to mirror that of upper-class laypeople. This impression is confirmed by detailed analyses of the large quantity and high quality of foods consumed.[63] In the meantime, however, another form of religious rule had taken root in Italy and France and spread through surrounding countries. The Franciscan and Dominican orders, named after their founders Francis of Assisi and Dominic, embodied a new type of religious rule. Benedict's Rule had been based around a principle of stability, with a key requirement being that members of the community remain living in one place rather than move between different communities. Francis and Dominic envisioned a far more fluid community which situated its members fully within ordinary society. Friars depended for alms on the people around them. This dependence extended to food, with friars relying for their subsistence on the hospitality of others and on gifts of food.

Temperamentally, Francis of Assisi emulated the itinerant monks whose unpredictable and often extreme behaviour Benedict had tried in his Rule to curb. Some smaller mendicant orders which grew up around this time, such as the Hermits of Saint Augustine and of Fonte Avellana, the Camaldolese and the Vallumbrosans, had sought to return to the dietary disciplines of these early Christian ascetics by modifying the Rule of Benedict to bring it into closer explicit conformity with this more rigorous discipline.[64] Yet in calling his followers to live within secular society and serve its members, Francis established a much closer relation between religious and secular life which itself had a moderating effect on dietary habits. Francis' food practices were also more explicitly related to the example of Jesus Christ than were those of Benedict, being developed during a period of increasing interest in Christ's historical life. When a guest in another's home, Francis followed Christ's example of being willing to eat foods from which he might otherwise have abstained. When welcomed into the house of a Christian in Lombardy, for example, Francis accepted his host's invitation to 'eat of everything set before him, in observance of the holy gospel', including capon (chicken) on toast.[65] He observed Jesus' instruction to his disciples in Luke's Gospel that 'when you enter a town and its people welcome you, eat what is set before you'.[66] This joyful acceptance of hospitality was a key part of Francis' imitation of the life of Christ, emulating the many instances in the gospels when Jesus was criticized, especially in the Gospel of the tax collector Matthew, for the meals he ate and the company he kept.[67]

Accounts of what happened during the meal in Lombardy suggest that, even during his lifetime, people did not expect Francis to eat meat. While the group was eating, a man presented himself at the door pretending to be a beggar, and Francis gave him a piece of the chicken. The following day, the impostor appeared at Francis' open-air sermon and sought to disrupt it by producing the gift in front of the crowd in order to cast doubt on the saint's holiness. Francis' eating of chicken would have contradicted the people's expectations on two counts. Members of the traditional religious orders were, as previously discussed, expected to abstain from meat. In contrast, the more relaxed practices of the new mendicant orders would have seemed undisciplined.[68] Moreover, Francis was well known for his kinship with animals, displayed in events like his sermons to birds, freeing animals caught in traps, healing an ox's leg and releasing fish from nets.[69] The Lombardian impostor's ploy backfired, however, when the chicken appeared to the crowd miraculously not as chicken but as fish. Instead of undermining Francis, the beggar ended up praising his sanctity. The chicken was later restored, again miraculously, to its real appearance.

The significance of this episode in the context of hagiographical narrative seems to be that, although Francis was not by eating the chicken committing a sin, one of the public signs of his holiness, made possible by divine intervention, was that he appeared to abstain from all meat including chicken. The narrative assumes and affirms this association of asceticism with holiness, while at the same time destabilizing it, because Francis does in fact eat the chicken. According to his contemporaries as well as later interpreters, Francis regarded all foods as acceptable in the sense that any food was, in theory, available for consumption. No potential food source was formally prohibited. This view contrasted sharply with the assumption of his audience that more rigourist dietary discipline should be pursued by a person called to such exalted levels of holiness as was he, with certain foods absolutely excluded. Francis' actual practice lay somewhere between seeing all foods as permitted, and many foods as forbidden, in ways which might initially seem curious. Although flexibility was fundamental to his mission, he did not wish dietary issues to occlude the message he preached. But neither did he want to circumscribe his freedom to accept hospitality or gifts, undertaking all these activities in imitation of the life of Christ. That the attempt to exploit the supposed infraction redounded upon Francis' accuser seems to have been intended by the various Franciscan authors who retell the episode to signal divine approbation of Francis' approach to this particular food dilemma. Part of the reason for the miraculous transformation of the chicken seems to be to shift judgment from accused onto accuser. The transformation also influences the crowd's perception of Francis and the message of his preaching by eliminating a potentially large cause of offence.

A similar concern about the expectations of onlookers is reflected in another account of Francis' response when offered meat as a guest. Julian of Speyer, one of his early followers, states that Francis would 'put his hand to his mouth, appearing to be eating the meat, but rarely tasting even a little bit of it, he would unobtrusively put the rest in his lap'.[70] This suggests that when the friars received hospitality their principal desire was to accept it, but without exploiting the freedom which the status of guest allowed.

The permission for friars to eat and drink whatever food was set before them became enshrined in both Franciscan Rules.[71] The inverse question also arose of how lay guests in Franciscan houses should be treated. At least one account indicates that food of higher quality than usual could be provided for visitors. According to this story, Francis invited the doctor who attended to his eyes to dine, and the doctor, familiar with the brothers' impoverished existence, reluctantly accepted. As the meal commenced, a woman arrived with a present for Francis comprising, among other items, fish and crab cakes, which he gladly received and shared.[72] Here are apparent both Francis' willingness to entertain frugally, and his willingness at times to exceed his normally low level of provision. There existed, however, the danger that occasions of hospitality would provide opportunities for greed by members of the community. To guard against this, Francis established a constitution that brothers should consume no more than three morsels of meat when dining with laypeople.[73]

The disciples of Dominic followed a life of poverty similar to the Franciscans, adopting the Rule of Saint Augustine. They amassed only sufficient food for the day, and accounts describe food being supplied in response to prayer or following other forms of divine intervention.[74] A key feature distinguishing Dominican houses from Benedictine monasteries was the requirement placed formally on the prior – who fulfilled the role of a monastic abbot in governance and discipline – to share the life of the ordinary community members. So far as dining went, he was not permitted to take meals outside the house and was required to render an account of journeys undertaken to the sub-prior, and to the whole convent if a journey was sufficiently important.[75] As with the Franciscans, concerns about the complete banning of meat consumption were apparent during the order's early years, with the 1234 chapter rebuking brothers who preached that it was a serious sin for members of religious orders to eat meat.[76]

Francis and Dominic were mendicants and therefore ministering to a society on which they were dependent for food and other bodily needs, while awaiting the expected consummation of that society by Christ. Their desire to live literally from hand to mouth was testimony to the spiritual hazards of excessive concern about maintaining a reliable food supply. This has been presented in Indian ascetic tradition as a 'downward spiral' of hoarding, cultivation, private land ownership, theft, violence and an aggressive state.[77] *Contra* Bourdieu, luxuries were seen not as providing a taste of freedom but were tastes of necessity from which these ascetics felt driven to liberate themselves.[78] Their flexibility over dietary practice was not, therefore, entirely voluntary at the point of consumption, being an inevitable consequence of larger decisions about the kind of life they wished to share with their followers. More consistent practices were required by the traditional monastic rules, but for Francis and Dominic, flexibility and ambiguity were corollaries of the exigencies of the social situation in which they chose to live. Pursuit of a much higher level of rigor by early Franciscan and Dominican communities would have limited the possibilities for social engagement. This is why Francis and Dominic actively resisted excessive dietary rigourism and sometimes ate meat.

Modern vegetarians might well lament a failure to espouse a more rigourist ethic closer to that of their own practice as well as the earlier Benedictine tradition. As G.K. Chesterton wrote, 'what St Benedict had stored St Francis scattered'.[79] This 'scattering' can be seen in different ways, however, not only as the dilution of a previously clear principle but equally as the incarnation of that principle into social life and its reconnection with the complexities of that life. The Franciscan and Dominican dietary option provides, in its flexibility, an alternative for people today who do not wish to espouse complete vegetarianism.

Food, body and identity: scholastic debates

It was not only through concrete engagement with secular society that the mendicant orders established a new basis for dietary discipline in religious orders. They rapidly became famed for their intellectual endeavour, producing from their earliest years scholars of tremendous intellectual distinction and breadth. Food and its relationship to bodily identity provided one focus for theological and philosophical debate, in an intriguing example of the ways in which theologies of food can shape material practices and be shaped by those practices.

The debates in question, explored by Philip Lyndon Reynolds, were rooted in the philosophy of Aristotle and bore implications for both biology and theology. The key controversy was about whether the human body really assimilated the food that it consumed, or whether this food was processed and then ejected while the matter composing the body persisted unchanged. During the twelfth century, many scholars had argued that, despite appearances, food taken into the body was not incorporated into what they termed the 'truth of human nature'. Rather, the matter ingested as food was simply converted into blood, or expelled from the body by a range of direct and indirect methods such as perspiration, and as fluids like spittle and mucus. A corollary of this position, counterintuitive to the modern mind, was that the physical core of the body did not require food in order to persist and grow. This view was defended by some of the most highly respected theologians of the age, including Hugh of St Victor, Gilbert of Poitiers and Peter Lombard.[80] Growth was seen instead as the result of the quasi-miraculous multiplication of an original 'seminal' or 'radical' substance analogous with the multiplications of loaves and fishes narrated in the Gospels.[81]

Knowledge of this theory of growth makes clearer how credit could be given to the accounts of extreme asceticism discussed in other chapters of this study.[82] A theoretical basis for extreme fasting was that the body was a closed system with no need of any of the nourishment which food might be considered to supply. Eating thus sustained, on this view, inessential and superfluous processes that the body could best do without. Hardline anti-assimilationists embraced a more extreme position, claiming that food 'adulterates the body, gradually weakening and poisoning it and eventually killing it'.[83]

The matter added to the body as a result of eating was, in any case, regarded as not fully assimilated into the core of human nature. For anti-assimilationists, if such matter were assimilated, then the body would become estranged from its own human species because its genetic core would no longer correspond to the universal human body that all people shared with Adam from birth. This was proven in part by reference to Matthew 15.17: whatever is taken into the mouth descends into the stomach and then leaves the body. The same idea is put slightly differently in Mark 7.19: food enters not the heart of a person but their stomach, from where it is ejected from the body. Even when the body's original seminal matter began to depart from it, and once all that original matter had disappeared, it could not be replaced by new matter derived from food. Indeed, it was precisely the gradual wastage of this matter which was seen as constituting bodily degeneration.[84] According to anti-assimilationists, therefore, it was impossible for food to become part of the resurrection body.[85]

The 'seminal reason' account of how the human body persisted across time was regarded as answering at least two key problems in philosophical theology. First, it allowed the resurrected body to be identified with the earthly body in all phases of its life right back to its birth and even conception. Second, the account gave a clear response to the perennial issue of the continuity of human identity by founding this in the material human body. Yet difficulties remained. As Caroline Walker Bynum explains, the problem of bodily identity at the resurrection was sometimes posed by imagining situations in which the human body became food.[86] For example, in a much earlier extract collated by the

Christian bishop Macarius Magnes, such a case had provided the basis for a Porphyryian critique of the Christian doctrine of the resurrection of the flesh:

> A certain man was shipwrecked. The hungry fish had his body for a feast. But the fish were caught and cooked and eaten by some fishermen, who had the misfortune to run afoul of some ravenous dogs, who killed and ate them. When the dogs died, the vultures came and made a feast of them. How will the body of the shipwrecked man be reassembled, considering it has been absorbed by other bodies of various kinds?[87]

In this story it is eating practices, and specifically the consumption of flesh, which pose the doctrinal problem of whether bodily resurrection is possible, and if so how. Christian theologians wished to refute this type of objection to a fundamental tenet of Christian belief that endured remarkably well in Christian imagination and doctrine. They sought to found their defence on a more robust theory of bodily identity.

Aquinas was one of the theologians who rejected the anti-assimilationist position, favouring instead a view close to that of Aristotle. He maintained that every part of the body suffered wastage and replacement, thereby contesting the notion that part of the body constituted a seminal core into which food could not truly be incorporated.[88] In the final question of the first part of the *Summa Theologiae*, following an extensive discussion, he wrote: 'The diversification of the human body cannot occur save by food being changed into the substance of human nature.'[89] In the course of this argument, Aquinas dismissed the idea that any real distinction existed between the seminal material constituting the truth of human nature and the nutrimental matter consumed as food.

It might be assumed that the assimilationist stance would have augmented the status of food and the act of eating. By refusing the notion that any part of the body persisted or multiplied itself without the nutriment that food provided, Aquinas made the entire body dependent on food. However, the kinds of objection previously raised in respect of bodily identity and continuity again presented themselves. In response, he proposed that the body was given these marks of consistency not by an element interior to it but by an external spiritual entity which would, at the resurrection, enable the original matter from which the body was generated to be recovered.[90] In allowing a more porous interpretation of bodily boundaries and the body's dependence on food, however, Aquinas did not accept a more mutable conception of human nature than his predecessors. Instead, he posited as a new unifying entity a soul that subsisted outside the physical body and which could be regarded as separable from that body, especially in purgatory.[91] In the rationalist climate of the thirteenth century, this scheme was seen as allowing a more plausible account of human nature, including processes of growth, than one dependent on the notion of the supernatural growth of a seminal core. Anti-assimilationist ideas did not entirely disappear, re-emerging periodically as commentators searched for explanations for apparently miraculous feats of women's fasting such as those which occurred in seventeenth-century England.[92] Yet the number of thinkers who entertained anti-assimilationism as a serious possibility dwindled.

The rise of an assimilationist theory of digestion coupled with an increasingly relaxed approach to diet sanctioned at the highest levels of the Church had the effect of further separating issues of diet from theology and spirituality. These different styles of embodiment and inhabiting the world are well illustrated in G. K. Chesterton's comparison of Aquinas and Francis. Chesterton depicts Francis as lean, lively, and little more than a 'thin brown skeleton autumn leaf dancing eternally before the wind'. Aquinas, by contrast, is presented as a 'huge heavy bull of a man, fat and slow and quiet'. According to his first biographer William of Tocco, he was described by his teacher Albertus Magnus as an ox whose bellowing would eventually fill the world.[93] Scholars have typically seen these comments as referring to Thomas's intellectual ability and shyness. But the two images point, if unwittingly, to two different ways of living and eating in the world: one physically vulnerable and materially precarious, and another based on a stable sense of self and body founded on interior intellectual and spiritual contemplation.

Paradoxically, the victory of the assimilationist position – making the body entirely dependent on food – directed theological attention away from both food and the body towards an understanding of human identity as abstract and spiritual. This scholastic idea of the spiritual soul emerged in the context of discussions about food and eating, and against a background of shifts in Christian dietary practice. These practical origins were soon forgotten, however, as the abstractions generated from theological reflection on material activities developed increasing complexity and coherence in isolation from the practical concerns that had originally produced them. Theologians less frequently engaged medical authorities and those in the other natural sciences.[94] Questions of diet, which pertained to the mutable physical body, were increasingly secularized.

The picture that has emerged from this chapter is of dietary disciplines predicated on a body set apart, whether the monastic community, the individual holy person, or the unassimilated seminal core of the physical body. These set-apart bodies are exposed to the unavoidable porousness of their boundaries and the consequences of radical dependence on other bodies. The monastery had to receive guests and gifts, and the mendicant friar needed to accept what he was offered. As different, restricted or problematic foods entered the set-apart body, dietary habits shifted. In the guest welcomed 'as Christ', in Francis' joyful acceptance of hospitality and in monastic attention to the needs of the sick, is revealed a capacity to accept and welcome bodily and dietary vulnerability. This made classic ascetic practices harder to sustain, but also allowed asceticism to be reframed as a way of joyfully living out one's dependence on the world. Yet theologians could regard bodily vulnerability, particularly in relation to food, as a threat, leading to an unintended theological neglect of the body.

4   Fasting by choice

By the fifteenth century, classic Christian patterns of dietary abstinence had been transformed. In monasteries, an inherent instability in the food rules resulting from abbatial discretion, caring for the sick, spatial differentiation and the presence of guests had changed greatly the patterns envisaged by Benedict. The newer mendicant orders had adopted a more flexible approach to diet, living as part of secular society by sharing its poverty and depending on alms. Their approach to dietary flexibility could be seen as more straightforward because it did not depend on the subtle distinctions of scholastic reasoning. Even so, as was seen in Chapter Three, friars were subjected to at least as much criticism as monks, perhaps because of their greater visibility.

This chapter will begin with an overview of Reformation critiques of traditional fasting practices, before focusing on modern Christian reflection on diet. As has already been seen and contrary to what might have been expected, the Reformation did not make fasting a matter of purely private choice. Public fasting, whether seasonal or occasional, remained for some time a significant means of ordering and reordering the body politic, and was given extensive theological justification. The Reformation dynamic was nevertheless towards individual liberty in fasting. It would be easy to assume that the decline or disappearance of public fasting that occurred during the seventeenth century meant that dietary practice ceased to hold significance for Christians. Yet instead, fasting became a matter of personal choice. Modern vegetarianism, also freely chosen, was fundamentally shaped by these Christian practices of dietary restriction.

Reforming the fast

Resistance to fasting in fact predated the Reformation. In England, the Lollards were a pietistic and anticlerical movement that grew up in the mid fourteenth century and who vehemently opposed what they saw as the corrupt priestly power and wealth of the Roman church. A key method of defying the Christian social establishment, practised by some Lollards, was the breaking of food rules, which they regarded as the arbitrary dictates of a corrupt institutional church.[1] Many admitted eating meat and even hunting animals on fast days, and stored and ate meat during the long Lenten fast.[2]

Opposition to traditional fasting practices began to be justified in greater theological depth in the writings of leading Reformation theologians, beginning with Huldrich Zwingli. In 1522, a member of his Zurich congregation who was also his printer was hauled before the civil magistrates, who enforced fasting regulations, for eating meat during Lent. Christoph Froschauer ate sausages with his workers, justifying his actions to the court on the grounds that he had an unusually large amount of work that Lent.[3] In response, Zwingli prepared a long sermon defending the principle that Christians were free to eat any foods at any time, even during Lent. Zwingli opens his exposition with a series of proof texts.[4] What goes into the mouth does not defile a person, rather the things that come out of a person.[5] In Peter's vision of the sheet at Jaffa, God makes all foods clean.[6] Both meat and the belly will eventually be destroyed, and so food makes no difference to a person's ultimate spiritual state.[7] People are neither worse nor better if they consume meat.[8] Any item bought in the market may be eaten.[9] No-one shall be judged on the basis of the foods they eat.[10] Meats were created by God to be received with thanksgiving, and only false teachers forbid them.[11] The heart is established by grace, not with meats.[12]

After presenting these proofs that a Christian may eat all foods, Zwingli proceeds to address critics who accept this general principle but argue that, at specific times or under specified conditions, particular food prohibitions should nevertheless be adhered to. First, how about those who argue that, although all foods are pure, they are not pure at all times?[13] He responds that the Sabbath is made for humankind, not humankind for the Sabbath, and that time is therefore subject to humans, who can use all foods in all seasons.[14] The kingdom of God does not come with the observation of works, and those who know God should turn away from the weak elements, i.e. the letter of the law.[15] Zwingli then turns to the objection that, if people are free to eat meat, they will never fast. He argues that the power of fasting is given by a desire to fast, not by external compulsion.[16] People who complain about the demise of fasting are typically from the leisured classes, he contends, and able to compensate the prohibitions of meat abstinence by the pleasurable consumption of alternatives such as fish. The real motivation for their complaint is an attempt to prevent common working people who do not fast from enjoying a standard of living closer to their own. Third, Zwingli considers the status of meat abstinence as a merely human prohibition.[17] It lacks scriptural warrant, he protests, depending on a small number of writers – 'as though one single mendicant monk had power to prescribe laws for all Christian folk' – and traditions that turn out, on close examination, to be recent inventions buttressed by a system from which people can gain exemptions by bribing clergy.

The fourth topic, to which Zwingli devotes most time, is vexation or offence (*skandalon*).[18] He begins by accepting that everyone should avoid offending their neighbour. Yet such consideration does not prevent the Gospel being preached or lived: 'Christ gives us strength not to consider the vexation of those who will not be convinced of the truth.' When a believer in liberty encounters a person of little faith who is convinced of the need for abstinence, he 'should yield the matter of eating meat in his presence, if it is not necessary'. By implication, the believer always remains at liberty in private. Nevertheless, the ultimate objective of the strong believer should be to instruct the weak believer and strengthen them by bringing them to a point where they are fully persuaded in their own mind of the rightness of liberty. Moreover, when a Christian is invited to another's house to share hospitality, they should follow the example of Christ himself by eating all types of food that are offered, although not any foods that the host regards as prohibited to them.

Christians should above all else not be weakened by the bishops and other clergy who seek to enforce abstinence. Zwingli compares these clergy with an eye, hand or foot that should be cut off and cast away in order to prevent the entire body perishing.[19] The weak in faith should be received into the pure and simple truth rather than be drawn into doubtful disputations and subtle arguments.[20] Approaches to rule observance will evolve over time: for instance, Paul had Timothy circumcised but not Titus.[21] Eventually, the minority who stubbornly adhere to inessential rules should be let go, just as Paul and even Christ himself did not care if a few Pharisees wished to be offended provided that most disciples remained 'unaffected and unsuspicious'.[22] In any case, no-one should be judged good on the basis of the foods they eat or be 'beguiled by those who pretend humility'.

Martin Luther also inveighs against fasting undertaken in obedience to arbitrary rules, which make no reference to ultimate ends. He nevertheless sees fasting as performing a crucial function in disciplining the flesh, describing this in terms of subjugation and even killing: 'It was solely to kill and subdue the pride and lust of the flesh that fastings, vigils, and penances were instituted. If it were not for lust, eating would be as meritorious as fasting.'[23]

Luther is at least as critical as Zwingli of formulaic approaches to fasting, on the grounds that they negate this stated objective. He complains: 'Some fast so richly with fish and other foods that they would come much nearer to fasting if they ate meat, eggs, and butter.'[24] Yet amid these candid judgements, sensitivity emerges: fasting is worthwhile only in so far as it is needed to discipline the flesh of a particular person. Any additional fasting is tantamount to murder, regardless of the justification given for it. For this reason, pregnant women and the sick should not fast, especially if life would thereby be endangered.[25]

Luther's insistence that the decision about whether to fast should be left to personal discretion was motivated by a desire to break the yoke of the ecclesiastical authorities in Rome, which he saw as borne by the whole of Christendom. He proclaims:

> They have bound us with their canon law and robbed us of our rights so that we have to buy them back again with money. In so doing they have made our consciences so fearful that it is no longer easy to preach about liberty of this kind because the common people take offence at it and think that eating butter is a greater sin than lying, swearing, or even living unchastely.[26]

These comments recall the elaborate 'Butter Tower' of Rouen Cathedral, reputedly funded from income generated by an archiepiscopal dispensation permitting the burning of butter in lamps during Lent in a year when oil was in short supply.[27]

Luther's critique of Lenten meat abstinence is complemented by an outspoken and disturbing assessment of the primary purpose of animals as being to provide meat for human consumption. He asserts that, following the Flood,

> animals are subjected to man as to a tyrant who has absolute power over life and death. Because a more oppressive form of bondage has now been imposed on them and a more extensive and oppressive dominion has been assigned to man, the animals are dominated by fear and dread of man[28]

God's words to Noah permitting human consumption of meat 'establish the butcher shop' and 'attach hares, chickens, and geese to the spit'. Indeed, God 'sets Himself up as a butcher; for with His Word He slaughters and kills the animals that are suited for food, in order to make up, as it were, for the great sorrow that pious Noah experienced during the Flood'. Thus the 'dumb animals are made subject to man for the purpose of serving him even to the extent of dying'. Luther also reasons that meat eating is necessary for human wellbeing on the curious grounds that the number of humans living on the earth exceeds the number that could be nourished on the fruits of the earth.

Calvin's views on public fasting were discussed in Chapter Two. In his *Institutes,* he accepts that fasting prepares the mind for prayer and promotes humility, self-deprecation, the sincerest confessions of guilt, and gratitude for God's grace, as well as disciplining lust.[29] Calvin undoubtedly sees particular acts of fasting as justified only in so far as they promote human virtue, and like Zwingli and Luther makes polemical use of the pronouncement that 'all foods are clean'. In his commentary on Acts, Calvin writes:

> As touching meats, after the abrogation of the law, God pronounceth that they are all pure and clean. If, on the other side, there start up a mortal man, making a new difference, forbidding certain, he taketh unto himself the authority and power of God by sacrilegious boldness.[30]

This scriptural interpretation is accompanied by the standard critique of the ecclesiastical hierarchy: 'rudeness and ignorance in the bishops, lust of power, and tyrannical rigour, with abundant exquisite delicacies replacing the excluded flesh'.[31]

A set of harsh oppositions and potential annihilations are apparent in these discussions, particularly in Luther's rhetoric: between flesh and spirit, individual believers and the ecclesiastical authorities, God and animals, and humans and animals. The Reformers' urging of liberty in fasting is nevertheless a further development of a medieval theme prominent in previous chapters. Fasting has no intrinsic merit, but serves and reflects a greater end. It is a medicine to be prescribed to each individual as appropriate and necessary, and therefore not an appropriate matter for universal prescription. The Reformers recognize the variation in fasting practices that in fact existed, due to differences of wealth and station and the ways in which existing pattern of fasts could maintain social divisions or even widen them. This was especially apparent in a context where new professions, such as that of Froschauer the printer, were subject to variations unconnected with the seasons.

What happened in practice, however, when fasting ceased to be a public undertaking? How did Christians unfettered by state regulation negotiate their liberty, prescribe to themselves the medicine of fasting, and make dietary choices? In the rest of this chapter, we trace how individuals and groups related themselves and their dietary practices to Christian tradition and scripture, and to their beliefs about body and society.

Liberty and method

In England, public fasting was abolished during the Commonwealth, having continued largely unchanged through the Reformation. In the mid seventeenth century, however, the Puritan 'Long' Parliament swept away the complex medieval pattern of fasts, instigating in its place a single fast on the final Wednesday of each month. But in April 1649, following the execution of Charles I, the Parliament terminated this innovation on grounds of neglect.[32] For the first time in many centuries, there existed in England no commonly accepted or legally enforceable rule of fasting. Jeremy Taylor's *Holy Living*, published in 1650, provides a good example of a theologian grappling with this new political and religious context. Taylor accepts that fasting is a 'duty nowhere enjoined or counselled. But Christianity hath to do with it,' he continues, 'as it may be made an instrument of the Spirit.'[33] This can happen in one of three ways: through prayer, in mortifying bodily lusts, and by repentance. Taylor instructs that all public fasts, including days of humiliation, should be observed, although argues that fasting needs to be enjoined on theological grounds such as those just listed. Drawing on Basil of Caesarea and other unnamed doctors of the Church, he commends fasting as the 'nourishment of prayer, the restraint of lust, the wings of the soul, the diet of angels, the instrument of humility and self-denial, the purification of the spirit, and the paleness and meagreness of visage', identifying the last of these qualities with the mark on the forehead observed by the angel in Revelation when he signed the saints to escape God's wrath.[34]

Taylor sought to salvage the Christian fasting tradition by means of great learning and exquisite prose, but how did ordinary faithful Christian make dietary choices in an age when fasting was no longer regulated by the state? While docked in Liverpool preparing for a voyage to West Africa, the slave trader, ship owner and sea captain John Newton resolved that once at sea he would establish a 'scheme of rules' to order his life. Newton had undergone a conversion four years earlier, and believed that he had been saved from death on several occasions by divine agency. The aim of his scheme was to promote

God's honour and glory, and the 'perfection of my nature in obedience to his commands'. One part of the scheme concerned fasting, and Newton outlined his rationale for adopting the practice in a diary entry of 30 July 1752, developing two strands of reasoning. First, he saw fasting as a means of acknowledging God's infinite perfections and contemplating his love.[35] This recognition of the benefits of fasting as a spiritual discipline were complemented by a second, eschatological perspective, in which he regarded fasting as anticipating the improvement of human nature and permitting a foretaste of the joys of the heavenly world to come. Importantly, he sees fasting as providing a means of affirming faith in the 'immediate gift and free grace of God', and as therefore made possible by the working of divine power in human beings to strengthen them, rather than by human achievement independent of God's grace. Newton possessed a strong, intuitive awareness of his unworthiness to fulfil God's call unless strengthened by grace. In his theology of fasting and associated spiritual disciplines like prayer and the reading of scripture, he wished at all times to exclude the possibility that good works were the product of successful personal effort.

In formulating his idea of fasting, Newton draws on both the Old and New Testaments. He discusses the tradition of prophets such as Daniel fasting in order to gain spiritual inspiration and foreknowledge of future events. Newton's interest in Israelite practice is complemented by his reading of the Gospels, in which he sees fasting as commended by both Christ and the apostles. He regards fasting as especially appropriate on occasions of solemn prayer and confession. This is partly for psychological reasons: fasting sharpens the 'faculties of the soul' and restricts the lusts and other natural infirmities of the fallible human body.

Innocent of much of the historical controversy surrounding fasting practices, their ecclesial regulation and the benefits that churches had reaped from granting dispensations, Newton embraces fasting as a personal choice, unencumbered by knowledge of historic theological invective. Nevertheless, in framing his scheme of rules he needed to confront at least one of the issues underlying those debates: the extent to which fasting should follow a regular pattern, even one personally chosen, rather than being observed spontaneously. Newton was undoubtedly aware, in broad terms, of the contemporary national controversies surrounding the state regulation of fasting. In the Commonwealth, the new absence of formal civil regulation provides the backdrop for his own scheme of rules. He writes:

> Upon the whole I would not constantly prescribe to myself a fast absolutely, of such a determined number of hours, or confine myself too strictly to forms, which often degenerate into superstition. I would rather habituate to a constant and orderly abstemiousness, and moderation in the enjoyment of all God's temporal blessings, thankfully receiving them and using them, but always with an eye to his glory, and to making them subservient to a more excellent end than they offer in themselves, and yet at

some times, when most agreeable to my temper, frame and opportunities, in order to the perfecting myself in this mastery over the fleshly appetites, to keep up a sense of my constant dependence upon God's bounty, and the just forfeiture I had often made of my share in the commonest of his favours, and the free grace of my Saviour who by his merits and sufferings has purchased for me a good title to all I can enjoy and hope for; for these reasons I would look upon fasting as amongst the means of grace and improvement which I enjoy, and in some measure or manner or other as a duty to be frequently observed. And for the most part I dare say I should find a profit in setting apart one day in every week for this purpose.[36]

Although Newton thus eschews forms of fasting that 'often degenerate into superstition', he concludes his consideration strikingly by resolving to set aside for fasting one day each week. Here are echoes of the persistent tradition of Friday fasting, even if this only entails eating fish instead of red meat.

Yet Newton did not seek to achieve 'mastery over the fleshly appetites' solely by means of a regime of weekly fasting. His contemporary biographer Richard Cecil states that, while on voyages, Newton abstained completely from animal flesh in order to 'subdue every improper emotion' towards the slave women under his command.[37] At some points in Newton's life, therefore, his practice of a weekly fasting discipline appears to have been complemented by a general discipline of meat abstinence similar to that enjoined in the Rule of Benedict.

Newton appears to have possessed little awareness of evangelicalism at this time, only learning of the movement and the work of John Wesley two years later in 1754.[38] He met George Whitfield the following year and was introduced to Wesley himself in 1757.[39] Wesley was by then already developing his own system of fasting, which exhibits some similarities to Newton's. Wesley's approach was quite different, however. Newton was a rough sailor who had been held captive and sold as a slave. He had also transported other people as slaves. He first went to sea aged eleven and had little historical or theological awareness of a scholarly kind. Wesley, in contrast, was a clergyman of the Church of England and a child of the rectory, educated at Charterhouse and Christ Church, Oxford.

As has already been seen, fasting was by this time not widely observed in England. The final proclamation of Lenten fasting had been made by King Charles II in 1664, and the last prosecutions for breaching the injunction occurred in the same decade.[40] Wesley believed that the recovery of fasting disciplines would spiritually invigorate the Church, and drew on ancient Christian writers such as Epiphanius and Tertullian to defend their permissibility and effectiveness.[41] Theologically, his espousal of fasting was the product of the confluence of two specific concerns: the contemporary significance and relevance for Christians of historic Church practices, and worries about personal bodily health. Each requires consideration.

Wesley had been impressed by the thought of William Law, the Anglican divine whose *Serious Call to a Holy and Devout Life*, published in 1729, was to exert profound influence on the evangelical revival.[42] Four years after this work appeared, Wesley met Thomas Deacon, another Nonjuror, who was the same year consecrated a bishop and was greatly concerned to restore various ancient Church practices including fasting.[43] In 1739, Wesley read Claude Fleury's *Manners of the Ancient Christians*, which examined early Christian asceticism, summarizing the volume for a tract in his series *The Christian Library*.[44] His links with such figures and texts confirm that his own mission and preaching were inspired by some of the much earlier manifestations of Christian dietary discipline previously explored.

The second preoccupation of Wesley's which led to his interest in fasting was the vulnerability of the human body. A key influence on his ideas about human embodiment was the Georgian physician Dr George Cheyne. As early as 1724, the year of his graduation from Oxford, Wesley wrote to his mother Susannah commending Cheyne's *Health and Long Life* and noting some of the prohibitions there recommended: salt and anything highly seasoned, pork, fish and stall-fed cattle.[45] Wesley also mentioned the daily quantity of foodstuffs that Cheyne permitted: eight ounces of meat and twelve of vegetables.

Cheyne was an enigmatic figure. In the words of one commentator, he stood 'at that critical juncture between religious and secular, magical and scientific, spiritual and psychological; he was both a man of science and a mystic at a time when the two may still have seemed contradictory'.[46] Cheyne inherited a Renaissance fusion of intellectual disciplines, having read George Herbert's 1634 translation of *Discorsi della vita sobria*, a treatise composed by the Venetian nobleman Luigi Cornaro.[47] Many Renaissance writers on diet drew on classical advocates of vegetarianism such as Pythagoras, Porphyry and Plutarch.[48] Yet both Cheyne's and Cornaro's interest in health stemmed, more directly, from their own illnesses precipitated by overeating. A sample menu from a lunch served to Cheyne by one of his patients includes almond soup, boiled pike, battered rabbit, calf's foot pie, veal ragout, goose, tongue, chicken, lamb ragout, gravy soup and salmon, with salad and cabbage the only vegetables mentioned.[49] He was eventually forced to change his ways after becoming so fat (32 stone in weight, or more than 200 kilos) that he could hardly walk. He regained some measure of good health by adopting a strict diet of milk and vegetables.

Cheyne recounted his return to health in various dietetic and spiritual writings. These followed a well-established pattern of spiritual autobiography originating in Augustine's *Confessions*.[50] Yet Augustine associated food rules with his early Manichaeism and following his conversion to the Christian faith gave them little consideration, as will be seen in Chapter Six. For Cheyne, in contrast, such rules became a primary source of personal discipline and salvation. Some of his speculations echo those of ancient writers, such as the view expressed in his *Essay of Health and Long Life* that God provided animal food after the Flood only in order to shorten human life. Echoing the biblical food laws discussed in Chapter Five, Cheyne urged those of his readers who chose to eat meat to opt for the flesh of animals that ate vegetables rather than those that preyed on other animals.[51]

Cheyne's ideas influenced Methodism deeply and were recognized by contemporaries, including critics, as among its distinctive features.[52] Followers of Wesley in his Oxford 'Holy Club' – which developed around him following his election to a fellowship at Lincoln College in 1726, and to which some of the origins of Methodism can be traced – accepted that diet was relevant to basic spiritual issues of sin and redemption and themselves promoted similar restrictions.[53] Moreover, Cheyne's conversion narrative shares many similarities with what would become the standard conversion testimonies of Methodism.[54] The spiritual significance of dietary ideas is highlighted by the mystical context in which they developed. Cheyne had assimilated the speculations of Jacob Boehme, which he communicated to William Law. Assisted by Boehme's theories, Cheyne came to regard worldly creatures in Neoplatonic terms as reflections, or embodiments, of God their creator.[55] This ontology suggested a view of the material realm as analogous with the spiritual realm. Bodily health could then by implication be seen as signifying spiritual health, 'in which self-purification of the soul through Christian practices runs parallel to self-purification of the body through strict dietary practices'.[56]

Cheyne had conceived his regimen for wealthy patrons suffering from excessive consumption, but Wesley saw its far wider relevance, developing its implications in his bestselling exposition *Primitive Physick*.[57] Although not ultimately adopting a wholly vegetarian diet, Wesley did, together with his brother Charles, abstain from meat for two periods each lasting two years: when setting sail for Georgia in 1735, and again in 1746, until seized by a 'violent flux' in Ireland.[58] During the first period of abstention, Wesley experimented with a diet consisting solely of bread and reported that he and his brother were 'never more vigorous and healthy than while we tasted nothing else'.[59] Much later in his life, when aged sixty-eight, he reflected on the reasons for his lasting health and identified moderate eating as key. He recalls that, between the ages of ten and thirteen, he ate little else except bread because of the poverty of his family, in which he was the fifteenth child.[60] He then attributes his continued modest diet to the advice of Dr Cheyne.

In a journal entry of approximately 1716, written when he was aged about thirteen, Wesley's mother Susannah recorded her own understanding of dietary abstinence. This suggests that she had a role in shaping her son's own early dietary practice and his theological interpretation of it. She saw the principal aim of abstinence as being to 'bring all the sensual appetites into a due subject to the superior powers of the mind', with several of its 'other excellent ends' including the gaining of time for spiritual exercises, prayer, penance, deprecating judgements, intercession, and acts of faith and love.[61] Of particular interest is Susannah Wesley's classification of fasting as a means to virtue and perfection rather than a moral virtue in itself. She states that 'strictly speaking, I think it no virtue at all, but rather a way or means to acquire the virtues requisite for the perfection of the Christian life'. Fasting can therefore be regarded as a 'positive command' and hence a practice with 'greater latitude' than a moral virtue. Susannah Wesley lists, like Luther, various types of person who should be excused fasting on the grounds that it might injure them: the sick, weak or infirm; nurses or pregnant women; the elderly; and the poor, 'who through extreme penury are compelled to a constant abstinence, that seldom or never taste delicious food or rarely have the pleasure of a full meal of the coarsest fare'.[62]

John Wesley delivered his own extensive exposition of the purpose of fasting in a sermon for the beginning of Lent. He commences his text by striking a characteristically Anglican balance between the notions that fasting is essential and that it is superfluous. Types of abstinence can range, he observes, from the complete elimination of all food from the diet, enabled by supernatural strength, to the refusal of specific especially pleasant foods. He then distinguishes 'stationary' fasts – those occurring on a fixed day each year – from 'occasional fasts appointed from time to time as the particular circumstances and occasions of each required'.[63] Wesley, as might be expected, follows Calvin's lead by expressing greater interest in these moveable observances. In his case, this is probably because they could be used to address individuals' specific spiritual conditions. He first identifies a 'natural ground for fasting' originating in a sense of affliction, sorrow for sin or deep apprehension of God's wrath. People with such feelings, he observes, indeed usually eat far less than normal. Another ground for fasting is for the Christian to 'refrain his soul, and keep it low', limiting the sensual appetites which harm body and soul and undermine interior mental discipline and attentiveness to the surrounding world.[64] Further motives for fasting include self-chastisement and the aiding of prayer. These means are not established merely by reason or the light of conscience, Wesley avers, but are taught in various portions of scripture such as the book of the prophet Joel.

Wesley proceeds to address several standard objections to fasting. These include the idea that personal faults such as pride, vanity and other weaknesses of personal character should be addressed before attention is paid to food issues. In response, Wesley presents a view of fasting which has intriguing resonances with sacramental theology. He states:

> We abstain from food with this in view, that by the grace of God, conveyed into our souls through this outward means, in conjunction with all the other channels of his grace which he hath appointed, we may be enabled to abstain from every passion and temper which is not pleasing in his sight. We refrain from the one that, being endued with power from on high, we may be able to refrain from the other.[65]

Fasting is thus a means by which divine grace affects the human soul. In this sense, it is an outward sign of a spiritual grace given by God. Wesley established the connection between the outward sign of fasting and the spiritual grace – being 'enabled to abstain from every passion and temper which is not pleasing' – at least in part through a better understanding of the body and its passions. Grace, in this sermon, works with and through the body's natural processes. In his advocacy of fasting, Wesley thus combines medical, scriptural and historical arguments in an attempt to understand how God's grace makes bodies holy and healthy.

Theologically, awareness of the importance of dietary discipline in Wesley's spirituality illumines some of the motivations for his well-known efforts to resurrect the Anglican Eucharist from widespread disuse.[66] He saw eating and drinking as deeply human acts usually performed in the company of others. From this perspective, it was entirely appropriate that the Eucharist, being a gathering centred on the sharing of food and drink, should also reassume a key place in Church life alongside everyday dietary discipline.

Christians and the birth of modern vegetarianism

It is strange that Wesley's considerable interest in dietary abstinence in general and vegetarianism in particular did not permeate British society more extensively. A prolific correspondent, traveller and preacher, Wesley was rarely out of the public eye and neither were his views. Yet until the mid nineteenth century, the epithet 'Pythagorean' was used to describe diets that excluded meat, suggesting inspiration from classical abstainers rather than Christian associations. The term 'vegetarian' dates from the decade leading up to the founding of the British Vegetarian Society in 1847 and the American Vegetarian Society in 1850. Vegetable diets had previously been referred to by means of a range of terms including 'Pythagorean' (Antonio Cocchi), but also 'primeval' (George Nicholson) and, anachronistically, 'Monasticall' (Francis Bacon).[67]

By unifying their terminology and establishing an organizational structure, vegetarians took a significant step towards forming a sense of shared identity. This would soon be visible in public. In London, the first vegetarian restaurant opened in 1876 and by 1886 twelve others had followed.[68] Yet for the next several decades, vegetarianism was limited to a small core of practitioners who mostly observed strict abstinence from all meat (including fish) and were likely to be allied with other radical social and political stances such as anti-vivisectionism, gay rights and sunbathing.[69] Radicalism of a religious variety formed part of this constellation, with Quakers and Unitarians including in their number a far higher proportion of vegetarians than the larger Christian churches. Charles Spurgeon, the famous Reformed Baptist preacher, became vegetarian in his later life, but vegetarianism did not ever become a mark of Baptist identity.[70] More important were the several radical Christian groups that espoused vegetarianism during the decade leading up to 1847 and thereby helped establish it as a modern dietary option. These included sacred socialists, concordists, Owenites, Chartists, Etzlerists and White Quakers.[71]

One Christian sect deserves special mention for its contribution to forging the modern vegetarian identity. The Bible Christian Church, founded in Salford in 1809 by William Cowherd, an Anglican clergyman, was notable in requiring its members to be vegetarian. Many of this Church's ministers and members occupied key positions in the Vegetarian Society.[72] Although the Cowherdites, as they were sometimes called, probably numbered less than two thousand people, they made a large impact on the town in the early nineteenth century by providing vital medical and social services, a burial ground and a kitchen serving onion soup. One minister, Joseph Brotherton, became a Member of Parliament, and many of the borough's senior police officers were members.[73] The vegetarian rule was reinforced by additional verses interpolated into hymns, and by reinterpretations of scriptural texts which posed problems for vegetarians' arguments. For instance, Cowherd asserted that the animal sacrifices of Leviticus were really animal skins stuffed with fruit and vegetables.[74] This type of interpretation of scripture was inspired by the theory of correspondences developed by the eighteenth-century Swedish seer Emanuel Swedenborg. This was founded on the belief that a new spiritual vision had been given to humanity via Swedenborg himself in 1757, and that the whole biological and social order should be interpreted as revealing this true spiritual reality. Vegetarianism was seen as fundamental in bringing humankind into conformity with this new enlightened condition.

Following Cowherd's death in 1816, the Bible Christian Church became more focused on promoting vegetarianism for its own sake, with its proselytising efforts bearing fruit in the founding of the British Vegetarian Society. Most of the Society's founding members were Bible Christians or Swedenborgians. As Peter Lineham notes, although the Society depended mainly on scientific and moral arguments to promote vegetarianism, its fundamental aim was nevertheless in clear continuity with that of the Bible Christian Church: the healing of humankind by means of a meatless diet.[75]

The direct link between the Bible Christian Church, Christian theology and the modern vegetarian movement in Britain is demonstrated by Brotherton's speech at the founding conference of the British Vegetarian Society held at Northwood Villa, near Ramsgate in Kent, on 30 September 1847. Following a late lunch, Brotherton, who was presiding, rose and addressed the assembled company, employing as a key part of his argumentative arsenal a selection of theological ideas. As a result of the laws of creation and of nature, he asserted, every human has implanted in them by the Deity an 'abhorrence to the shedding of blood', which should rightly be consulted as a guide to conduct.[76] He noted that, in the 'early ages, we find that persons lived to a far longer period than they do at the present day' – an apparent reference to vegetarian Old Testament patriarchs. In practical decision making, Brotherton saw vegetarians as having in their favour the 'command of God, in addition to all that he has written in His works, and all that we experience in ourselves'.[77] He then addressed interpretations of several biblical passages commonly taken as sanctioning or even requiring meat eating, demonstrating how a more reasonable reading in fact lends support to the case for abstinence.

The Bible Christian Church was small and relatively isolated. Later in Britain, the largest Christian group recommending vegetarianism was the Salvation Army. Its Methodist founder and first general, William Booth, wrote in the Orders and Regulations for its officers in 1886: 'It is a great delusion to suppose that flesh-meat of any kind is essential to health.'[78] This order proceeded to note that much of the world's work is done 'by men who never taste anything but vegetable, farinaceous food, and that of the simplest kind', repeating a popular vegetarian argument of the British Imperial era. Booth then enumerated several foods in which, he claimed, there are 'more strength-producing properties' than in meat or other animal foods. His list reads like a list of the staples of early Christian anchorites: seasonal root vegetables, raw fruit and salad vegetables in summer, wholemeal bread, peas, beans, lentils and oatmeal. In fact, he continued, the 'use of flesh-meat may be abandoned at any time without loss in either health or strength'. Such a diet would save money, he argued, which could be diverted to Christian mission and promote a simplicity of living that would free his officers from earthly human concerns.[79] Booth also connected abstinence with fasting and the ability to cast out demons. These various theological benefits were additional to the advantages for personal health and wellbeing which he also recognized. A vegetarian diet was still commended in the 1925 Orders and Regulations, which directed that 'an Officer's diet should consist chiefly of products of the vegetable kingdom'.[80] This order contradicted historic Christian practice on one important point, however, by rejecting fish alongside beef, mutton and other animal foods. Booth's classification was made on nutritional grounds, revealing that his dietary injunctions were motivated more by a theory of health than by a desire to connect his movement with historic Christian practice or even with biblical food practices.

Despite extolling the advantages of meat abstention, Booth had presented the 'vegetarian system' as optional even for field officers.[81] Although his son Bramwell was vegetarian, William himself gave up the practice because of the difficulties it brought him in his 'wandering life, especially as it seemed to involve those around [him] in extra labour, a little vexation, and always an amount of unprofitable controversy'.[82] Like Francis and Dominic, Booth gave priority to accepting hospitality. Moreover, in his blueprint Farm Colony, where the unemployed and homeless would be trained in agriculture before being despatched to cultivate foreign soils, rabbits and poultry would be raised alongside fruit and vegetables, as well as pigs, the usefulness of which for manure and waste disposal, as well as meat, Booth was well aware.[83] Dietary practice was, as in the Rule of Basil discussed in Chapter Two, to be shaped by local conditions. Expressed in contemporary terms, Booth aimed to create a sustainable pattern of food production and consumption.

Other vegetarians of the second half of the nineteenth century were associated with a range of marginal social and political causes. Secular moralists as well as spiritualists and theosophists stood alongside Christians in this curious alliance. Latent evangelicalism can be identified as a common basis. Julia Twigg identifies the ambivalent nature of this inheritance, showing how in many cases it functioned as much as a foil as a positive religious identity. She argues that evangelicalism produced an 'intense reaction against its doctrines and its heavy psychological demands to believe, at the same time as creating a cast of mind still receptive to the broad form of religious ideals and emotions'.[84]

As if to satisfy a residual requirement for a firm scriptural basis for vegetarianism, the former Anglo-Catholic priest Gideon Ouseley 'discovered' and published in 1904 a vegetarian gospel, which he claimed to have translated from an Aramaic codex in the custody of Buddhist monks in Tibet.[85] The case of Ouseley shows just how precarious vegetarianism's relationship with doctrinal and scriptural orthodoxy had, by the later nineteenth century, become. In the Bible Christian Church, the historic Christian scriptures remained the central source of authority, even when subject to idiosyncratic interpretations. Moreover, the Church's burial service attested that its teachings did not include reincarnation.[86] Nevertheless, vegetarianism was more likely to be cast alongside Gnosticism, spiritualism or other marginal forms of belief in opposition to classic mainstream Christianity.[87] When the Bible Christian Church closed in 1932, its remaining members joined a Unitarian congregation.

Although the Bible Christians exhibited various traditional markers of Christian orthodoxy, the same cannot be said for another group with Christian origins, the Order of the Cross. Founded in 1904 by John Todd Ferrier, a Scottish Congregationalist minister, the order combined a belief in the normative status of personal religious experience with an affirmation of the central importance of the person, teachings and voluminous writings of its founder, which were based around his esoteric interpretations of Christian scripture.[88] Jesus Christ was believed to have been a member of the Jewish Essene sect, to have died in 49 CE and to have been reincarnated forty times since then. The Order continues today with groups in Britain, North America, Australia and New Zealand, comprising a total of about 400 members. A structurally similar group has been founded more recently in Germany following revelations by the Prophetess Gabriele in 1975, placing strong reliance on its founder's teaching, writings and interpretation of the Gospel – including reincarnation – but also undertaking a range of social and charitable enterprises.[89]

Christian vegetarians and new food products

The legacy of the Bible Christian Church was its impact on vegetarian diet in the United States. In 1817, Bible Christian minister William Metcalfe had departed from England with a small congregation to establish a new community in Philadelphia. The church they founded was never large and faced financial challenges and encroaching urbanization. In 1890, it was effectively forced off its premises by the adjacent sausage factory, whose machinery disturbed worship and emitted steam that discoloured the tombstones. On the congregation's departure to a new site, their agent sold the church to the pork packer and before long the sanctuary had been ignominiously converted into a storehouse for hams.[90]

During the eighteenth century, at least two other Christian vegetarian communities had grown up in the United States: the Ephrata cloister of Seventh-Day Baptists in Pennsylvania, and the Dorrellites in Vermont.[91] These had mainly local appeal, were centred on the direct leadership of their founders and did not endure much beyond the end of the century, at least in their original vegetarian forms. Vegetarianism had also been promoted in some Shaker communities in the 1840s, partly as a result of health concerns about meat diets.[92] But Shaker communities did not generally adopt the practice, even though many experimented with it.[93] The Bible Christian Church made a greater lasting impact on American dietary consciousness by spreading its vegetarian gospel among more active publicists. In 1830, Presbyterian minister Dr Sylvester Graham was working as a temperance lecturer and was introduced to some Bible Christians. Metcalfe took the opportunity to strike up a correspondence with him and also with another dietary reformer, William Alcott.[94] During the following decades, these men founded two journals to promote vegetarianism: the *Moral Reformer* and the *Graham Journal*. Graham was particularly well known for his opposition to white bread, which he regarded as lacking in nutrition.

A similar complaint had been voiced many centuries earlier by Clement of Alexandria, that gluttons 'emasculate plain food, namely bread, by straining off the nourishing part of the grain'.[95] Clement had objected to this process partly because he saw it as an example of unnecessarily complex and dainty food preparation. But Graham, more concerned than Clement about the health consequences of this procedure, went a step further by promoting in place of white bread the wholemeal loaf baked with his own branded flour, which included coarsely ground bran and germ. Graham also developed the cracker biscuit which took his name. Made using the same flour, this had a taste and consistency similar to a digestive biscuit, with its dryness intended by Graham to curb sexual urges. A perennial concern of Christian promoters of abstinence from the desert fathers onwards thus resurfaced yet again, now influencing the development of new food products in an era of mass production and marketing.

The most important of these products were cornflakes, and breakfast cereals generally. Dietary reformers, by focusing their energies on the first meal of the day, confronted the pork, beans and pie breakfasts which had become standard in years characterized by prosperity, the stockyards and railroads centred on Chicago, and extremely high levels of meat consumption nationally.[96] It is little realized today that the production of crisp cornflakes was a major technical achievement. Granola, billed as the 'first cold breakfast food', needed rehydrating for at least twenty minutes and was therefore often too time-consuming to prepare first thing in the morning before work, whereas early cornflakes had the appearance of toasted breadcrumbs because they could not be made to stick together. John Harvey Kellogg discovered by accident that the flakes, once rolled, kept their consistency if left to rest for several hours in a process known as 'tempering'.[97] These cereals, being marketed as health cures, became closely identified with their promoters: granola with James Caleb Jackson, shredded wheat with Henry D. Perky, and cornflakes with the Kellogg brothers. William Keith Kellogg's signature, still on the packet today, reminds breakfasters of the personality cults which surrounded the various cereal recipes and the health benefits they were believed to effect, particularly in the context of acquisitions, mergers, and battles over patent rights.[98] In the case of the Kellogg brothers, such rivalry escalated into a decade of lawsuits not finally resolved until 1920 followed the shortening of the famous signature 'W.K. Kellogg' to just 'Kellogg's'.[99]

Interestingly, the idea of a personal seal of authenticity was not new, having been in use in the United States at the beginning of the twentieth century to label kosher foods, following difficulties ensuring that foodstuffs labelled as kosher truly were kosher. In the case of meat, when slaughter took place in large private abattoirs or carcasses were transported long distances for sale, the scope for dissembling about sources and slaughter methods was extensive. Respected rabbis therefore allowed their seal to appear on packaging to show that meat and other foods originated from a trusted source.[100]

Initially, the Christian context of breakfast cereals was proclaimed by their names, which included Food of Eden, Golden Manna and even Elijah's Manna. In 1908, however, the last of these was renamed 'Post Toasties' after its inventor C.W. Post, in response to fundamentalist protests about the use of Christian imagery in marketing. Moreover, export to Britain would have been difficult because it was not permitted to register biblical names there.[101] Quaker Oats, although not invented or ever produced by members of the Society of Friends, presented an image of simplicity and integrity. Being allied to this Christian context of breakfast foods could only reap commercial benefits. The continuing Christian context of vegetarianism was alluded to by popular vegetarian writers such as Dio Lewis, who quoted classic Christian vegetarian sources like Cornaro, Cheyne and John Wesley.[102]

A key impetus to the development of Kellogg's breakfast cereals was Seventh Day Adventism. This movement's founding teachings were established by the visions of Sister Ellen White, received in 1863 during the American Civil War. These included the importance of eating no more than two meals a day and abstaining from meat, lard, cake and spices. Positively, White's visions commended fruits, vegetables and Graham bread.[103] John Harvey Kellogg had worked as superintendent of the huge Adventist headquarters, the Battle Creek Sanatorium, which each year welcomed thousands of guests for health treatments and rehabilitation. In conjunction with his business-minded younger brother Will Keith, he had founded the Battle Creek Toasted Corn Flake Company to market his invention. The company also pioneered other meat substitutes such as peanut butter. The brothers' close relationship with White soured, however, as a result of rivalry and the brothers challenging key Adventist tenets such as sabbatarianism and White's infallibility. The consequence was that, in 1907, Will Keith was expelled from the Church.[104] Thus was severed the most important concrete linkage between Christian vegetarianism and twentieth-century mass food production, with the ancient mystical and spiritual basis for dietary discipline being superseded by modern scientific justifications.

Christian vegetarianism: a revival?

In the Battle Creek Sanatorium, dietary discipline was seen as assisting the recovery of a level of health which had previously been lost as a result of poor eating. In the 'muscular Christianity' movement in both the United States and Britain, however, good health in men was regarded in supererogatory terms as part of a spiritual striving whose results would be exhibited in the gymnasium, on the athletics track and through imperial conquest.[105] The place where good dietary habits could most reliably be inculcated in society's future leaders was, of course, the boys' boarding school. These institutions were seen by Eustace Miles, a classics lecturer at King's College, Cambridge, as providing opportunities to establish a new form of dietary regime in opposition to the meat-based orthodoxy upheld in the domestic sphere and buttressed by the medical profession.[106] Other commentators of the time were concerned to establish the dietary regime of adult males on a superior footing. A notable example is the transcendentalist Ralph Waldo Emerson, who saw dietary abstinence as a source of Christian self-mastery and the triumph of willpower over the sensual desires to avoid pain and seek pleasure.[107]

Yet for Christians concerned with diet, vegetarianism was no longer regarded as the only viable option. It came more frequently to be seen, contrary to long-standing Christian tradition, as a sign of weakness. As a result, some evangelistic movements distanced themselves from meat abstention and other traditional Christian practices for fear that these might detract from their 'pure' Gospel message. Of particular note is the Men and Religion Forward Movement, founded in New York in 1910 to promote a new style of evangelism which favoured heroic and aggressive conceptions of faith above what its leadership regarded as the privatized, feminized and enervated culture characteristic of too much modern Protestantism. *Collier's Weekly* tellingly described the movement's thirty programme experts as 'all hearty meat eaters'.[108] This description no doubt implied criticism of the vegetarianism associated with Seventh Day Adventists. Yet they had related their dietary prescriptions clearly to Christian tradition, rather than basing them on an aesthetic appeal to perceived secular norms. Moreover, they saw improved dietary discipline as a means of acquiring new physical and spiritual strength by reducing the deleterious effects on the body of consuming excessive quantities of meat.

In recent decades, the Roman Catholic and Orthodox Churches have both continued to promote fasting according to classic seasonal and church patterns.[109] One recent interpreter, Tito Colliander, has drawn on the desert fathers to commend moderate fasting on the grounds that it promotes freedom, a sense of emancipation and clarity of mind.[110] But although fasting disciplines are followed by some of the many members of these churches, they have not permeated wider society and have not been part of a wider advocacy of vegetarianism.

Some mainstream Christian churches have, in recent decades, tried occasionally to encourage their members to eat less meat as part of a lifestyle change in response to world hunger. Notable in this regard in the United States are the resolutions passed in the later 1970s by the United Reformed and Presbyterian Churches.[111] These had little traceable lasting impact, however, either within those Churches or in wider society. Indeed, in the public mind, vegetarianism is no longer associated with Christian observance. In religious terms, it is more often seen as indicating alignment with one of the world's four 'vegetarian religions', as Ryan Berry has described them – Jainism, Buddhism, Hinduism and Taoism.[112] Carol Adams, for instance, draws inspiration from Buddhism and yoga for her vision of vegetarianism as, among other things, a form of witness and celebration, and an experience of grace.[113] Alternatively, vegetarianism may be employed as a focal practice for combining and fusing elements from different religious traditions, as in Donald Altman's multi-faith vegetarian vision which draws in successive chapters on a succession of different religious traditions. Aspects identified by Altman as Christian include community and communion, fasting, and monastic attention or 'mindfulness' in food preparation and consumption.[114]

Alternatively, vegetarianism may be cast as one of a range of ethical concerns that have sprung up since the 1960s, 'with which,' in the words of Callum Brown, 'Christianity and the Bible in particular are perceived as being wholly unconcerned and unconnected'.[115] Sometimes it is linked with New Age spiritualities, which can share various structural similarities with historic Christianity, including narratives of personal conversion, cosmological doctrines and even fasting practices.[116] Yet any dietary discipline associated with them is unlikely to be related to Christian scripture, tradition or spirituality.

In the United States, the social importance which vegetarianism has come to assume as an independent quasi-religious movement was illustrated by a 1996 ruling of the federal Equal Employment Opportunity Commission in response to the sacking of Bruce Anderson, a vegetarian bus driver, for refusing to distribute coupons entitling his passengers to free hamburgers. The Commission ruled that his beliefs, although not religious in the classic sense, were just as strongly held as traditional religious beliefs and should, therefore, be respected and protected, and the lawsuit was settled by Anderson being awarded $50,000.[117] At the same time, it has been plausibly argued that even though vegetarianism frequently exhibits taboo and avoidance behaviour, reverence for life, denial of an ontology of death, and systems of personal discipline, it cannot ultimately be regarded as religious or even quasi-religious because it does not by itself entail belief in a deity.[118]

Some vegetarian groups are not unaware of the strong Christian tradition of meat abstinence and have identified churches as places potentially sympathetic to their message. In 2003, representatives of the 'Veg4Lent' campaign, sponsored by the Christian Vegetarian Association, wrote to nearly sixty Anglican and Roman Catholic bishops in Britain inviting them to support its initiative by abstaining from meat for Lent.[119] Only one quarter of the bishops contacted responded, and only one third of these considered that the campaign raised significant ethical or spiritual issues. The most prominent bishop to respond positively was Richard Chartres, the Bishop of London, who later became vegetarian.[120]

Although this conversion was by no means a big event, it points to a change in the perception of vegetarianism in the historic churches of Britain. In 1747, Chartres' predecessor in the See of London, Edmund Gibson, had used his visitation charge to accuse Methodists of 'extraordinary strictnesses and severities' and 'pretences to greater sanctity' on the basis of their distinctive material practices including diet.[121] His successor's choice has been explained ecologically, as a response to global warming, and ecumenically, as drawing on traditions in Orthodox Christianity with which he enjoys close links. At no point has his vegetarianism provoked serious accusations of heresy, 'pretences' or other unsoundness. Current concerns about the sustainability of food production have brought vegetarianism back towards what have come to be seen as mainstream Christian ethical and spiritual issues – and even, increasingly, back into newly emerging practices of Lenten fasting. For example, in 2009 the Christian relief and development charity Tearfund advocated eating less meat as part of a Carbon Fast for Lent.[122] Renewed interest in sustainability can in turn be related, as shown in Chapter Two, to a long Christian tradition of reflection on the place of diet in the natural, social and economic orders.[123]

We should be wary of 'baptizing' contemporary vegetarians either as Christian or more generally as religious. But it is also highly problematic to categorize them as 'secular' and hence to cut them off from the traditions which we have been exploring. In the opening years of the twenty-first century, increasing levels of concern in historically Christian cultures with a wide range of issues related to diet – health, obesity, genetic modification, food miles, anorexia – could be seen as replacing Christian belief in the role which it formerly played in shaping and defining personal identity. Alternatively, they could be regarded as a sign not of the end of Christian religion but of what Pierre Teilhard de Chardin called 'unsatisfied theism'.[124] This displays itself in a yearning for more organic forms of belief than those prominent in recent decades, and forms which address more convincingly the reality of human life as materially embodied.[125] Modern Western food spiritualities arise on sites evacuated by historic Christianity, and present it with immense challenges and opportunities to rediscover and articulate the historic dietary disciplines intrinsic to it.

5 Clean and unclean animals

In our first four chapters, we have shown by means of a broad historical survey that dietary issues have been vitally important to Christian identity and discipline, and that Christian reflection on dietary practice has often promoted general themes and aims, such as simplicity. Yet dietary practices always involve decisions about specific foods, and in the case of meat, about specific species of living being that are slaughtered and prepared for consumption as meat. What counts, or can be made to count, as meat has been a perennial question in the formation of dietary practices. Some animals are rarely classed as meat because they are rarely eaten. Alternatively, as will be seen, if there are rules against eating meat, various animals or parts of animals have even been excluded from the category of meat and therefore deemed edible.

This chapter and those which follow will focus on cross-historical themes that have shaped Christian dietary consciousness. In this chapter, we shall examine the relationship between dietary practices, categorizations of living beings and ethical and theological claims. In particular, we shall consider Christian uses of the Hebrew Bible, which is the source of food rules that is most deeply embedded in Christian thought. Some general comments on the relationship between food practices and beliefs are first appropriate. One of the principles that emerges from our study so far is that food rules are not the direct product of beliefs. Indeed, the frameworks of belief within which dietary practices are located develop partly in order to make sense of particular practices. Principles of classification and general rules emerge from reflection on historically contingent particularities. Yet conversely, specific practices are produced when general principles are applied to new situations. In some cases, these two movements are likely to conflict and generate contradictory results. Such clashes usually develop over time, as one set of cosmologies and practical justifications shifts and becomes overlaid by another. Single explanations for particular dietary practices, whether theological, biblical, economic or some other, usually fail. Furthermore, as practices persist and are transmitted through history, they seem to call for explanation and generate new explanations.

The meaning of biblical classifications

A substantial and well-known body of scholarly literature has developed to address the themes of order and separation in the Hebrew Bible's priestly literature and how this determines the classification of living beings and food rules.[1] Some explanations emphasise cosmological and cultural-historical explanations. Consider the best-known prohibition, that against eating pork. Mary Douglas' famous early account of why the pig was regarded as 'abominable' was founded on the idea that it failed to fit into a clear set of categories. Although it possessed a cloven hoof, it did not chew the cud.[2] Other explanations for pork avoidance have related the practice to Israel's national and religious self-definition: pork was the cheapest of the sacrificial animals and therefore offered widely to pagan gods; or it was regarded as demonical, and offered to infernal or secret deities. A once-popular biological explanation was that the pig carried trichinosis.[3] This explanation is particularly hard to justify: the symptoms of the disease are not mentioned in the Hebrew Bible or other Hebrew texts, and other animals apart from pigs are also carriers and transmitters.[4] Each of these explanations points to something important about how food works. Certain foods and certain food practices indeed pose greater health risks than others, food practices are key to forming and strengthening group identity, and ambiguous animals which elude categorization are troubling, especially when presented as food. Yet any single explanation would, if taken as a complete explanation, explain away the food rule in question, making its continued observance meaningless. This would render insignificant the wider theological context in which the particular rule is situated.

When Douglas revised her interpretation of the Levitical food rules, she described how her original analysis had been motivated by a concern to argue, in defiance of fashionable 1960s anti-structuralism, that order and patterning were fundamental to human life and not merely the accretions of bureaucratic late modernity from which enlightened people should or could liberate themselves.[5] In her reassessment, Douglas presents abomination as part of a wider theological cosmology of creation, covenant and fertility. She sees the regulation of Israel's use of animals as a mark of respect for them, which in turn results from the divine patterning of the universe according to the precepts of justice and mercy.[6] When discussing the meaning of abomination, Douglas then states that 'though contact with these [unclean] creatures is not against purity, harming them is against holiness', concluding that the 'animals classified as unclean turn out to be not abominable at all'.[7] Our discussion in this chapter will follow Douglas in seeking to understand the interrelationships between food rules, systems of classification and wider theology and ethics. Christian rereadings of the Hebrew Bible's food rules have sometimes been quick to explain them away and render them theologically irrelevant, but the history of Christian dietary restriction suggests that such interrelationships have continued to exert strong influence in Christian societies. In Douglas' own case, her long-standing interests in the ritual aspects of food dated from childhood, when as her biographer comments she 'learnt to read off the days of the week from the lunchtime menu' when staying at her grandparents' house while her parents were working in Burma with the Indian Civil Service, before later experiencing the strict mealtime regime of convent school.[8]

In the Hebrew Bible, living beings are classified primarily by the spaces they inhabit. The birds of the air, the animals of the land and the fish of the sea acquire their status as birds, animals or fish primarily by association with their habitats. These different locations are fundamental in the primordial ordering of the world described in Genesis 1, which presents the sky being created to separate the heavens from the waters of the earth, and then the waters of the earth being gathered together into one place in order that dry ground may appear.[9]

This spatial classification of living beings generates some marginal cases. The bat, for instance, is classed as a bird because it flies in the air and exhibits behaviour suited to this space, such as nesting.[10] The ostrich, in contrast, has more in common with land animals than with birds, despite possessing wings, because it cannot fly.[11] Other birds, such as the heron, stork and cormorant, live in close proximity to water and thus appear more naturally associated with it than with air, even though they have birdlike physical characteristics including wings and beaks.[12] Also ambiguous are shellfish, which live much of their life submerged under water yet cling to rocks or bury into the sand.[13] Similarly problematic are 'flying insects that walk on all fours', as the description tellingly puts it, pointing to their ambivalent situation as neither birds nor land animals.[14] According to Jean Soler, the common feature uniting the various living beings just mentioned is that, because they transgress one of the three boundaries between air, land and sea established at the creation, they are classed as unclean and therefore inedible. Classification by physical attributes impinges on the spatial categorization of animals. A method of locomotion is needed to inhabit the sea, land or air, and if this is absent from a particular living being, then that being cannot be regarded in any strict sense as inhabiting any of these three spaces. This is most clearly apparent in the case of fish, which in Leviticus are defined as creatures with fins and scales – in other words, as creatures able to swim through the water and flourish independently of the land.[15]

The quadruped

For the people of Israel, the most problematic living beings potentially available as food were land animals. Physically located close to human habitats, these were quite literally the 'animals with which in the most tangible sense we live on an equal footing'.[16] As in many societies, they were frequently stabled on the ground floor of the family house, especially during cold winter nights.[17] It is unsurprising, therefore, that land animals appear in various places in the Hebrew Bible to be under God's covenant and subject to the law.[18] They are required to rest on the Sabbath, when they may not perform any work such as ploughing.[19] Firstborn animals are in need of redemption and must be dedicated to the Lord.[20] Crucially, land animals pose greater purity problems than birds or fish due to their blood.[21] This physical and biological closeness of animals to humans brings them potentially closer in status than any other living beings to humans, and thereby calls into question humanity's sense of its unique place in nature based on its difference from other living beings. Categorizing land animals as edible and consuming them as meat is a clear means by which humans continually re-enact this distinction.

Medieval Christian usage of the quadruped category shows continuities with the Hebrew Bible.[22] Discourse from this period draws on the biblical texts to reflect on the perennially problematic status of the quadruped – the nonhuman animal that lives alongside humans and bleeds as humans do. As Ambrose of Milan states: 'There is in the nature of quadrupeds something which the language of the prophetical books exhorts us to imitate.'[23] But general exclusions of quadrupeds from Christian diet went well beyond any previous Jewish legislation, which had allowed quadrupeds regarded as clean to be eaten virtually all year round by all people, even Nazirites, provided that ritual requirements were met. In Christian tradition, the absence of any generally accepted sacrificial system for declaring a particular animal clean seems to have contributed to greater concern about all animal flesh. Most notably in the Rule of Benedict, which fundamentally shaped Western monasticism and was discussed in detail in Chapter Two, the consumption of quadruped flesh in monasteries was completely prohibited. Secular fasting laws also banned the wider populace from consuming meat during the long season of Lent and on many other fasts.

The Christian category of the quadruped was not formally defined in scripture, with the result that considerable disagreement arose about what it encompassed. The Benedictine legislation in particular, as a result of its brevity, set the parameters for a debate that would run for centuries over precisely which varieties of meat monks were permitted to eat. Some monasteries went to considerable lengths to classify as fish certain living beings that most people would regard as land animals. The best-known example was the beaver, notable for its wide furless tail. Gerald of Wales, whose critiques of monastic discipline have already been encountered, reports:

> In Germany and the northern regions, where beavers are plentiful, great and holy men eat the tails of beavers during fasting times – as being fish, since, as they say, they partake of the nature of fish both in taste and colour.[24]

Gerald relates a similar story about barnacle geese, which were popularly believed to grow on logs: 'In some parts of Ireland bishops and religious men eat them without sin during a fasting time, regarding them as not being flesh, since they were not born of flesh.'[25] Puffins were also regarded as fish in this period.[26] In these three examples, the living beings' boundary status becomes the reason used to justify their consumption by humans, rather than to account for their avoidance. This is because, in the scholastic context of these debates, attention is focused on food categories rather than on the boundaries separating those categories, with opportunities sometimes taken to exclude particular foods from prohibited categories.

Another line of argument concerned how far Benedict had intended to extend dietary restriction when compiling the Rule. What was his intention, some interpreters asked, in prohibiting consumption of the flesh of four-footed land animals (*quadrupeda*)? Some argued that eating game and chicken was a matter of indifference, given the absence of any specific prohibition. Others believed that Benedict had intended to promote a dietary regime similar to that of the desert anchorites, and regarded fowl as equally injurious to spiritual contemplation and on these grounds as effectively excluded.[27] In the East Syrian Church, fowl was prohibited on the ingenious grounds that, at Jesus' baptism, the Holy Spirit had descended in it.[28]

In general, it is not fanciful to draw connections from the Hebrew Bible's recognition of land animals as human neighbours and medieval avoidance of quadruped flesh to contemporary arguments for vegetarianism based on the idea that humans and other animals share certain characteristics. Within the wider biblical picture of creation, recognition that humans share their particular space, the land, with animals, shows that all creatures participate in a divinely ordered cosmos created for justice and mercy. Recognition of these imperatives leads us to a second, more extended, example of a Christian rereading of a biblical food rule: the blood prohibition.

Blood and predation

As has been noted, part of what makes land animals problematic is their blood. Killing an animal makes it consumable, but the blood shed in the act of killing shows the animal's closeness to humanity. In the Hebrew Bible, the entitlement to shed blood and its right exercise are tightly circumscribed. The draining of blood from a carcass marks the boundary between life and death, and the presence of blood indicates the presence of life. It is therefore a key requirement of biblical food rules, and established in the Noachide covenant, that the blood be drained from the carcass prior to consumption.[29]

This ritual system provided a means of negotiating the purity issues provoked by blood without requiring complete abstinence from animal flesh. It also defined a specifically human way of eating, and humans who failed to observe it could be regarded as little better in their eating habits than predatory animals. This point is developed in a commentary by Nachmanides, the thirteenth-century Catalan Jewish scholar, on the Israelite despoliation of the flocks and herds of the Philistines after their routing of the Philistine army. Saul's army, by 'flying' upon the spoil, slaughtering it on the ground and eating it with the blood 'before its life had entirely left it', behaved like a flock of predatory birds. Nachmanides protests of the Israelites' slaughter of these animals: 'Their blood was spilled on the ground. They tore off their limbs and ate them before life had entirely left the animals.'[30] Similarly, in order to highlight its uncivilized barbarity, the Assyrian army is compared in scripture with a lion, which 'tears' and 'strangles' its prey.[31]

Concerns about the shedding of blood have wider but less obvious implications for the food rules. Four quadrupeds are specified individually as unclean in both Leviticus and Deuteronomy: the camel, the rock badger, the hare and the pig.[32] In Leviticus, an additional list of prohibited animals includes the weasel, the mouse, the crocodile, the chameleon and various lizards.[33] Although these are quadrupeds, they are here all classified as animals that 'swarm' in language which emphasizes their closeness to the ground and the appearance of their movement to humans towering high above.[34] The reason given for the uncleanness of three of the quadrupeds – the camel, rock badger and hare – is that, although each of these animals chews the cud, it does not possess a split hoof. The pig, by contrast, although possessing a completely divided hoof, does not chew the cud.

Why are these features decisive in determining uncleanness? A clue is offered in Leviticus, where it is stated that all quadrupeds that walk on their paws are unclean.[35] The difference in function between a hoof and a claw is clear: whereas a hoof is hard and immovable, enabling an animal to stand upright and aiding stability in mud, a paw can be flexed and also contains claws or nails for catching and killing prey. In other words, if an animal is predatory, it is regarded as unclean. This account finds a parallel in the list of birds regarded as unclean, the majority of which are birds of prey that would feed on quadruped flesh: the eagle, the vulture, the buzzard, kites, ravens, hawks, and owls.[36]

The idea that land animals possessing the physical characteristics of predators are unclean is reinforced by the specific requirement that animals eaten by humans must be ruminant, chewing the cud rather than obtaining food by predation. In the case of birds, although no signs of uncleanness are mentioned in scripture, these were developed by subsequent rabbinic interpretation in order to aid recognition. A fowl with one more talon than normal and with a crop (food-storage cavity) and gizzard (stomach) that may both be peeled was fit to eat, on the grounds that birds possessing all three of these features are not predatory.[37] All birds possessing only one or two of the features were, in contrast, regarded as potential predators and therefore forbidden. There are, as usual, exceptions – the bearded vulture and the osprey – but, as Maimonides states, 'these two are not found in inhabited localities but only in the deserts and in the distant isles of the sea which are beyond human habitation'.[38] He here reads the biblical texts practically, as regulating potentially available foods, rather than cosmologically, as encompassing all known living beings. A similar system of animal classification based on diet is identifiable in the seven-volume *Book of Animals* of the Arabian polymath Al-Jahiz. There, land animals are divided into humans, non-carnivorous quadrupeds, and carnivores, as well as insects without wings or feathers.[39] Flying animals are similarly distinguished as either carnivorous or non-carnivorous.[40]

This typology of animals as clean or unclean on the basis of their diet makes sense in the case of the birds previously listed, which possess claws and the obvious capacity to capture, kill and consume prey. Furthermore, among the prohibited land species the camel, hare and pig are all known to scavenge smaller mammals, and in extreme cases human flesh. Pigs are recognized in several cultures to be indiscriminate scavengers and therefore effective waste-disposal systems, sometimes being bred for this purpose.[41] A notable example has been their use by the Zabbaleen community of Coptic Christians in Cairo, who have for the past century been primarily responsible for refuse disposal and recycling in the city.[42] Despite increasing competition from new waste disposal companies, which employ modern technologies, the Zabbaleen have continued to inhabit shanty towns near the dumps outside the city and perform this role. In a dominant Muslim culture, their use of pigs has contributed to forming their identity as a distinct community engaged in unclean work. This confirms the truth of Xavier de Planhol's observation that peoples who eat pork within the zone of Islam's influence are considered impure.[43]

The notion that animals are unclean if they are predatory is lent credibility by the first Genesis creation narrative, in which animals are, like humans, given green plants for food. God intends animals to be herbivorous.[44] Human diet is subsequently modified to include meat, but no such change is granted to animals. Predatory animals and scavenging animals are therefore both regarded as contravening divine dietary law. The divine dispensation granted to humans as part of the new covenant following the Flood is presented clearly, with God blessing Noah and his sons with the words 'Everything that lives and moves will be food for you. Just as I gave you the green plants, I now give you everything.'[45] In the next verse, they are required to drain the lifeblood from a carcass before consuming its meat. But animals are given no such permission. No further covenant is made with them after the Flood, and they would in any case be incapable of draining the blood from their prey before devouring it.

The practical import of the dietary rules about predation is not confined to the distant past. For example, bovine spongiform encephalopathy (BSE) spread among cattle in Britain during the 1980s because normally herbivorous animals were fed on the remains of other animals in the form of rendered meat and bone meal. Disease, in the form of (new) variant Creutzfeldt-Jakob disease (vCJD), spread to humans who had consumed infected beef, which was, in effect, the flesh of a predatory animal.

Christian diet: Jerusalem and beyond

Walter Houston argues that the food rules of Leviticus and Deuteronomy, such as those concerned with blood and predation, were in broad continuity with wider cultural notions of cleanness and uncleanness. What was distinctive about the practices was not that they existed but that they were formalized into a ritual system that impinged on people's daily lives, which could as such be taught, internalized and passed on to future generations. Yet he asserts and argues at length, in continuity with later Christian self-perception, that 'early Christianity abandoned the law of forbidden food'.[46] The Christian picture is, in fact, more complicated. A key moment in the Christian acceptance of some of the dietary laws of the Hebrew Bible was the Council of Jerusalem, described in Acts 15. The Council's president was James, the brother of Jesus, identified by Hegessipus as a strict ascetic who avoided all meat.[47] Believers from Antioch, Syria and Cilicia (now southern Turkey) were urged by public letter from the Council to abstain from blood and from the meat of strangled animals – from which the blood could not have been properly drained – as well as from food sacrificed to idols.[48] This text was cited by a council of Eastern bishops held at Constantinople in 652, which instructed:

> The divine scripture commands us to abstain from blood, from things strangled, and from fornication. Those therefore who on account of a dainty stomach prepare by any art for food the blood of any animal, if he be a clergyman, let him be deposed; if a layman, let him be cut off.[49]

The edict of Jerusalem echoes, as has often been noted, the prescriptions of the Noachide covenant, which is regarded in Jewish theology as applying to the whole of humanity. Its adoption by subsequent councils may be simply due to its presence in the Christian scriptural canon, as the instruction suggests. In this case, no wider implications follow for Christian thinking about the consumption of blood. But the problematic status of blood is a notable theme in subsequent Christian reflection, which draws clearly on the Hebrew Bible.

The best-documented and most extensive Christian observance of biblical food rules relating to blood is in Celtic Ireland, with the Canons of Adamnan being particularly noteworthy. Adamnan was Abbot of Iona from the year 679 until his death in 704, and the biographer of St Columba.[50] These canons give extended consideration to situations in which animals have been killed accidentally or by an unknown means, because it is difficult in such cases to establish whether their blood has been properly drained. Canon 2 states:

> Cattle that fall from a rock, if their blood has been shed, are to be taken; if not, but if their bones are broken and their blood has not come out, they are to be rejected as if they were carrion.

Adamnan pursues the implications of this requirement to drain the blood from a carcass, proscribing in Canons 3 and 14 the eating of drowned animals on the grounds that their blood remains within them. He also bans, in Canons 17–19, the consumption of flesh eaten by predatory animals, because the blood in the flesh has been shed by beasts. Another unidentified Irish penitential forbids the consumption of cat's vermin on penalty of a bread and water fast lasting one hundred days, while the Preface on Penance by Gildas lays down forty days' penance for eating carrion, even in cases when the offence is committed unwittingly.[51]

Regarding carrion, similar requirements are found in the Penitential of Archbishop Theodore of Canterbury, also dating from the seventh century. Animals 'torn by wolves or dogs' cannot be eaten, on pain of a penance lasting forty days, and stags and goats may not be consumed under any circumstance unless it is reliably known that they were killed by a human being.[52] Moreover, at his accession in 731, Pope Gregory III issued a general prohibition against the consumption of blood and of strangled animals on pain of forty days' penance.[53]

This suggests that blood avoidance was not an issue confined to the Irish church. Indeed, the preservation in some Orthodox churches of the blood prohibition, even into the early modern period, contrasts sharply with evolving Western practice, and has sometimes produced conflicts when Western missions have rediscovered Orthodox churches and their practices. For example, counter-Reformation Catholic missionaries in Egypt strongly objected to the Coptic conviction that all meat eaten must have been slaughtered in accordance with the requirements of the Old Testament.[54]

One feature of Irish monastic food rules which cannot be traced to the Jerusalem edict, but appears to be more directly related to the Hebrew Bible, is the problematic status of predatory animals as potential food sources. Adamnan instructs in Canon 8: 'Hens that taste the flesh of a man or his blood are in a high degree unclean, and their eggs are unclean; but their chicks are to be preserved.' The issue of the possible contamination of animal offspring is also discussed in the preceding Canon 7, in which pigs that have tasted human flesh or blood are deemed unclean, but their young are permitted to be eaten. A related intriguing dilemma is raised in Canon 6: what to do with a pig that has eaten carrion. Does the uncleanness spread throughout the entire body of the pig, and does it persist for the remainder of the pig's life? The latter would seem an unfeasibly rigorous interpretation and be likely to contribute to food shortages in times of hardship. Adamnan offers a practical response:

> swine's flesh that has become thick or fat on carrion is to be rejected like the carrion by which it grows fat. When, however, [the swine] has grown smaller and returned to its original thinness, it is to be taken. But if it had eaten carrion [only] once or twice, after this has been ejected from its intestines it is to be taken in good faith.

Theodore of Canterbury grapples with a similar question, ruling that if pigs or hens merely taste human blood they remain clean, but that if any 'tear and eat the corpses of the dead, their flesh may not be eaten until they become feeble and weak and until a year has elapsed'.[55] The desire to prevent one human consuming part of another human body probably motivated such reasoning. This would have been seen as presenting problems for the resurrection of both human bodies for the reasons discussed in Chapter Three.

Once again, the biological aspects of the concern about eating carnivorous or scavenging animals should not be discounted. Adamnan directs in Canons 12–14 that no food which has come into contact with pigs, crows or leeches be eaten, on the grounds that these animals are likely previously to have consumed contaminated flesh. Ann Hagen identifies concerns with health and hygiene as underlying Christian ideas about uncleanness in Anglo-Saxon England as early as the eighth century, with mice and weasels, both well-known scavengers, regarded as especially problematic.[56] Dogs and cats were also considered to be agents of contamination, with various of the Irish penitentials previously cited imposing penances on people who consumed food touched by these animals.[57]

They were at best useful means of catching vermin, and in this earlier medieval context it would have been unthinkable that such animals would one day acquire privileged domestic status with owners expending time and money providing them with good food.

This ambivalence about consuming blood persisted alongside a catholic sacramental tradition in which, in the Eucharist, the blood of Christ shed on the Cross provided a primary focus. According to a range of theological interpretations, this blood is symbolized in the wine, which is offered to the people gathered at the Eucharist to be consumed in accordance with Christ's commandment at the Last Supper. Yet the deeply ambiguous nature of this practice that is central to Christian worship and spirituality is today rarely recognized.[58] The biblical prohibition on consuming blood extended not only to the people of Israel but to all foreigners living among them.[59] In the Gospels of Matthew and Mark, the prominence given in the Eucharistic institution narratives and associated theological expositions to the drinking of blood can be seen as constructed in order to present a complete rupture with Jewish legal tradition and cultural practice.[60] Indeed, from this perspective it is only in John's Gospel – the one Gospel lacking a formal institution narrative – that the scandalous nature of the idea is fully expounded: that, in the Eucharist, flesh and blood are somehow really consumed. This is taught by Jesus, provocatively, in the synagogue at Capernaum.[61] Yet the blood has often been relegated to second place, with long-standing traditions of congregations receiving the flesh but not the blood, and of reserving only the flesh. Moreover, while what appears as bread is normally referred to as the body of Christ, what appears as wine is frequently designated via elliptical reference to its receptacle, the cup or chalice. Drinking blood remains, it would seem, more problematic than eating flesh.

Eating moral and spiritual animals

Despite the often neglected history of Christian observance of food rules, Christian interpretations of the Hebrew Bible have generally assumed or argued that the rules need not be taken literally. Such rereadings have had obvious implications for dietary practice. Yet it proves difficult to escape these texts' concern with real food, especially when Christians interpret them alongside observant Jewish communities. In Chapter Seven, we shall examine in greater depth the ways in which Christian food practices have functioned to contrast Christianity with Judaism. In the remainder of this chapter, we shall focus on interpretations of food texts in the Hebrew Bible by Christian theologians.

The Epistle of Barnabas provides a good early example of a Christian text that moves from the claim that Moses 'spoke with a spiritual reference' when laying down the food rules to a detailed rereading of clean and unclean animals in moral terms. Fish with fins or scales signify endurance and self-control, whereas the forbidden fish, which lack these, are swept away by the current. Reptiles, wriggling along on their belly, represent people who are motivated by greedy desires and passions. Creeping things able to leap serve as an allegory for successful moral effort. By contrast, pigs recognize their master only when hungry, and so represent people who remember the Lord only when in need.[62] Birds of prey signify people who sit idly waiting to seize on the flesh of others rather than procuring their food by work and toil. Christians should not, Barnabas warns, associate with such people. The food rules thereby define the boundaries of a moral community, even in their spiritual use.

The epistle could be read as a supersessionist attempt to replace Jewish definitions of identity with Christian definitions.[63] However, allegorical rereadings of biblical food rules were not confined to Christianity, being also a significant strand of Jewish tradition.[64] Indeed, the positive allegorical meanings Barnabas presents for clean food are very similar to those proposed by Philo, who complains that the sophists 'divide as it were the hoof by making hairsplitting distinctions but do not smooth the roughness that has accrued to their soul by chewing the cud', which itself symbolizes the 'method best suited for acquiring knowledge ... memorizing again and again what one has learned'.[65] Allegorical and literal interpretations of these rules are not opposed, therefore, but mutually confirming.

This chapter has shown how the idea that some potential foods are clean and therefore available for consumption, while others are unclean and should be avoided, has a long history in Christian practice. In medieval Christendom, however, the practice of categorizing certain foods as unclean came to be regarded as fundamentally and uniquely Jewish. Literal adherence to the food rules of the Hebrew Bible became, for Christians, a sign first of Jewish 'hardness of heart' and then of Jewish irrationality. The literal sense of the food rules was, it was claimed, rendered obsolete by the coming of Christ, and in later medieval interpretations the literal interpretation of the food rules was condemned as intrinsically irrational.[66] As Abigail Firey shows, as early as the ninth century Carolingian theologians developed the tradition of reading the food rules allegorically in direct and polemical opposition to Jewish interpretation.[67] Agobard of Lyons presented the chewing of the cud as a form of interminable mastication which pointed to the open-ended, self-generating and for him indiscriminate character of Jewish scripture and teaching.[68] He also suggested that Jews effectively consume the very animals from which they claim to abstain by exhibiting their immoral characteristics:

> In a spiritual sense the Jews imitate and eat the camel ... Figuratively, they consume the owl and the bat, from their cunning the fox, from their strength the ass, from their ignorance the ox, from the filth of their mouths the pig and all the impure reptiles and birds.[69]

This inversion was based on Christian taboos against particular animals, turned against the tradition from which Christians had inherited them. It was a common polemical tactic to argue that the Jews in fact no longer observed the law as handed down to them by the prophets, having replaced this with superstitious and superfluous observances. Notions of cleanness and uncleanness were, it was argued, part of the oral tradition – both as recorded in scripture and as developed in subsequent interpretation – which contradicted the true teaching of the Old Testament. Christian polemicists thereby sought to use Jewish dietary practices as a means of wresting ownership and interpretive control of the Hebrew Bible away from Jews and into their own possession.

Aelfric of Eynsham, in his late-tenth-century tract on the Passion of the Maccabees, states that

> clean beasts who chew their cud
> betoken those men who meditate in their mind
> about God's will, after that they hear his word
> from teachers' mouths, as if they chewed their meat.
> And those are unclean which chew not their cud,
> because they betoken those who desire not rightly,
> neither will learn what may be pleasing to God,
> nor revolve in their minds the Saviour's commands,
> and they are therefore unclean just like the wicked beasts.

The cloven hoof is also assigned a spiritual meaning, signifying

> the two testaments,
> the old and the new, that is Law and Gospel;
> and that we ponder in mind the Almighty's behest;
> and he who forsakes either, he liveth unclean[70]

Aelfric's text reflects Christian ambivalence about food laws. He deploys a comprehensive rereading of the Maccabean text to undermine his Jewish contemporaries' continuing refusal to eat pork yet claims spiritual kinship with the Maccabean martyrs, who before the advent of Christianity died rather than agree to eat pork. He affirms the principle that 'all things are clean to all men', while acknowledging that 'some were then foul, which now are also foul'. Aelfric is unable to escape the facts that choices are made, and continue to be made, about which foods are acceptable, and that there is some continuity between Christian and Jewish food practices. His discussion ends with the rather unsatisfactory assertion that

> it will be too tedious to discourse here fully
> concerning the clean beasts or concerning the unclean
> in the old law, which one eats now nevertheless.

In the later medieval period, mendicant preachers such as the Franciscan Ramon Lull further developed the tradition of reading the Hebrew Bible's food rules against Jews. For Lull, the significant point about chewing the cud was that it entailed rumination, which is a double digestive process. Animals such as cows only digest food after eating it a second time, which implied for him that the new Christian law surpassed the old, regurgitated Israelite law as a path to virtue and truth because it was new food.[71] Similarly, he regarded a split hoof as signifying the distinction between bodily existence and spiritual existence, an interpretation which again undermined the literal Jewish food practices with its implication that those practices were based on a misguided conflation of spirituality with materiality. Christian disputational literature from this period proclaims not merely the supersession of Jewish practices, including food practices, but also their inherent irrationality.

This exclusion of the literal sense of scripture in favour of allegorical senses is highly problematic. It is also difficult to reconcile with Christian exegetical practice when faced with other moral topics such as sexual relations. In the words of Henri de Lubac, allegory 'does not eliminate the literal sense or add something else to it but rather rounds it out and gives it its fullness, revealing its depths and bringing out its objective extension'.[72] Even Augustine's case for abolishing Christian dietary asceticism did not rest on this contestable exegesis of Hebrew scripture but on an unease with Manichean cosmology and spirituality which pervaded his Christian theology. For Augustine, the allegorical sense of scripture was always dependent on its literal sense.[73] This was because, if the facts are not accepted as really existing, the allegories inferred from them possess no reference in the concrete world and therefore remain speculative. Furthermore, texts describing food rules – like food practices themselves, including those discussed in preceding chapters – have oddities, inconsistencies and unexpected effects which prove difficult to encompass within a single explanatory framework. Some Christian interpretations of the Hebrew Bible, as well as Jewish interpretations, have understood the food rules in ways which neither dismiss them nor domesticate their strangeness.[74]

Claudine Fabre-Vassas suggests that medieval European Christians justified eating or avoiding certain foods, especially around the time of major Christian festivals, by extrapolating from scripture. For example, the conger eel was thought a desirable food because it had plugged a hole in Noah's ark; John Dory and skate bear the imprint of Jesus' hand or the instruments of his Passion, or of Mary's face; chickpeas were grazed at the Temple doorstep by the donkey carrying Jesus to Jerusalem on Palm Sunday, and are eaten on that day in Catalonia.[75] Conversely, Catalans avoided the onion on the grounds that Judas was weaned on onion omelette.[76] Desirable and undesirable foods, and seasonal patterns of diet, were given additional levels of meaning by being located within Christian narratives, but without ceasing to be 'real' food. Here, local and traditional dietary practices, the origins of which were probably entirely obscure, performed a function similar to the food laws of the Hebrew Bible. They were, in their very oddness and superfluity, a spur to theological and moral reinterpretation. As long as the practices themselves continued, they were open to new explanations that did not explain them away, just as the preservation of the literal sense of the scriptural text left open the possibility of multiple future reinterpretations.

Christian reflection on animals and the lessons they taught humanity, especially via the moral characteristics imputed to them, was also sometimes used to support dietary exclusions. The arguments employed could be bizarre, particularly in the case of the hare. Owing to its natural associations with fertility, the hare had functioned as a totem animal and was even regarded in some cultures as divine.[77] This might have been why early Christian writers subjected it to moral critique. Timotheus of Gaza recorded that the hare was, like the hyena, alternatively male and female.[78] Clement of Alexandria reported in greater depth, drawing on Aristotle by adding that it possessed an insatiable sexual urge and that the doe was polygamous, able to mate each month and give birth each month even while suckling previous offspring. Even more fabulously, he alleged that the hare each year acquired a new anus, and as a result possessed an orifice for each year of its life. By not consuming the hare, he argued, Christians reject violent desires, uninterrupted sex, sex with pregnant women, homosexuality, pederasty, fornication and sexual licence.[79] The hare has also been regarded as problematic by some Muslims, especially Shi'ahs.[80] The fourteenth-century theologian Ad-Damîrî offers a similar description, adding that the hare, like the bat, menstruates, before concluding bemusedly, 'Praise be to Him who is capable of performing all things!'[81]

In the case of fish, which recur as a symbol of sexual and spiritual purity, the influence of the moral bestiary has persisted into the present day, providing part of the background to the consumption of fish on fast days and the use of a fish in schematic form as a Christian symbol. People commonly believed that fish did not reproduce by intercourse but were born spontaneously. Hence Basil the Great observed in a sermon that the unions of fish were 'not like those of mules on the land' because the 'water receives the egg that falls and makes an animal of it'.[82] Augustine went further, believing that bees, frogs and 'many other creatures' were not generated by sexual intercourse.[83] The Cathars, discussed in Chapter Six, are the most obvious example of a group with Christian links for whom the supposed sexual purity of fish made them a permissible food.[84] Furthermore, it is unclear in biblical interpretation whether fish were rendered extinct by the Flood. If they were not subjected to the same punishment of drowning by inundation by which all land animals and birds perished, they were by implication free from sin. This possibility helps to explain why Christians have consistently regarded marine life as less problematic food than land animals or birds of the air. They appear unaware of the opinions of some rabbis that the floodwater was hot and therefore dissolved the bodies of fish – or of the possible escape routes also mooted in Midrash, such as diving to deeper, cooler waters or migrating to the Mediterranean Sea, which the floodwater was believed not to have reached.[85] Representations of fish as pure, as well as Jesus' cooking of fish for his disciples on the beach following the Resurrection, lent support to the idea that they were an appropriate Christian food.[86] Furthermore, although fishing involves the killing of a living being, it is generally a peaceful occupation which does not entail the noise and other commotion of killing land animals.[87]

A further interesting dimension of the interplay between literal eating and its religious interpretations can be found in some of Christianity's unexpected positive food metaphors. These are, in modern terms, countercultural. For example, the metaphor of God as sweet has been recurrent in Christian spiritual imagery. This sweetness has, like any sensory experience, been not abstract but concrete, dependent on real sweet foods for its meaning and evoking the Song of Songs imagery of the bride's lips dripping with honeycomb as well as the land flowing with milk and honey and God's word tasting sweeter than honey.[88] In this context, sweetness represents natural purity and spiritual devotion, reinforced by the belief, discussed previously, that bees conceive miraculously. The metaphor draws at least some of its power from a cultural context in which the experience of tasting 'sweetness' was fairly rare, and associated with foods, such as honey, which were not products of human manufacture. That the source of the taste of sweetness is natural is important here. By contrast, most sweet foods eaten today are highly processed, available in large quantities, and rightly deemed unhealthy if consumed in such quantities. In any case, paying greater attention to the basis of Christian food metaphors in people's experience of real food might prompt a reconsideration of dietary choices.

A structured gift

Food is the paradigmatic consumer good. It has, by definition, no role in human culture apart from being eaten, at which point it ceases to exist as food. It is no accident that the imagery of eating is used to portray a wide range of other types of consumption: digesting information, devouring books or feasting the eyes. Imagery is sometimes inverted so that a person becomes the food being eaten, such as when being 'consumed' by envy, anger or passion. Human perceptions of food and eating thereby exemplify and illumine other activities that come to be seen as consumer acts. Food and eating are important in themselves, but also possess wider significance.

The idea that the world and its provisions are gifts from God to humankind is prominent in current theology. The implications of this idea for a theology of eating are, however, ambiguous. Frequently associated with the gift are concepts like excess, abundance and overflow. So far as food is concerned, however, these quickly become problematic when deployed to suggest that resources have been given to humanity without any structure of rules or traditions limiting their use. At their worst, notions of excess can unwittingly buttress a view of the world as little more than the legitimate object of progressive annihilation driven by advanced consumer capitalism.

Some of the beliefs and exclusions examined in this chapter are weird, such as those surrounding the hare, and there is no good reason for present-day Christians to accept them. Nevertheless, they point to a view of specific animals eaten as meat or rejected as meat as inhabiting a world imbued with moral, symbolic and theological meaning. It is this world which humans eat. Moreover, the difficulty of rationally justifying the avoidance of some foods points to the possibility of placing a greater burden of justification for consuming particular land animals, birds and fish as meat on consumers than has become common. Among the people of Israel, exclusions were not regarded as requiring an over-poweringly convincing justification. Rather, if the range of species of living beings defined as clean and available for consumption was sufficiently wide to provide the population with enough food of these kinds, there was no reason to classify any further species as clean. A similar motivation seems to be at work in the preservation of these rules by modern Diaspora Jews, especially those living in the United States. There, an advanced consumer society both celebrates the free, undifferentiated availability of food products and establishes a dynamic of assimilation into those practices, but in so doing intimates their superfluity and provokes resistance.[89]

The world's food resources are not only structured but finite and exhaustible, as classical liberal economics, with distant origins in scholastic natural law theory, correctly recognized in its founding concept of 'scarcity'. Theologians need to embrace anew the concept of scarcity, especially when thinking about food – not least because they have distinctive intellectual resources to offer to its redefinition as humankind encounters ever more closely its ecological limits. An adequate theological response to ecological scarcity cannot, of course, be to quantify the gift purely in terms of its exchange or money value. But it would be equally inexcusable for theologians to dismiss altogether the idea of scarcity as a conceit of 'secular' economics. Its cosmological and spiritual dimensions need to be rearticulated, and theologians have a distinctive contribution to make to this task.

In this chapter, we have shown that the world is indeed presented by God to humans as a gift for their consumption. Yet it is, crucially, a gift intrinsically patterned by structure, boundaries and rules. This patterning does not fit neatly with a modern consumerist 'logic' that everything in the world is comprehensively or completely available for consumption. It is far more complex, being unfolded in Christian scriptural, moral, theological and sacramental traditions, and exhibiting a real respect for the animal creation and its variety. Such respect needs to be reaffirmed in our own day, however different the choices we make and the reasons behind them may be from those of the past. Furthermore, various rules seem to demonstrate underlying good sense identifiable in modern terms. This includes the potential for some animals that eat other animals to carry diseases like BSE, and the likelihood that predatory or scavenging animals will pose greater hygiene risks to humans than will herbivorous animals. Yet the example of the Zabbaleen in Cairo showed how the keeping, feeding and eventual eating of scavenging animals, especially pigs, can provide one part of an ecologically sustainable system of recycling other products of human consumption. It cannot be overlooked, however, that in this case the positive ecological function is in the context of a life lived in poverty as a small and increasingly oppressed Christian minority.

It is no mere coincidence that Christian traditions of food and eating have been handed on from one generation to the next along with the world's actual resources, because they are essential to understanding and sustaining those resources. The structured differentiation by which the gift of the world's resources to humankind is characterized is, as has been seen in this chapter, described in detail in the Hebrew Bible. Christians and all humans are called to acknowledge that the natural world of which they are part exhibits structure and that rules, followed obediently and with appropriate self-sacrifice, are needed if its resources are to continue to be handed on.

6 Community, orthodoxy and heresy

A key thread running through this study has been the function of dietary practices in identifying people as Christians. In some cases, diet has situated individuals within a continuing ascetic strand of Christian tradition exemplified by particular figures such as John the Baptist, hermits in the Egyptian desert, and well-known personalities of the modern era like John Newton and John Wesley. More frequently, dietary practices have been located in a community context, with individuals adopting particular disciplines in order to identify themselves as members of a specific Christian group. For example, the Rule of Benedict required abstinence from quadruped flesh, the Bible Christian Church imposed vegetarian discipline on its members, and the entire adult population of Reformation England was enjoined to abstain from red meat during Lent in obedience to its new royal head King Henry VIII and his successors.

Christian communities, like other religious communities, define themselves partly by contrasting their own dietary practices with those of the majority culture or of other communities, especially those with which they are competing for the label of doctrinal orthodoxy. Hence the relationship which develops between diet, community membership and orthodoxy is dynamic, with dietary discipline contributing to the construction of doctrinal boundaries between different religious groups. This suggests that Christian communities will have different food practices in different places, even during the same historical period, depending on which other religious groups are present in their locality.

This chapter will explore in greater depth the role of food in defining and reinforcing doctrinal boundaries. But a prior possibility, frequently voiced by Christians, first needs to be considered: that food rules of any kind are in fact inimical to Christianity, that much of the material so far presented in this book is an aberration of true Christian belief and practice, and that the identifying feature of Christianity distinguishing it from other religions is and should be its lack of concern with food, eating and diet.

Augustine's Manichaean shadow

For nine years before his Christian conversion and baptism, Augustine of Hippo had been a Manichaean 'hearer'. The widespread and powerful religion of

Manichaeism had been founded during the third century by its prophet Mani and was inspired by his writings. Among its key features were the distinctive food practices to which its higher, elect members were required to conform, and the reasons given for these. The food of the elect was picked and prepared for them by the hearers, some of whom functioned as their servants, so that the elect did not themselves inflict pain on the divine light particles which they believed to be mixed with the food. Augustine himself performed this service, 'supplying food to those whose title was the Elect and Holy, so that in the workshop of their stomach they could manufacture for us angels and gods to bring us liberation'.[1] He would, like all hearers, have been rewarded for his troubles with a ritual cursing then absolution for the pain he had caused the food, followed by intercession for his spiritual health.

Paradoxically, although food preparation was thus regarded in profoundly negative terms, tremendous theological value was attached to the act of eating. When eating, the elect were believed to separate the light particles from the matter imprisoning them, releasing these particles by ingesting the matter into their bodies.[2] The particles represented the reincarnated souls of the dead, which were then freed to return to the spiritual realm. This abstruse cosmology led to the conclusion that it would be sinful to feed a person dying of starvation if this disrupted or in any way diminished the food supply to the tables of the elect, who at their daily common meal were engaged in a theologically and metaphysically far superior enterprise.[3] As Augustine comments acerbically, according to this reasoning belching has greater moral worth than feeding the poor, with more mercy shown to a cucumber than to a human being.[4]

In one Manichean confessional prayer from Turkey, all harming of five categories of animals – humans, quadrupeds, flying animals, water animals and creeping things – was forbidden: they were not to be frightened, scared, beaten, angered, pained or killed.[5] The destruction of all living beings was thus prohibited because this would further imprison in matter the pure elements of light, and would pollute the bodies of the elect. At their daily common meal, the foods regarded as acceptable were those considered to possess a high light content. Apart from cucumbers, these included melons, wheat bread, beans, lettuce, herbs, oil, water and fruit.[6]

The boundary between Manichaeism and Christian orthodoxy was sufficiently contested that many Manichaeans saw themselves as a Christian sect, characterized not by heresy but by the seriousness with which they pursued their philosophic and ascetic endeavours.[7] Accusations that he remained a closet Manichee dogged Augustine long after his Christian conversion. Around the time of his consecration, his senior bishop Megalius of Calama accused him of being a crypto-Manichaean.[8] In Augustine's old age, Julian of Eclanum charged him with holding a Manichaean view of evil as a permanently existing force, and sought to demonstrate the Manichaean character of his views on issues such as salvation and the ubiquity of unmerited worldly suffering.[9]

In the context of a Christian empire and the evolving concept of Christian orthodoxy, identifying an opponent as Manichaean was a standard form of abuse, with wandering monks and ascetics providing especially easy targets.[10] Augustine played a key role in the forging of Christian orthodoxy, and after turning his back on the Manichaeans therefore needed to demonstrate his antipathy to their movement and doctrines in the clearest terms possible. As Veronika Grimm states, 'using the issue of their food customs, especially their vegetarianism, he attempted to expose and ridicule the speciousness of their beliefs in the transmigration of souls, the entrapment of pieces of God in vegetation, and the like'.[11] This was an especially important task in his coastal see of Hippo, which was a key centre for Manichaeism and potentially for its diffusion via trade routes both northwards and inland.[12] Augustine was particularly critical of the hierarchical organization of the Manichaean diet, which had permitted hearers such as him to consume meat while requiring the elect to abstain. Because none of the animals killed by the hearers could therefore be offered to the elect for consumption as meat, no pardon could ever be gained by a hearer for an act of killing.[13] This meant that hearers who ate meat lived in a permanent state of damnation.

Moreover, Augustine undermines the idea that humans would ever require a pardon for killing living beings by arguing that no 'community of rights' [*societatem juris*] exists encompassing humans, animals and plants. This is 'shown by Christ', he contends, who sent devils into the herd of swine and withered the fig tree with a curse.[14] In the case of animals, another reason why no such community exists, Augustine claims, is that they lack a rational soul. The fact that humans 'see and hear that animals die with pain' is, he contends, ethically irrelevant.[15]

Augustine's refusal of the idea that all sentient beings are bound together in a community of rights could be regarded as part of a deeply problematic trajectory within Western thought which excludes the nonhuman creation from the moral community. Yet it seems that his principal reason for resisting this idea was his objection to the Stoic and Manichaean cosmology of the unity of all beings. This led, in his view, to repugnant conclusions. If the Manichaean version of this cosmology is correct, he protested, and trees weep when picked and vegetables experience pain as they are pulled from the earth, then it would appear that nothing can be eaten.[16] He rages:

> Surely it is great madness to make a pretence of piety in not slaughtering animals, while you hold that the souls of animals inhabit all the food you eat, and yet make what you call living creatures suffer such torture from your hands and teeth.[17]

Augustine also attacks more specific Manichaean abstention from animal flesh by targeting its justification on the grounds that such flesh is peculiarly unclean. This was based on the teaching that the first animals to have inhabited the earth had been the live aborted offspring of heavenly women precipitated when the sky began its rotation. Augustine argued, however, that animals should therefore be seen as superior to other non-sentient elements of the world, not inferior; and by implication more clean, not less clean, due to their heavenly origin.[18] Vegetables, in contrast, come out of the earth, and so are generated from a lower principle. Following Manichaean logic, he argues, they should in fact be seen as less edible than meat.

Arrangements at the daily meal of the elect, Augustine complains, encouraged overeating, contrasting sharply with the Christian practice of moderation. Too many provisions were often brought to the meal, he recollects, but because the surplus could not be thrown away or distributed to others, the elect ate huge quantities, and when sated, allegedly forced boys in the community to do the same. He goes so far as to accuse the elect of child murder by this practice.[19] In contrast with the disciplines of orthodox Christian ascetics, this was outrageous gluttony. Augustine avers:

> Is it not the greatest absurdity that one, who stuffs and loads his stomach every day to gratify his appetite with mushrooms, rice, truffles, cake, mead, pepper, and asafoetida, and who fares thus every day, cannot be transgressing … the rule of sanctity; whereas another, who seasons his dish of the commonest herbs with some smoky morsel of meat … be doomed to certain punishment?[20]

This behaviour was a perfect example of concupiscence, which he sought to extirpate from the spiritual life.[21]

Augustine is not being entirely fair here. The basis for the Manichaean belief that the elect possessed the ability to release the particles of divine light from the food they ate was that the elect were themselves spiritually pure, gaining this status through rigorous spiritual practices including fasting, which was organized partly to commemorate the life of Mani.[22] Manichaeans fasted for specific periods totalling one hundred days per year, including a single span of thirty days.[23] The fasting of each elect member was believed to vanquish all the archon spirit within them, refine and sift out the darkness bound up with their food, and on Sundays to generate seven angels.[24] Moreover, hearers were required to fast for fifty days of the year and were also regarded as able to produce angels when fasting on Sundays.[25]

Augustine was also abstemious following his Christian conversion, like the Manichaeans during their periods of fasting. Possidius states: 'His table was frugal and sparing, though indeed with the herbs and lentils he also had meats at times for the sake of his guests or for some of the weaker brethren.'[26] Augustine certainly respected ascetic Christians, praising the monks of the Egyptian and Palestinian deserts as well as city-dwelling ascetics. Yet he saw their abstinence as motivated by very different factors from those influencing the Manichaeans. After discussing Paul's dietary advice in Romans and 1 Corinthians, he states:

> The people I was describing know and observe these things; for they are Christians, not heretics … Him that eats not, no-one despises; him that eats, no-one judge; he who is weak eats herbs. Many who are strong,

however, do this for the sake of the weak; with many the reason for so doing is not this, but that they may have a cheaper diet, and may lead a life of the greatest tranquillity, with the least expensive provision for the support of the body ... Thus many do not eat flesh, and yet do not superstitiously regard it as unclean.[27]

A key indication, for Augustine, that Christians do not abstain from foods because they believe particular foods to be unclean is that many confine their abstinence to specified days or seasons, and then retain a degree of personal choice over the degree of abstinence observed.[28]

Leo Ferrari shows convincingly that Augustine had an abiding spiritual concern with food. The *Confessions* abound with food imagery, especially when describing the Manichaeans: rumination, by which food is brought up from the stomach, as an analogy for memory recollecting thoughts from the subconscious; being led astray by secret doctrines as like consuming forbidden food; estrangement from God's word as similar to starvation, or like that of the prodigal son, who was forbidden even the food of pigs; the name of Christ as like his mother's milk; the words of Faustus as an exquisite but insubstantial dish; himself as a hungry person awaiting food from God at the appointed hour; Manichaean falsehoods as vomit; and many others.[29] Yet Augustine's Manichaean past effectively constrained him from following the same ascetic path as many of his Christian predecessors and contemporaries, despite his admiration for them, as Ferrari shows in another important article.[30]

Augustine's obsessive desire to dissociate himself from the food of the Manichaeans or of any group not considered to maintain Christian orthodoxy is revealed by his assertion that it would be preferable to die of hunger than to consume food sacrificed to idols.[31] His unwillingness to extend flexibility to this particular issue suggests that his underlying concern was not in fact to render all foods lawful but to distinguish Christian spirituality and practices as clearly as possible from those of other religious groups, especially the Manichaeans, by means of dietary discipline. Augustine's idea that starvation was better than consuming idol food became incorporated into Gratian's *Decretum*, the founding text of Western canon law.[32] Through quotation and commentary, it was used to promote the social segregation of Christians from other religious groups, especially Jews, by means of food. Augustine's assertion even found its way into the now infamous *Malleus Maleficarum* manual for the identification of witchcraft and the interrogation and conviction of people accused of practising it, in which it was used to help establish an inalienable link between belief and practice by excluding the possibility that a person might be engaged in outward acts associated with witchcraft, such as by eating foods associated with it, but not giving their interior assent to those practices.[33] This inflexibility did not extend to the avoidance of any particular food type, however. No food was in principle excluded from Christian diet. Rather, the reason it had been killed or originally prepared as food required close scrutiny.

Food issues therefore continued to be a major preoccupation of Augustine's, even if they ran deeper and were less visible than his concerns with sex. Veronika Grimm, although disagreeing with Ferrari over the relative priority of Augustine's concerns with lust and gluttony, states: 'Even if he had felt the need for ascetic self-restraint in eating, he could not have advocated a strict vegetarianism or extreme fasting, lest this should be held as another proof of his Manicheanism.'[34] Augustine was, as has been seen, willing to eat meat when the occasion demanded.[35] Moreover, in Book Ten of the *Confessions* he deploys biblical evidence to argue that meat abstention is a matter of spiritual indifference. From a moral viewpoint, he argues, vegetable food can tempt just as much as meat, as shown by the examples of Esau, who sold his birthright for lentils, and even Christ himself, who was tempted in the wilderness to eat bread.[36]

By presenting dietary discipline as marginal to Christian life and doctrinally ambiguous, Augustine played a significant part in sidelining it as a matter for serious theological debate and spiritual reflection, presenting arguments the force of which was still felt many centuries after Manichaeism had ceased to exist. Yet his view that vegetable food presents as many moral problems as meat is, setting aside anti-Manichaean cosmological biases, contestable. Meat can only be eaten if the animal whose flesh becomes meat is first killed. Indeed, as shown in Chapter Five, the carcasses of animals that have died by natural or unknown means are typically not regarded as available for human consumption. Neither are live animals seen as 'meat', as suggested by the clear rules in several religious traditions demarcating the boundary between life and death, and thus between a live animal and dead meat.

Yet Augustine rightly suggested that Manichaean cosmology did not give sufficient grounds for discrimination among foods. Food rules of any kind will produce marginal cases and inconsistencies, also as seen clearly in Chapter Five, but this does not mean that theological or ethical choices about food are impossible or undesirable. The idea that meat eating poses no major theological problems has helped to lay the foundations for a modern culture of large-scale meat eating by humans, buttressed by assertions from nutritionists that meat is a necessary foodstuff for everyone. In a curious way, this modern insistence in the West that meat must be eaten regularly is a parody of the Manichaean assertion that it should be avoided completely.

Regulating orthodox diet: rules, councils and inquisitions

Augustine was not the only Christian to distinguish himself from Manichaeans by means of dietary discipline or lack of such discipline. By the late fourth century, monastic communities in Egypt were under scrutiny from bishops trying to extirpate Manichaean tendencies. Eutyches, who was condemned at the Council of Chalcedon for maintaining that Christ was composed of a fusion of divine and human elements, reported in the 380s that monks and bishops were permitted and even required to eat meat on Sundays in order to identify closet Manichaeans.[37] The implication of his account is that monks holding

Manichaean doctrines would either refuse, or their submission would amount to de facto conversion to doctrinal orthodoxy. Occasional meat eating was therefore an important means of preventing oneself being polemically consigned to a heretical group.

The visible effects of fasting on the body could also be used to impute a belief in Manichaean doctrines. For instance, Jerome complained in a letter to Eustochium that a pale or sad face gave sufficient reason for a person to be labelled Manichaean.[38] This supposition was repeated much later by Anselm of Canterbury in advice for identifying Cathars.[39] As Teresa Shaw observes, the close link between orthodoxy and dietary flexibility helps to explain why the giving and receiving of hospitality, and being sure not to cause offence to others, become such key requirements in ascetic texts of this period. Strict fasting, although still recommended, was increasingly tempered for doctrinal reasons.[40] The theological significance of hospitality therefore came to lie just as much in its role as a doctrinal signifier as in the intrinsic ethical or Christological value of hospitable acts. The curious situation thereby arose of Christian groups allowing their dietary practices to be determined indirectly by doctrines they deemed heretical in order to confirm themselves as doctrinally orthodox.

From a historical perspective, such compromises were unnecessary. As was seen in Chapter One, dietary asceticism and even prodigious acts of abstention had a well-established place and commonly understood functions in early Christian practice, being founded on scripture and personal discipline. Yet as Augustine Casiday comments: 'Catholic fasting habits were responsive to the possibility of misinterpretation – and in some cases were, in fact, deliberately (one might say *polemically*) intended to distinguish Catholics from others.'[41] It is a sign of the tremendous extent and pervasiveness of Manichaeism during the period when the idea and content of Christian orthodoxy were being forged that Christians sought so determinedly to distinguish themselves from it by their dietary teaching.

The practice of meat abstention thereby acquired an enduring ambiguity as a result of its potential significance as a marker of unorthodoxy. On the one hand, abstention can be seen as a continuing element of the ascetic practice essential to a disciplined, embodied Christian life. Yet meat was also refused in various increasingly marginal sects, such as by the Pythagoreans, who believed in reincarnation.[42] Christian writers on vegetarianism were able to justify the grounds for their belief carefully: for example, Origen insisted that Christians should not eat meat although explicitly excluded a Pythagorean basis for the practice.[43] But in practical situations, suspicions could easily remain. These conflicting imperatives weighed on the mind of Basil of Caesarea, who has already been encountered as a key figure in the development of monastic communities and dietary rules in the fourth century. Basil stated in his own Rule:

> Self-control is indispensable for all contestants for piety, for every contestant is self-controlled in all things. But in order to avoid falling in with the enemies of God who are seared in their conscience and thereby refrain from

foods [*cibis/bromaton*] which God created to be partaken of by the faithful
with thanksgiving, we should taste each food as the occasion presents itself,
to show observers that to the pure all things are pure ... Even so we must
continue to keep self-control as the goal, satisfying our need with the
cheaper foods and those necessary for life – while in these too we avoid the
harm of satiety and refrain altogether from what fosters pleasure.[44]

This complex instruction is ambivalent. Basil appears to recommend that, for
the sake of public appearance, community members should in principle be willing to eat anything. Yet his concluding sentence restates a norm of abstention,
especially by warning against that which 'ministers to pleasure'. Revisionist
work by Philip Rousseau suggests that Basil should be seen not as having composed 'rules' for 'monasteries' but rather a set of guidelines for a range of communities possessing varying markers of monastic identity.[45] At least some of
these communities enjoyed close links with wider society and shared many of its
practices, and would therefore have needed the kind of robust yet flexible
guidelines that such living requires. Indeed, Basil's recommendations and reasoning resemble those of Francis of Assisi and the mendicant orders discussed
much earlier, which operated in a similar social context.

   Earlier in his life, Basil made considerably stricter recommendations. In a
letter written during his grand tour of monasteries shortly before his ordina-
tion, he suggested that a diet of bread would suffice for a healthy man, perhaps
accompanied by some vegetables to give the body strength to discharge its
functions.[46] Indeed, on the basis of such recommendations, one writer has gone
so far as to portray Basil as engaged in a « lutte contre la gourmandise ».[47] Yet
in a letter composed around the same time, Basil praises the abundance of the
land surrounding his abode and the high quality of hunting it offers, especially
as entertainment for guests. He enthuses that the area 'abounds in game',
feeding 'herds of wild deer and wild goats, hares, and animals like these'.[48]

   Such inconsistencies may be explained by Basil's concern to refute the doctrines of the Armenian bishop Eustathius of Sebaste. Around 350, when Basil
was composing his Rule, the bishops of the province of Caesarea gathered at
the Council of Gangra. The Council's main purpose was to condemn Eustathius
and his followers for various excessive ascetic practices, including diet, pursued
contrary to Christian custom. Eustathians were condemned on the grounds that
'they observe fasts on Sundays, despising the sanctity of the free days, whereas
they make light of the fasts ordained among the churches and eat on them'.
Moreover, the charge continued, 'some of them revile the partaking of meat for
food'.[49] In response, the Council pronounced in strong terms:

> If anyone condemns him who in all piety and faith eats [flesh] while
> abstaining from blood, things offered to idols, or things strangled, as if by
> such partaking he has no hope, let him be anathema ... If anyone, from
> supposed asceticism, fasts on a Sunday, let him be anathema. If any of the
> ascetics, not from any bodily necessity, but from arrogance, as if he were

possessed of a more perfect understanding, disregards the traditional fasts observed by the Church in common, let him be anathema.[50]

Yet Basil had been a disciple of Eustathius, and the two remained friends until well after the date of the council.[51] It is far from clear that Basil ever accepted the Council's position, although he evidently needed to tread carefully in order to reduce the likelihood of being branded a heretic himself.

The concerns displayed at Gangra about meat abstention as an indicator of heresy are evident around the mid fifth century, when the Rule of the Master was composed. These concerns are again coupled, however, with a conviction that a norm of abstention is spiritually desirable. The community envisaged by the Master had more clearly demarcated boundaries with the outside world than did Basil's communities, and flexibility therefore needed to be implemented more proactively. The Master invites the abbot to permit meat eating during the two principal festal seasons: from Easter to Pentecost, and the shorter period of Christmas until Epiphany.[52] By eating meat, members of the community celebrated these feasts and the Christian doctrines they represented: Christ's incarnation, manifestation, death and resurrection, and the sending of the Holy Spirit.

The 'Master', whose identity is unknown, seems to have encouraged his community to eat meat at Easter and Christmas partly because, in his context, meat eating was still considered a sign of orthodoxy in the face of Manichaeism. Manichaeans were deported from Rome by three different popes, Gelasius, Symmachus and Hormisdas, in the period from 492 to 523, just before the Rule was composed, and their books and images were burnt.[53] Gelasius was from North Africa, and so likely to have been well acquainted with Manichaeism. Moreover, the First Council of Braga, held in 563 in the Galician metropolitan see, instructed that clergy who chose to abstain from meat should cook their vegetables with meat in order to eliminate suspicion of Priscillianist sympathies.[54] Priscillian, who in 385 had become the prototypical Christian heretic-martyr, defended meat abstention on the grounds that it helped prepare the soul to receive immediate inspiration from the Holy Spirit. This teaching was also condemned by another sixth-century council held at Toledo.[55]

Priscillianist fasting on Sunday, contrary to the practice of most Christians, was also seen as highly contentious.[56] Augustine writes to his fellow priest Casulanus refuting an argument that he attributes to them, which defended this custom based on a view that Paul's address to the apostles on the first day of the week narrated in Acts 20 took place during a fast. This would have given Sunday fasting scriptural warrant. In fact, retorts Augustine, the gathering omitted to eat solely because of the importance of the discourse being delivered by Paul prior to his imminent departure, and for no other motive connected with doctrine or observance.[57]

The Rule of the Master is notable for its harsh condemnations of monks guilty of faults, especially if impenitent, condemning them as heretics and offspring of the devil.[58] Yet the Master's prescribed arrangement for the Easter and Christmas feasts casts doubt on his true motives. He suggests:

> Let those brethren of a deanery who are going to eat meat be seated beside
> one another at their own tables, and let the specially cooked meat courses
> be brought to them in separate dishes, lest the purity of the abstainers seem
> to be sullied, and in order that the eaters may notice how great the distance
> is between them, those who cater to their desires and those who master the
> stomach.[59]

This seating arrangement establishes a degree of segregation at meals, but one
that members of the community are given considerable freedom to negotiate.
The Master clearly envisages the possibility that this freedom might lead to a
collapse in dietary discipline of a kind associated with much later medieval
feasting. He therefore advises in the same chapter that, when the feast approaches, the monks be guided in their choice, stating: 'As to eating the flesh of
[flying] birds [*volucres*], winged land animals [*pinnae terrenae*] and quadrupeds
[*quadrupes*], let the abbot tell the brethren that it is good to want to eat it, but
advise them that it is better to abstain.' This rather unclear passage suggests
that consumption of the flesh and blood of land animals (*carnes sanguinarias
terrae*) would in any case not be permitted, but that birds and winged land
animals, including insects, might be allowed. The key assumption seems to be
that at least some monks will feast on permitted meats, and thus perform the
important vicarious function of showing the monastery to be a place where
meat is eaten, and by implication a place in which doctrinal orthodoxy is
maintained. The bodily purity of the abstainers therefore depends, in unac-
knowledged ways, on those who literally cater to their desires. The monastery
itself was, of course, situated within a larger, omnivorous lay Christian community, and meat eating within the monastery also reinforced links with this
wider community.

The Rule of Benedict is roughly contemporaneous with the Rule of the
Master. It is much shorter, however, and offers less detailed dietary prescriptions. Benedict is apparently more explicit than his forebears in prohibiting
meat, asserting: 'Let everyone, except the sick who are very weak, abstain
entirely from eating the meat of four-footed animals.'[60] This indicates that meat
could not ever be eaten by ordinary healthy adult members, as discussed in
Chapter Three. By the ninth century and later, this was a point of contention
among interpreters, with the question of whether poultry and game could be
eaten, especially at Easter and Christmas, provoking disputes between rigourists
and reformers.[61]

As with the Master, possible reasons for Benedict's approach may be identified in his community's wider doctrinal context. He does not appear as constrained as either the Master or Basil by the need to present a united front
against Manichaeism. At Monte Cassino, south of Rome, where Benedict founded his community, Manichaeism had by the mid sixth century been successfully
reduced and virtually eliminated by the decrees and persecution of Christian
imperial power. Benedictine meat abstention could, therefore, be seen as signifying the successful establishment of Christianity as the civic religion. In

isolated and far-flung regions of the Empire, in contrast, Manichaean tendencies persisted. Indeed, Rufinus, the translator and robust editor of the Latin version of Basil's Rule on which Benedict and his European contemporaries depended, seems to have judged the whole discussion of meat as lacking relevance to them. He omitted this chapter from his edition, originally prepared for Italian monastic usage by the community at Pinetum near Terracina, on the coast south of Rome, under its abbot Ursacius.[62]

The early Christian concerns with dietary discipline as a possible signifier of heresy associated with Augustine and the monasteries of Egypt, Palestine and Syria re-emerged in later medieval Europe in the suppression of Catharism. The practices of the Cathars were somewhat similar to those of the much earlier Manichaeans. One key feature was abstention from meat and from all animal products, linked with a belief in reincarnation, and adherents in the highest rank of 'perfect' members had an assistant, known as a believer, to prepare food for them.[63] Yet the degree of similarity between the Cathars and the Manichaeans should not be overstated. The Cathars did not hold the light-liberating cosmology of the Manichaeans, and did not fast on Sundays.[64] Indeed they could, like ascetics of earlier ages, be regarded as exemplary Christians who took certain aspects of Christian practice more seriously than most others.[65] For instance, they observed the traditional Christian fasts with particular rigour, consuming only bread and water during their first and last weeks.[66]

What made the Cathars' dietary discipline seem unacceptable was not the practices themselves but their use to signify separation from Church institutions. Total abstention from red meat became the key indicator of this separation, and was so contentious that even a convinced ascetic like Bernard of Clairvaux could preach vehemently against it. In three successive sermons on the little foxes who ruin the vineyards in Song of Songs 2.15, Bernard compares the 'heretics' to these foxes, in one place attacking their 'excessive and superstitious abstinence ... which makes them a burden to themselves and everyone else'.[67] The Dominicans' approach to Catharism was also from the standpoint of their own strict fasting regime, at least initially, with Dominic's own approach focused on preaching to Cathars and attempting to bring them fully into the Church rather than to condemn them.[68] Yet for Dominican inquisitors of the later thirteenth and early fourteenth centuries, like Moneta of Cremona and Bernard of Gui, meat abstention served as a key means of identifying Cathars as well as providing a device by which their conversion back to orthodoxy could be tested.[69] For inquisitors, this reasoning achieved perfect logical consistency: anybody who refused to consume meat was a heretic, because Christians did not observe food prohibitions of any kind.

The doctrinal ambiguity of vegetarianism again became apparent in the seventeenth century: although part of the Enlightenment impulse to self-improvement, it was also seen as religiously significant. Francis Bacon argued for the benefits of a vegetarian diet, and his disciple Thomas Bushell actually became vegetarian as part of a hermit existence. This was a potentially hazardous choice in a Puritan age, and Bushell was at pains to show how ascetic diets were common in scripture and the early church, and that they did not necessarily signify assent to a heretical creed such as Manichaeism or Catharism.[70]

Condemnations of meat abstinence based on its association with heresy and Gnosticism re-emerged once more in some nineteenth-century polemics against the nascent vegetarian movement. A good example is some of the writings of the independent minister Robert Govett, who saw vegetarianism as a key sign that the last days of the earth's destruction had arrived, when God's covenant with humankind after the Flood would be annulled, the order of nature ended, new scourges unleashed on the earth, and a large part of humanity eliminated. He concluded a pamphlet on the topic by warning gravely: 'How will the faith of those be shaken by the Great Apostacy, who have been led to expect that the world is about to be converted to Christianity!'[71]

Converting the world to Christianity and to meat eating was certainly a feature of numerous Christian missions in the modern period. The idea that Christians did not abstain from meat was used to distinguish Christian missionaries from the populations they evangelized. But even this generated controversy, especially in the case of the Jesuits, whose willingness to adopt the dietary and other customs of the surrounding populace sparked consternation among their superiors in Rome. In India, missionaries espoused vegetarianism partly in order to accommodate themselves to the caste system, through which they needed to work if they were to make progress in converting people living within that system. If missionaries were to eat beef and other kinds of meat, they would lose the respect of the local population. Equally, requiring converts to eat meat would complicate and retard the whole conversion process. Disputes about what should happen raged for two centuries. St Francis Xavier had developed the accommodationist approach and this had been broadly endorsed in 1623 by a bull of Pope Gregory XV. Yet in 1704 a new attempt was made to terminate accommodationism by the apostolic delegate to India, who overruled the allowances previously granted.[72]

Issues surrounding diet and conversion in India erupted again as late as 1857, when the British Imperial government forced Indian sepoys to use new rifles greased with beef and pork fat, which deeply offended both Hindus and Muslims.[73] This was a major contributing factor to the Sepoys' Revolt, otherwise known as the Indian Mutiny, which almost toppled the British occupation and engulfed the region in months of bloodshed. In India, beef eating remains a marker of Christian identity, with Kerala, the main Christian state, one of the few in which cows may legally be slaughtered for meat.[74] Such exceptions are likely to remain an important feature of Christian identity in India, in a context of ascendant Hindu nationalism in which vegetarianism is both promoted and contested.[75]

Christians, Jews and their food

The idea that some potential foods are clean and therefore available for consumption while others are unclean and to be avoided persisted for many centuries in Christian practice, as explained in Chapter Five. In the early Church, the imposition of some Mosaic food rules on Christians – as classically expressed at the Council of Jerusalem in Acts 15.29, where idol food, blood and strangled meat were all banned – had been a means of demonstrating neighbourly love by avoiding causing offence, and had helped maintain civil peace.[76] The rules did not necessarily imply a high degree of respect for the Jewish religion, because a key justification for Christians continuing to eat with Jews was that hospitality provided possibilities for conversion. Indeed, for much of Christian history, Judaism was the 'other' against which Christianity was most frequently and insistently defined. As suggested in Chapter Five, food practices have also been a major locus for negotiating and defining the place of Judaism in relation to Christianity, whether as unwilling witness to Christian truth, as heresy, or as a threat to the Christian body politic.

The food forbidden by Jews which has made the most complex and enduring impact on Christian food practice has been pork.[77] Avoidance of the pig was a key marker of communal identity in medieval Jewish culture, being traced in scripture to the defiance of the Jewish mother and her seven sons who were all tortured and killed in the same day, along with the elderly teacher Eleazar, after refusing the demands of the Seleucid King Antiochus IV that they eat pork.[78] These events sparked the Maccabean Revolt. As Walter Houston states, 'it is not just that being a Jew entails not eating pork, but that eating pork in a certain sense entails ceasing to be a Jew'.[79]

Claudine Fabre-Vassas has traced how pork consumption sometimes became a feature of Christian observance and celebration, with massive pig slayings held at Easter and benedictions of ham and bacon featuring in some French provincial liturgies. Hence Christian celebration of Christ's resurrection implied polemical critique of the Jews, who were deemed to have murdered Christ, by means of food practices. By consuming what was, for Jews, the primary unclean food, Christians could demonstrate the obsolescence of their system of rules which they believed Christ's Resurrection had brought about. Indeed, practices even arose by which the pig and its flesh could be used in popular folk observances surrounding the Lenten and Easter cycle to represent the body of Christ.[80] Hams were buried in ash for the duration of Lent and exhumed on Holy Saturday, and pigs were killed on Maundy Thursday and eaten on Easter Day. The association between the flesh of Christ and the flesh of the pig is made explicit in one late-thirteenth-century description of the body and blood [sic] of Christ as 'flesh taken from the larder of the Virgin, cooked in the salt of the Passion on the gibbet of the Cross'.[81] In the conclusion to her study, Fabre-Vassas states:

> The pig is a creature divided. It incarnates the sins of lechery and gluttony; demons take up residence within it. At the same time, it is Christian flesh. Endowed with a soul of blood, called upon to appear at the meals of Christmas and Easter ... It leads ... from Jewish oldness, from which it originates, according to the myth, to young Christianity, which chose it as a tangible mark of the New Law.[82]

The anti-Jewish associations of pork consumption were exploited even more disturbingly in Nazi ideology as part of romantic, back-to-nature primitivism. One of this movement's many apologists, Richard Walter Darré, proclaimed the pig to be the archetypal animal of the German nation, unsuited to nomads owing to its relative immobility, thriving on acorns of the forests, and providing the large volumes of fat needed to survive long cold winters. Moreover, it had been the preferred sacrificial beast of ancient Aryans.[83] The pig was thus presented as naturally rooted in the German soil just like the modern Aryan race who ate it as meat, in a fusion of territory and diet from which Jews were excluded. Unsurprisingly, on occasions when meat was provided in concentration camps, it was very often pork.[84]

Christian inversion of Jewish notions of uncleanness was pursued to an extreme degree in medieval Provence and Iberia, where legislation was enacted prohibiting Jews from touching foods in the market without buying them.[85] The Christian motivation for these rules seems to have been a refusal by Jews to consume foods that had not been prepared according to the rules of kosher. Nevertheless, the practical effects of the ban were very different when targeted on a small minority by a majority with no spiritual reason for applying them, and provided yet another means of alienating Jews from Christian society. The supposition that Jews regarded Christian foods as unclean was thus manipulated by Christian jurists and theologians in order to develop the idea that Jews as a people were unclean. From a theological perspective this was another inconsistent transposition, given that Christian theological opposition to Jewish food rules was predicated largely on the notion that Christ abolished the principle of uncleanness.

Even in a region like Provence, where various discriminatory legislation was in force, Jews were permitted to continue to slaughter lambs during Lent – although not pork, beef, mutton or veal – when Christians were prohibited from so doing.[86] Christian legislators objected not to the act of consuming meat but to such consumption taking place in public.[87] Exempting Jews from the Christian Lenten fast served to recognize religious diversity, but also isolated them from the realm of public observance and consigned their food culture to the private realm. Slaughter by Jews of lambs in the period before Easter could also be interpreted by Christians as a re-enactment of the slaughter of Christ the lamb of God, for which Christians of this period typically held Jews responsible.

In the Spanish Inquisition, people who appeared to observe some Jewish practices, even if they did not claim or admit Jewish ancestry, were classified as 'Judaizers'. They were identified as Jewish often on the basis that they observed similar dietary rules to Jews. After the slaughter and sale of kosher meat had been outlawed, animals and poultry could be killed according to the correct methods only at home. This made the domestic sphere a key site for state religious regulation and resistance to such regulation. Alternatively, an animal might not have been slaughtered according to kosher methods, but could nevertheless be prepared in broad accordance with them by allowing blood to drip out of the slaughtered carcass and cutting off the fat.[88] Sheriffs were empowered to enter houses at any time to check that food was being prepared with lard rather than oil.[89] It was extremely difficult to prevent food rules being observed, however, because they were taught and preserved, primarily by women, through informal domestic education.[90]

Other medieval injunctions were designed to limit and even eradicate Christian consumption of Jewish meat. Again, the overriding aim was the elimination of Jewish food practices from the public and social realm. In 1267, a provincial council at Vienne banned Christians from buying meat from Jews or from dining with them, and similar measures were implemented elsewhere.[91] Yet it is unclear how successful such injunctions were. In the case of the sale of meat, Jews benefited from a market for those parts of the animal they were forbidden from eating, while Christians had access to what was, in their view, good meat.[92] Moreover, Christians in France had been instructed not to share a table with Jews as long ago as the Council of Agde in 506, which had commanded:

> All clerics and laity should henceforth avoid the meals of Jews, nor should anyone receive them at a meal. For, since they do not accept the common food served by Christians, it would be unbecoming and sacrilegious for Christians to consume their food. For that which we eat with the permission of the Apostle would be judged impure by them; moreover, Catholics will begin to be inferior to the Jews, as it were, if we consume what is served by them while they disdain what is offered by us.[93]

Agobard of Lyons, writing about three centuries later, suggested that Jewish food and hospitality might have been regarded as particularly desirable by Christians in consequence of the superior social status which Jews enjoyed.[94] Moreover, the strict rules surrounding the preparation of Jewish meat might well have resulted in a superior product. As with the Lenten meat prohibitions preserved in Reformation England, which were discussed in Chapter Two, economic considerations seem to have played a key role. Surpluses of Jewish meat were often available for general sale, with more animals slaughtered and butchered according to kosher methods than were needed by Jews themselves. By preventing Jewish merchants from selling their meat and the large Christian majority from purchasing it, legislators sought to restrict Jewish markets.[95]

Christians, Muslims and their food

Christian dietary discipline exerted formative influence on developing Muslim dietary practices. Muhammad is reported to have admired Syriac monks – who, as discussed in Chapter One, were known for their exceptionally ascetic lifestyle – and traded with them while employed by his future wife Khadijah.[96] Perhaps to emulate them, Muhammad developed an ascetic discipline in his youth while working as a herdsman.[97] This tradition of voluntary abstention persisted in Sufi mysticism, as shown in the work of Al-Ghazali, who permits some meat eating while emphasizing the importance of moderation and the goal of achieving a point of equilibrium.[98] More widely, the Muslim fast of Ramadan probably had some origins in the Christian Lenten fast. The rigour with which Ramadan continues to be undertaken today has similarities with the widely diffused lay observance of fasting by early Christians.[99]

Very soon, however, Ramadan came to be governed by the lunar cycle, with the result that it now begins about eleven days earlier each year. The different timings of Christian and Muslim fasting practices thus became an early key marker distinguishing the two communities. Like Judaism and Manichaeism before it, Islam presented, to Christian communities, issues of doctrinal identity that required them to define boundaries by a range of practical measures including fasting practices. Most obviously, although a complete fast is observed in Ramadan during the daylight hours, food including meat may be eaten after sunset. This led some Christians to ridicule the apparent laxity of the Ramadan fast when compared with Lent, during which meat could not be consumed at all. Moreover, Islamic women have often been permitted, with good reason, to break the fast while menstruating and while pregnant, compensating the days lost with additional fasting after the end of the collective fast or during the preparatory period the following year.[100]

For several centuries, Christians regarded Muslim food differently from Jewish food. Until the late twelfth century, Muslims (then called Saracens by Christians) had typically been viewed as pagans and had lived in relative harmony with Christians. During the twelfth century, however, the age of the Crusades, Christian jurists began to reclassify Saracens as 'Judaizers' on the grounds that they were circumcised, observed food rules and imitated Jewish rituals.[101] Muslims, like Jews, also abstained from pork, and sometimes identified pork consumption with Christian conversion or heresy.[102] Contemporary critics frequently suggested that these were recent developments in Saracen doctrine and practice. This assertion is difficult to support, although it undoubtedly provided a useful explanation for the hardening of Christian attitudes to Muslims. In any case, the effective recategorization of Muslim foods as 'Jewish' rendered those foods more problematic because it was primarily all things Jewish that Church authorities expected Christians to avoid. Commensality between Christians and Muslims thereby declined, with Muslims increasingly likely to be accused by Christians of superstition and contempt for scripture.[103]

The consumption of camel flesh has been associated by Christians with Islam. In Ethiopia, Christians have avoided camel flesh in order to distance themselves from Muslim pastoral peoples, by whom it is commonly eaten, and have only ceased to abstain on abandoning the Christian faith.[104] Yet some Muslims have claimed that eating camel flesh is permissible because Jesus abrogated the Israelite prohibition against its consumption.[105] The camel is referred to several times in the Qu'ran, moreover, and is the beast used by Muhammad 'the camel-rider' in clear distinction to the ass preferred by the Jewish and Christian messianic traditions, or, in the book of Revelation, the horse.[106] These textual attestations have been confirmed archaeologically, with more camel bones uncovered on Muslim sites than on those predating Islam. In Spain and Hungary, moreover, camels existed during the Ottoman settlement but are found no longer.[107]

Heresy and counterculture

The association of vegetarianism with heresy has persisted. Contemporary Western Christians arguing in favour of vegetarianism might still feel compelled to demonstrate their orthodoxy by, for example, distancing themselves from 'New Age' religions. Thus Stephen Webb advocates Christian vegetarianism in explicit opposition to both secular and New Age accounts of vegetarian diet, and anticipates his Christian readers' concerns about vegetarianism as a signifier of non-Christian religious beliefs.[108] In this chapter, although we have emphasized the Christian doctrinal history of these associations, we should not ignore the persistent association between dietary abstinence, particularly meat avoidance, and cultural protest. The practical and symbolic force of meat avoidance as a form of such protest is easy to understand. Withdrawal from the common table constitutes a refusal to maintain or contribute to existing patterns of social relations, even before the reasons for this withdrawal are expressed in negative ethical and theological assessments of the existing system. Moreover, meat is an expensive food with a complex production process which requires killing. Modern society's high symbolic investment in meat corresponds to its high economic and social investment, so the refusal of meat is a potent gesture.

Even within Christian history, and particularly in places where Christianity formed the dominant culture, tremendous importance has been attached to maintaining a literal or imagined common table, at which all can eat and at which the diet served is omnivorous. The ambiguous place of the ascetic, or the person who refuses certain foods, in this common space is seen very clearly in the Rule of the Master, which seats him in the same room as the meat eaters and praises him for a superior attitude to food and the body, and in so doing calls into question the choices of omnivorous fellow diners.

The countercultural refuser of meat could be understood, in Christian terms, as a prophet whose life and actions pronounce judgement on the failures and injustices of a particular social order. Can such a prophet be heard and recognized within a community whose self-definition has historically been tied so closely to omnivorous dining? The history we have recounted suggests that there is also a Christian tradition of transformative reflection on eating practices. This reflection has affected not only the eating habits of exceptional individuals and communities, but also the common table.

In this chapter, we have seen how abstinence from particular foods, especially meat, has signalled doctrinal difference and provoked fury in opponents. Of course, the times when Christians and others were able to follow their dietary disciplines unmolested by authorities and without the fear of being charged with heresy hanging over them are less well known. At some times and in some places, particular food cultures are more likely to be constructed as countercultures and thus to be seen as threatening a prevailing norm of doctrinal, political and social reasoning. The refusal of mass-produced meat has the potential to become a stance that ordinary people can, in their everyday lives, adopt against a dying technocratic, industrialized, desensitized food economy.[109] Yet socially, such refusals seem to be fairly comfortably assimilated into Western societies, with classically liberal commitments like vegetarianism existing uncontroversially alongside reactionary political agendas, rather than being part of an 'oppositional identity' and 'consciousness-raising process'.[110] Some people will lament the weakening of the relationship between dietary discipline and wider public commitments. Others might just be glad to eat their food in peace.

7   Sacrifice and slaughter

In modern Western societies, animal sacrifice is typically regarded as primitive, superstitious and barbaric, an uncivilized and unenlightened practice from which we have, thankfully, long since progressed. Sacrifice and associated religious slaughter methods have been attacked by many animal rights advocates, who regard them as inferior to modern slaughter practices. Christian attitudes to pre-Christian sacrificial practices have contributed to this negative assessment of animal sacrifice. Just as Christians have often defined themselves as people who do not follow food rules, so they have frequently categorized themselves as people who do not perform animal sacrifice. The outcome of these self-definitions has been a situation in which animals are eaten and their slaughter is a matter of religious indifference. Meat, when classified as one food among many, can be thought of without reference to the animals which become meat. Despite a long Christian history of meat abstention, it is striking how infrequently concern about the lives of animals has been invoked as the primary factor motivating such abstention.

In this chapter, we shall take a closer look at sacrifice and Christian practice, and especially at Christian practices of sacrifice. In some Christian contexts, animal sacrifice has been treated as a form of worship which can be directed towards either false gods or the Christian God. In any case, one important aim of this chapter is simply to present evidence of a Christian tradition of animal sacrifice, thereby disproving the widespread assumption that no such tradition exists. Jean-Louis Durand, for instance, accuses Christianity of 'theological arrogance' because it 'excludes from the domain of the sacred' the 'death of animals, which in other religious cultures has religious significance'.[1] In fact, Christians have sacrificed animals in order to express respect for life, praise God as giver of life, and highlight humans' ambiguous kinship with animals. We shall examine this little-known tradition, and consider the significance of the history of sacrifice for a modern society in which sacrifice is rejected and mass animal slaughter accepted as normal.

Early Christianity: beyond sacrifice?

The development of the early Christian churches in the later first century coincided with the fall of Jerusalem and the ending of the sacrificial system of the Jerusalem Temple. In Christian accounts, the idea that Christ came to abolish sacrifices could then conveniently be added to the various other super-sessionist interpretations of the relation between Judaism and nascent Christianity.[2] Early Christians also distinguished their practices from those of sacrificial cults, which for the next three centuries formed part of the religious landscape in which Christian communities were situated. Once Christianity became the official imperial religion sacrifices were outlawed, because of their close association with paganism. In 341, Emperor Constantius ordered that the 'madness of sacrifices shall be abolished', and five years later stipulated that anyone caught sacrificing would be put to death.[3] In 391, Emperor Theodosios moved decisively to ban animal sacrifice throughout the Roman Empire as part of his efforts to establish Christianity as the privileged religion and abolish the pagan cults competing with it.[4] Animal sacrifice thus became synonymous, in the minds of both pagans and Christians, with pagan religion. As the Roman Christian poet Prudentius urged the pagan senator Symmachus:

> Leave these heathen divinities to pagan barbarians; with them everything that fear has taught them to dread is held sacred; signs and marvels compel them to believe in frightful gods, and they find satisfaction in the bloody eating that is their custom, which makes them slaughter a fattened victim in a lofty grove to devour its flesh with floods of wine.[5]

Images of bloodshed, fear and gluttony here coalesce around the practice of sacrifice. The 'bloody eating' of the sacrificial victim is troubling both because of its association with violent death and because of the immoderate consumption of food and wine which follows. Sacrificers are presented as acting under the compulsion of 'signs and marvels' and 'custom'. Living under the sway of 'frightful gods', they are victims of the 'madness of sacrifices' along with the animals they slaughter.

The prohibition of animal sacrifice was reinforced by at least six emperors in the period 341 to 435: Constantius, Gratian, Valentinian, Theodosius, Arcadius and Honorius.[6] Animal sacrifice was by then seen increasingly as inimical to urban civilized religion.[7] Nevertheless, these successive bans suggest that animal sacrifice was, in practice, difficult to extirpate from all parts of the Empire, especially from its more remote and rural areas. This could have been due solely to the ongoing attraction of paganism. Yet such a simple explanation fails to take account of the specific features of animal sacrifice, including its cross-cultural character. It is possible that the attraction of sacrifice lay not in pagan religion as such, but in an impulse to offer thanks for meat and perhaps to deflect the guilt experienced for killing by situating the act cosmologically. Prudentius' comments to Symmachus hint at what is for him the strange and persistent attraction of sacrificial ritual. He lingers with fascination over its non-rational excesses, and in so doing suggests indirectly why it might persist. His objections to its 'bloody' and 'fearful' character and associations with excessive consumption refer to more than just the explicit association of sacrifice with pagan religion. For Prudentius, the 'madness' of sacrifice was synonymous with the 'madness' of pagan worship, and abolition of the latter would necessarily lead to the elimination of the former.

Christian rituals of animal sacrifice

In fact, sacrifice became assimilated into Christian practice in many regions. We shall now survey various places where it has flourished. Our first example is the oldest Christian nation on earth, Armenia, whose ruler King Tiridates was healed and baptized a Christian in 301 by St Gregory the Illuminator. In the Armenian Church, an ancient sacrificial liturgy known as the *matal* (or *madagh*), meaning 'something tender', has persisted to the present day. This was a continuation of pagan practice promoted by Gregory and later church leaders following the country's conversion to Christianity, but in revised Christian form. The sacrifice has typically been offered on several occasions through the year: Easter, all other dominical feasts, the feasts of famous saints, and to commemorate the faithful departed. At Easter a lamb has traditionally been offered, while at other times cows, bulls, goats or sheep have also been used, and even doves or pigeons in cases of scarcity or poverty.[8]

Nerses Shnorhali, an Armenian bishop and future catholicos, despatched an intriguing epistle in the mid twelfth century to his priests in the Hamayk province of Syrian Mesopotamia defending the *matal* against its detractors. It appears that Syriac Christian critics in the area had accused the Armenians of following Jewish practice, especially in the case of the Easter sacrifice of the lamb. Nerses' apologia therefore proceeds by distinguishing various ritual points of the Easter *matal* from those of the Passover sacrifice of the Jews. He writes:

> They selected a lamb a year old, and a male: our lamb is one month old, or, as a rule, more or less; and we never consider whether it is male or female. They carried it five days beforehand to their houses: we take ours on the same day or whenever occasion suits. They sacrifice at eventide on the old Pascha: we at dawn of the new Pascha. They ate it standing up, and by night: but we sitting down, and by day. They ate it with unleavened bread and bitter herbs: we with leavened bread and without herbs. Likewise the rest of their victims were offered for the living: but those which we offer are in memory of the deceased, in order that by feeding the poor, we may find the mercy of God.[9]

Later in his epistle, Nerses warns his priests: 'Let no one venture to smear the upper lintels of his door with the blood of the lamb ... for that is a Jewish custom, and the person who does it renders himself liable to an anathema.'[10] Although the rebuttal of accusations of Judaizing occupies most of Nerses' text, he also is at pains to distinguish the *matal* from the old pagan sacrificial rites. In a passage inveighing against both Jewish and pagan traditions, he states that the *matal* was not indeed according to Jewish tradition, God forbid! For he who shares their practices shall be accursed. But instead of the vain ingratitude of offering sacrifices of the creatures made by God to the demons, as the heathen were used to do, it was made lawful to transfer the sacrifices into the name of the true God, and to devote to him as the creator his own creatures, in the same way as the first fathers had also done prior to the law, I mean, Abel, Noah and Abraham.[11]

Nerses here locates sacrifice 'prior to the law' as a universal human activity continuous with worship. It is not therefore to be rejected but rather offered to 'the true God'. The three Old Testament readings appointed for the *matal* are instructive in this regard: although the first two, Leviticus 1.1–13 and 2 Samuel 6.17–19, situate sacrifice in Israelite context, the third passage, Isaiah 56.6–7, proclaims that the sacrifices of 'foreigners who bind themselves to the Lord' will also be pleasing to God: 'Their burnt offerings and sacrifices will be accepted on my altar; for my house will be called a house of prayer for all nations.'

   Nerses' appropriation of pre-Christian sacrifices was motivated partly by economic and political considerations. If animal sacrifice had been banned in the new Christian state, the clergy would have been deprived of their livelihood through being deprived of their portion of the sacrificial meat. The nascent Christian church had a clear interest in retaining these reformed priests, who provided it with native and comparatively well-educated leaders, and therefore enlisted the support of future generations of the historic priestly families.[12] Pagan priests were deemed eligible for Christian baptism, and once baptized were permitted to continue to officiate at sacrifices and receive their historic portion. Indeed, under the new dispensation this portion increased to include various limbs and organs. All that many pagan congregations had apparently left their clergy was skin and backbone.[13]

   In his defence of the *matal*, Nerses also appeals to similar practices elsewhere in Christendom, referring to a lamb sacrifice made in the Roman Church as well as 'all over the Church of the Franks, with greater care and diligence than we exercise'. In Gaul, Nerses claims, the reservation and consumption of the lamb sacrifice happened as part of the Eucharistic celebration itself. He describes the proceedings as follows:

> After they have roasted the lamb, they lay it in the tabernacle under the sacrifice on the day of the Pascha; and after they have communicated in the Mystery, the priest divides, and gives a portion to each; and they eat it up in the church itself before they partake of any ordinary food.[14]

Other accounts confirm that a ceremonial meal of lamb was taken at the papal court during the twelfth century.[15] The Frankish practices enthusiastically described seem unlikely to have been widespread, however, although at least two ninth-century writers refer to them.[16] Yet it is clear that similar transformations of pagan sacrificial practices had been a feature of other earlier medieval

Western Christian regions, including Britain. In 601, Pope Gregory the Great wrote to Mellitus, the missionary French abbot to Britain and future Archbishop of Canterbury, to advise him how best to deal with animal sacrifices. Gregory reasoned:

> I have long been considering with myself about the case of the Angli ... Since they are wont to kill many oxen in sacrifice to demons, they should have also some solemnity of this kind in a changed form ... Let them no longer sacrifice animals to the devil, but slay animals to the praise of God for their own eating, and return thanks to the Giver of all for their fullness, so that, while some joys are reserved to them outwardly, they may be able the more easily to incline their minds to inward joys. For it is undoubtedly impossible to cut away everything at once from hard hearts, since one who strives to ascend to the highest place must needs rise by steps or paces, and not by leaps. Thus to the people of Israel in Egypt the Lord did indeed make Himself known; but still He reserved to them in His own worship the use of the sacrifices which they were accustomed to offer to the devil, enjoining them to immolate animals in sacrifice to Himself; to the end that, their hearts being changed, they should omit some things in the sacrifice and retain others, so that, though the animals were the same as what they had been accustomed to offer, nevertheless, as they immolated them to God and not to idols, they should be no longer the same sacrifices.[17]

Once again is evident the comparison of the continuation of contemporary pagan sacrifice, in a new form, with divine approbation of the sacrifices of the people of Israel. Yet despite this comparison, Gregory demands surprisingly few changes to the practices themselves, with his principal requirement being simply that the animals be offered to the one true God rather than to other deities.[18] Moreover, even though the sacrifices of the Angles are certainly identified as provisional, the explicit comparison with Israelite sacrifices suggests that their imminent eradication was neither expected nor required.

Gregory's policy of permitting the traditional British sacrifices to continue, provided they were situated within the new Christian context, contrasted sharply with the approach adopted in the following century by the first German national synod, presided over jointly by Karlmann, Prince of the Franks, and Archbishop Boniface in 742. Germany, unlike Britain, had not formed part of the Roman Empire and so had not by then fallen under Christian influence. Paganism remained a powerful religious force there, presenting an increasingly serious obstacle to Christian mission in Saxon territory during the eighth century once this area was threatened with invasion by the Christian Franks.[19] At the synod, every bishop was enjoined, with the support of the Frankish court, to

> see to it that the people of God perform not pagan rites but reject and cast out all the foulness of the heathen, such as ... offerings of animals, which

foolish folk perform in the churches, according to pagan custom, in the
name of holy martyrs or confessors, thereby calling down the wrath of God
and his saints.[20]

It is notable that the decree condemns sacrifices despite reporting the invocation
of Christian saints during the ceremonies. Animal sacrifice is regarded not as a
form of worship which can be directed either towards the true God or towards
other gods, but as inherently problematic for Christians and irredeemably
pagan. The synod's robust approach elicited strong approval from Pope
Zacharius, who in a letter to Boniface six years later condemned

> sacrilegious priests who, you say, sacrificed bulls and cows and goats to
> heathen gods, eating the offerings of the dead, defiling their own ministry,
> and who are now dead, so that it cannot be known whether they invoked
> the Trinity in their baptisms or not.[21]

His baptismal reference highlights the problems which sacrificing caused for full
inclusion in the church. In a culture of competing and overlapping religious
commitments, sacrificial practices did not simply mark out some Christians
from other Christians, but contributed to identifying who was a Christian and
who was not, and thus to establishing the boundaries of the Christian community. In the Germanic context of combating paganism, Christian boundaries
were drawn particularly tightly.

The continuation of animal sacrifice by Orthodox Christians in several other
countries has been noted sporadically. These include Georgia, Bulgaria, Palestine, Jordan, Syria, Egypt and Ethiopia.[22] Of special interest, however, is the
more recent work of Stella Georgoudi examining the persistence of sacrificial
rituals in twentieth-century Greece.[23] The sacrifices are offered on particular
Christian festivals, notably those of Saints Athanasius (18 January), George (23
April), Elias (20 July) and Paraskevi (26 July). The sacrificial animal might be
presented before an icon of the saint for whom it is to be offered, or even left
inside the church to sleep the night before its sacrifice, and blessed by the priest
before its departure. The sacrifices are made outside the church building, often
during mass or immediately afterwards, or during the vespers marking the
beginning of a festival. The animal's head is turned towards the east, just as
churches are oriented by their altars. Following the slaughter, participants dip a
finger in the blood and trace the sign of the cross on their forehead. All inedible
body parts are buried to prevent scavenging by animals, especially dogs, who
according to Matthew's gospel must not be given what is sacred.[24] Before the
meal begins, the priest or sometimes the bishop stands over the boiling cauldrons to bless the meat.[25] Then the climax of the proceedings is reached: a lavish
feast served from the cauldrons 'bubbling with meat, spices, grains and vegetables, including rice, wheat or gruel, garbanzo beans, onions, garlic, and
tomatoes', supervised by the churchwardens and heralded by the tolling of the
church bells.[26] Although these multiple ritual elements are not all formally

codified, they point in combination to a ritual patterning of the slaughter and an understanding of the slaughtered animal as an offering to God. The slaughter can therefore reasonably be described as a sacrifice, even though no part of the animal is burnt as a direct offering to God.[27]

This Christian animal sacrifice diverges from the *kourbánia* of classical paganism on several points. The fire is used purely for cooking purposes and has no spiritual significance. No portion of the cooked meat is set aside to be offered to the saint. Priestly mediation occurs primarily through words rather than ritual action.[28] The cooking of the meat is a shared task, and the common practice of stewing ensures that everybody receives a helping of similar quality.[29]

The social dimension of this 'sanctified slaughter' is particularly noteworthy. Preparing and serving the meat is a communal task. Georgoudi highlights the pre-eminent importance of the shared meal that follows the distribution of the sacrificial meat, which forms the 'heart and essence of the festival'.[30] An interesting comparison may here be drawn with the *matal*. Michael Findikyan has complained that, among the modern Armenian diaspora in the West, the *matal* ceremony has become 'abbreviated and ritualized to the point of meaninglessness'.[31] Some of the sacrifice might be offered to neighbours, but he complains that the bulk of the meat is frequently consumed behind closed doors as the centrepiece of a large private party. Yet quoting the ceremony's epistle and gospel readings, Findikyan shows that the ceremony's essentials are praise and hospitality. In Hebrews, the *matal* is likened to a 'sacrifice of praise to God – the fruit of lips that confess his name'.[32] The final text from Luke's gospel makes clear that it must be shared with the 'poor, the lame, the maimed and the blind', because these people cannot repay the giver.[33] Indeed, there is a tradition that no part of the *matal* may be consumed by the person who has offered it.

In both Armenia and Greece, sacrifices are located at the boundary between church and society. In Armenia, sacrifice was traditionally offered on the church steps or in the courtyard. In Greece, the sacrifice typically happens in the square outside the church, with the priest perhaps blessing the animal about to be sacrificed in the narthex.[34] This boundary location of the sacrifices points to their liminal position between Christian and non-Christian ritual, and between the Eucharist and everyday practices of slaughter and eating. The theological ambiguity of sacrifices points, of course, to the intrinsic liminality of meat itself, which is in Bryan Turner's words 'located mid-way between nature and society, between nature and culture, between the living and the dead'.[35] It also, however, emphasizes their social character. The distribution of food that follows the 'sanctified slaughter' can be seen, in these contexts, as a means by which God's peace and generosity proclaimed in the church's liturgy is made real in society.

Despite Georgoudi's well-founded aversion to classical 'survivalist' accounts of modern Greek animal sacrifice which neglect its obvious Christian context, she rightly argues, as do scholars of classical Greece, that animal sacrifice displays the deep connections between everyday food practices and understandings of the sacred.[36] It is a fundamental part of human culture, cosmology and religion, and performs vital functions in these fields of human experience.[37] This suggests that Christians who have insisted on the elimination of animal sacrifice, especially in the Roman Empire, risk disengaging Christian belief from a fundamental part of human culture. A positive Christian reappraisal of animal sacrifice is also possible by, for instance, requiring that the poor enjoy a privileged share in the meal which follows, as in the case of the Armenian *matal*. This instruction places fellowship at the heart of the sacrifice, and has been restated at different times in several pronouncements directed against clergy or households who have reserved sacrificial meat for themselves.[38]

There are other examples of Christian practices of animal sacrifice in which fellowship is central. Sacrifice has been used in South Africa to promote reconciliation across hostile community boundaries. In the township of Mpophomeni, it played a key part in resolving a long-running war between different tribal groups allied with the Inkhata Freedom Party and the African National Congress. In 1996, the people of the township celebrated a rite of reconciliation which included the slaughter of cows by the chiefs of the seven main tribes, Christian worship, and a large public feast open to all. The rite drew on elements of Zulu religion by including an offering of meat to the participants' ancestors (*ukutelelana*). Nonetheless, Jone Salomonsen insists that the rite was not simply a mix of Christian and Zulu practices but given meaning by the sacrificial death of Jesus on the cross, bringing reconciliation, forgiveness and new community, and also reinterpreted in light of Hebrew scripture.[39] In this example, animal sacrifice should not therefore be viewed as a simple continuation of ancient Christian practice, but as an appropriation by Christians of an existing cultural practice.[40]

A similar doctrinal context is suggested by Samuel Britt in his discussion of animal sacrifice in the United Church of Salvation in Liberia. Britt adopts the motif of 'ritual struggle' in the context of an agonistic universe within which sacrifice serves to resolve personal and social tensions. As in Armenian tradition, the person offering the sacrifice is not allowed to consume any portion of the meat, which either goes to the priest or is cooked in a hot, peppery stew and eaten by other church members before midnight, depending on the category of sacrifice.[41] In this Liberian Christian context, strong emphasis is placed on the role of sin as the cause of the breakdown of fellowship, and so the collective context of fellowship is accompanied by a narrative emphasizing substitutionary atonement in which the animal is exchanged for the sin of the sacrificer, or even for his life in cases where this was seen as threatened by accidents, plots or bewitchment.

In some ancient accounts, animals are even presented as sacrificing themselves voluntarily. Porphyry reports a shortage of sacrificial victims during the siege of the sanctuary of Herakleion of the Gadeiroi by Bogos, king of the Maurousioi. This was alleviated by a bird flying down to the altar to present itself to the high priest for sacrifice. Similarly, during the siege of Cyzicus by Mithridates, the time for the festival of Persephone drew near, at which a cow had to be sacrificed. The cow, marked for sacrifice before the siege had begun, lowed and swam across the river, ran through the city gates opened by the guards, and thus to the altar ready for sacrifice.[42] Plutarch rightly questions the somewhat contrived nature of these 'voluntary' sacrifices, discussing the practice of pouring a drink offering over an animal selected for sacrifice to make it shake its head as if to communicate assent.[43] Such narratives persisted in some Christian accounts. For example, the Christian priest Paulinus describes such an instance at the shrine of Felix of Nola in southern Italy, in which a heifer vowed for sacrifice guided her owners to the shrine to present herself with them.[44]

By recovering some key elements of historic sacrificial practice, such as confining meat eating to particular days, making slaughter visible to the community, and having greater regard for animal welfare, Christians would bear witness to a redeemed and realistic fellowship between humans, but also between humans and animals, and humans and God. Sacrifice provides a context for slaughter in which thanks is given for the life of the animal as a gift from God. It enables rites of passage or other special events in human lives to be celebrated: anything from the birth of a child to safe return from the Mir space station.[45] Above all, the meal is shared, especially with the poor and needy.

Bloody eating

Yet is it not a conceit to endorse and thereby perpetuate the cycle of ritualized bloodshed which is the reality of animal sacrifice, even to the extent of suggesting that animals volunteer themselves for sacrifice? Why should peace and fellowship among all members of society, and the offering of praise to God for the gift of life, require repeated bloodshed? Furthermore, can the killing of animals really be regarded as the right worship of the God of Jesus Christ? One twentieth-century writer saw very clearly the continuities between Christianity and sacrifice. Her response was to reject both. Rebecca West, in her evocative account of her 1937 journey through Yugoslavia, describes attending a dawn sacrifice of lambs in Macedonia. In the area she visits there was a folk tradition that sacrifice on a particular rock, known as the Cowherd's Rock, will bring good fortune and fertility. West describes approaching this large rock, gleaming red-brown with the blood of animals offered during the night, smeared with wool and wax from the candles burned there, and with cocks' heads strewn around.[46] The two sacrifices she witnesses are both thanksgiving offerings for newborn children. These require the infant to be placed on the filthy, stinking rock alongside the lamb, as its throat is slit, and then to be marked on the forehead with some of the lamb's warm blood. West reflects:

> On the Sheep's Field I had seen sacrifice in its filth and falsehood, and in its astonishing power over the imagination. There I had learned how infinitely disgusting in its practice was the belief that by shedding the blood of an animal one will be granted increase; that by making a gift to death one will receive a gift of life. ... Now that I saw the lamb thrusting out the forceless little black hammer of its muzzle from the flimsy haven of the old man's

wasted arms, I could not push the realisation away from me very much longer. None of us, my kind as little as any others, could resist the temptation of accepting this sacrifice as a valid symbol.[47]

West is appalled by the ontology which the sacrifices represent. The whole of Western Christian thought, she protests, has developed in the shadow of the Cowherd's Rock, born from the atonement theology of Paul through Augustine's granting to the devil of rights over humanity, Luther's hatred of reason and Shakespeare's sickly longing for the disgusting and destructive. Western civilization has been founded on a scheme in which, through sacrifice, death may be exchanged for some share in life. For West, the Christian God is now the 'frightful' God enforcing the custom of 'bloody eating'. Also motivating her abhorrence of the sacrifices seems to be their whimsical character, and lack of order and dignity. The squalor of the rock thus becomes, for West, a metaphor of human life and the chaos into which the Balkans would imminently be plunged. In contrast with the sense that humans sacrifice animals through compulsion, as a particular pattern of thought gains power over their imagination, West insists that sacrifice is unnecessary. She states that goodness 'must be stable, since it is a response to the fundamental needs of mankind, which themselves are stable'.[48]

West's poetic and polemical attack draws attention back with a jolt to the Plutarchian challenge to meat eaters: that their eating habits are cruel and inhumane, and that a corollary of the human violence to animals on which they are predicated is human violence to other humans.[49] Plutarch suggests that, far from promoting fellowship among humans as previously suggested, animal sacrifice is emblematic of practices which breed violence and conflict. Reflecting on the historical development of meat eating, he writes:

> When our murderous instincts had tasted blood and grew practised on wild animals, they advanced to the labouring ox and the well-behaved sheep and the house-warding cock; thus, little by little giving a hard edge to our insatiable appetite, we have advanced to wars and the slaughter and murder of human beings.[50]

Plutarch links this degeneration with the atrophying of the virtue of sensitivity caused by meat eating, through which the 'brute and the natural lust to kill in man were fortified and rendered inflexible to pity, while gentleness was, for the most part, deadened'.[51]

In modern Britain, the idea that meat eating sets humanity on a path to violent confrontation was developed by opponents of the First World War. The impulse to war has been pictured, especially by feminists, as issuing from accumulated oppression, subjection and violence both latent and explicit in apparently civilized Western culture.[52] The renewed interest in vegetarianism around this period mirrors that in the later seventeenth century, when its adoption often formed part of a general pacifist commitment engendered by revulsion at the bloodshed of the Civil War.[53] Yet over previous centuries, foodstuffs other than meat have also been seen as provoking wars: for example, Clement of Alexandria attributed the Persians' invasion of Egypt in 525 BC to their desire for the splendid figs that grew there.[54] Nevertheless, in the case of meat eating a two-stage dynamic is identifiable in which an impulse is generated to acquire more land on which to grow the crops needed to feed the cattle which will eventually be killed for meat. An increased desire to eat meat therefore results in a disproportionately large increase in the need for arable land.[55]

This reasoning can be traced back at least to Plato's *Republic*, in which Socrates explains in his dialogue with Glaucon that, in a luxurious state, pigs and cattle would be required in great numbers, with the result that a territory of previously sufficient size will become too small and need to be enlarged by military seizure of a neighbour's land.[56] This theme was developed by the American post-war social critic Henry Stevens, who argued that meat eating was founded on food scarcity and originated during the last Ice Age among northern European tribes, for whom plant cultivation was impossible due to adverse climate.[57] Once the ice receded, the northern hunters migrated southwards and subjected the land to intensive animal cultivation with lasting negative effects on its crops and inhabitants. In these terms, the story of the killing of Abel, the keeper of flocks, by his jealous brother Cain, tiller of the soil, can be seen as representing the final, failed act of resistance by agrarian peoples against encroaching pastoral domination.[58] Abel is literally banished from the land, not simply by an arbitrary divine decree but by an encroaching meat-based polity whose products God accepts.

This association of meat eating with the control of land and the exclusion of existing inhabitants from their land is highly pertinent in the British context, when the enclosure of open common land into small individually owned plots impeded the grazing of animals by peasants. Beef, which remains the most costly meat to produce in terms of the quantity of vegetable protein required per unit of meat, thus became the defining feature of the table of the landed yeomanry.[59] 'British beef' came to represent a comfortable, domesticated, male-dominated social superiority to which, in time, many would aspire, retaining these class associations until the late nineteenth century.[60] This nexus of control over animals, land and other people was perfectly expressed in the ritual of the male head of the household carving the hunk of flesh in the centre of the table surrounded by his wife and family, a scene that Mrs Beeton revealingly expected to provoke 'envy' in others.[61] In the twentieth century a similar development can be traced in the United States, with meat eating becoming a sign of success among wealthier working men: three times a day, including steak for breakfast.

Rebecca West's account of the sacrificed lamb, like more recent feminist critiques of meat eating, identifies Christianity with the meat-centred system of domination and violence. For West, Christianity perpetuates the myth that life or goodness come about only through untimely death and violent killing. She sees in the practice of animal sacrifice a replication of the logic of the crucifixion.

Her work here intersects with a perennial area of controversy and reflection within Christian theology, showing its relevance to everyday decisions about eating.

Sacrifice and the cross

Where is the cross in animal sacrifice? In Greece, the tree – suggestive of the cross – has often assumed several important roles: the victim can be tied to the trunk, the roots receive the animal's blood, the carcass is hung from a branch while being skinned, and the boughs provide shade and shelter during the meal which follows.[62] These multiple functions echo descriptions of the cross of Christ as both the place and means of his death, but also as the tree of life – evoking the wood of that tree in the Garden of Eden – from which Christ reigns triumphant. Developing these associations in one of his *Homilies on the Resurrection*, Gregory of Nyssa describes the ram caught in the thicket that takes the place of Isaac in Abraham's sacrifice in strikingly literal terms as 'hung from wood, caught by the horns'.[63]

The Epistle to the Hebrews develops the implications for sacrificial practice of the sacrifice wrought by Christ on the cross, proclaiming this to be the one perfect and sufficient sacrifice for sin which establishes a new covenant between the Lord and his people.[64] Yet René Girard's highly influential account of the meaning of the crucifixion sees in Hebrews the roots of a fateful misinterpretation.[65] For Girard, the crucifixion 'abolishes' sacrifice not by being the perfect sacrifice, but by exposing the error of the sacrificial system, especially of the system of sin-offerings. If the cross has been used to support a system of violent sacrifices, this is due to a basic misunderstanding of Jesus' mission.

Girard's argument, like the Hebrews text he finds problematic, focuses on sacrifice as a sin-offering. This point is important, despite a blurring of the historic distinctions between the different types of sacrifice in both first century Jewish theology and early Christian discourse.[66] Hebrews presents Christ's once-for-all sacrifice as being primarily for sins, and secondarily for the removal of guilt. Yet in the Old Testament there are other types of sacrifice and several purposes for which sacrifice may be offered.[67] Notable among these is fellowship, which is, as has been seen, an important dimension of the *matal* sacrifice and of Christian sacrificial rituals in Greece. It could be argued that the Christian 'abolition' of sacrifice – whether through a Girardian unmasking of falsehood or through the final perfect sacrifice of Christ – relates only to sin-offerings, and leaves open the possibility of other functions of animal sacrifice. In the Liberian context, for instance, there is a rich interweaving of the themes of atonement and communal solidarity. The animal sacrifice makes effective the fellowship between people which is made possible by the forgiveness of sin.

This does not, however, fully answer West's critique. Nor does it satisfy at least one contemporary Christian theologian, who develops a cross-centred advocacy of Christian vegetarianism. Stephen Webb argues that, to the extent that the sacrifice of Christ abolishes animal sacrifice, it calls Christians to abstain from eating meat. For Christians to act otherwise would be nothing less than to continue the crucifixion of Christ. Webb avers:

> When Christians partake of the body of God in the eucharist, it surely is not a commemoration of animal slaughter but as an admission to our own guilt in slaughtering and destroying others, our own identification with Jesus in all of his animal cries and pain, and our own affirmation of the struggle to work to overcome such pain. Literal meat-eating, then, is a parody of the vegetarian supper of the eucharist, and giving thanks to God for servings of dead flesh is an affront to the suffering of God in Jesus Christ.[68]

Webb's powerful critique exposes the contradiction underlying standard interpretations of the Eucharist – it abolishes animal sacrifice, but is regarded as having no theological implications for animal slaughter or human consumption of animal carcasses as meat.

Israelite animal sacrifice served as the legitimating exemplar of all animal slaughter and meat eating. Through sacrifice, the people of Israel acknowledged the gifted character of animal life, originating from God and being offered, in part, back to God. The importance of this awareness is shown by the requirement that any animal to be sacrificed on festivals be one year old.[69] Moreover, all animals sacrificed had to be unblemished.[70] Such an animal was a significant offering. It would have attained optimal weight for the level of investment required, whereas the slaughter of a newly born animal would leave more milk from the mother available for human use. Alternatively, killing a much older animal would have amounted to convenient disposal of an increasingly unproductive beast.[71]

The gifting was represented above all by the blood, identified with the life of the animal, which consequently needed to be shed in all acts of slaughter rather than consumed by humans. The implication of the gifted character of all animal life is that, if Christ came to abolish sacrifice, then he came to abolish slaughter and meat eating too. As Issa Khalil puts it, Christ 'died *in place* of animals, thereby liberating and reconciling them to himself and to human beings'.[72] This notion is lent support by evidence from bread stamps that some early Eucharistic loaves were imprinted with images of animals.[73] The bread, representing the body of Christ, was thus seen as replacing the former animal sacrifices.

If, alternatively, animal sacrifice continues to be theologically justifiable within a Christian context, then meat eating might also be justifiable in this context. In this case, the supposition that Christ's sacrifice necessarily abolished animal sacrifice needs fundamentally rethinking. Such an understanding of animal slaughter as sacrifice is developed by Karl Barth, who goes so far as to argue that Christians can understand slaughter *only* as sacrifice, i.e., as a 'substitutionary sign for the forfeited life of man'. He states: 'The slaying of animals is really possible only as an appeal to God's reconciling grace, as its representation and proclamation.'[74] For a human being to presume to kill an animal on his or her own authority would, Barth contends, be murder. The only authority on which animals may be killed legitimately is God's, which means that moral and spiritual submission to God are required of humans engaged in slaughter. Barth asserts:

> The killing of animals in obedience is possible only as a deeply reverential act of repentance, gratitude and praise on the part of the forgiven sinner in face of the One who is the Creator and Lord of man and beast. The killing of animals, when performed with the permission of God and by His command, is a priestly act of eschatological character.[75]

The theological implications of this understanding of slaughter as sacrifice extend to the eating of the meat which follows. Barth affirms: 'A meal which includes meat is a sacrificial meal. It signifies a participation in the reconciling effect of the animal sacrifice commanded and accepted by God as a sign.'[76] In such a meal, the animal's life becomes a substitutionary sign by which human participation in the reconciliation is signified.

Support for this association of Christian reconciliation with animal sacrifice can be found in a long tradition of reflection on how, on the cross, the body of Christ becomes meat. In early Latin Easter hymns, Christ is described as the 'innocent lamb which is killed and roasted on the altar of the cross', and as 'hung on the spit of the cross and roasted by the fire of love and sorrow'.[77] This imagery, initially disturbing to the contemporary reader, recalls the various ways in John's Gospel in which the rules for the Passover sacrifice are observed in the sacrifice of Christ, the lamb of God. In fulfilment of the requirements of sacrificial ritual, no bone of Christ's body is broken, his blood is shed and scattered, and his body is removed before morning.[78] The sponge soaked in wine vinegar, which Christ is offered to drink, is raised on a stem of hyssop, the plant also used to spread the blood of the Passover lamb on the door frames and lintel of Israelite houses.[79] The paschal lamb was, like Christ, also pierced with a shaft of pomegranate wood, which served as a spit for roasting.[80] We noted in Chapter Six the links identifiable in some medieval Christian folk devotion between the killing of pigs and the death of Christ. This association might now be seen as susceptible to interpretation against itself, with the injustice and cruelty which Christ suffers in order, in Stephen Webb's terms, to become meat giving an insight into the injustice and cruelty of animal suffering.

Whatever one concludes about the justifiability of Christian practices of animal sacrifice, it is clear that they are very far removed from contemporary practices of animal slaughter. The theological association of meat eating with the crucifixion and the Eucharist might make the suffering and death of animals visible in a context where meat eating is connected with sacrifice. Such linkages are impossible, however, in the present-day context of mass slaughter.

Sacrifice and the slaughterhouse

In Eastern Orthodox churches, sacrificial ritual has maintained far greater continuity with Israelite practice than in Western churches. This analysis is supported by the understanding of Orthodox liturgy developed by Margaret Barker, who sees it as fundamentally continuous with Jewish Temple worship.[81] Barker does not, however, give any attention to liturgies of animal sacrifice. This is understandable, because her interest is to read modern mainstream Western liturgy through the lens of Temple worship. Yet their relation can also be viewed in reverse perspective, with the Temple tradition calling Christian theologians and liturgists to reappraise which practices count, or could count, as liturgical. In the case of the slaughter of animals by Christians, conceiving this as a potentially ritual act in continuity with Israelite sacrificial practices illumines what should be some of its underlying motivations and restraining factors, especially the limitation of the pain experienced by the animal. In the case of the Armenian *matal*, several marks are identifiable which have the combined effect of minimizing the suffering caused to the animal, including rule observance, attentiveness and reverence.

The Armenian and other Orthodox rituals of slaughter display obvious links with *shechitah*, Jewish kosher slaughter. Various Jewish scholars have argued that animal welfare is of key importance in the theory of kosher slaughter, and that minimizing the animal's suffering is a theme in rabbinic discourse.[82] Dan Cohn-Sherbok points out, for example, that the shochet who performs the killing must be pious and sensitive, and well instructed in the Law, animals and the method of slaughter. He must not be mentally or physically impaired, nor a drunkard, and must have steady hands. His knife must be sharp, clean, and at least twice as long as the diameter of the animal's neck. The act of slaughter itself should take no more than a second, and render the animal immediately senseless. Five prohibitions are formulated to ensure that the slaughter is as swift and painless as possible, and infringement of any of these renders the animal non-kosher. Comparable requirements are found in Islamic halal slaughter, with the difference that the cut must sever the trachea and oesophagus as well as the jugular veins. Furthermore, there is a Muslim tradition that nothing be done to the slaughtered animal until the body is completely cold, in order to avoid any possibility of mutilation while it is still living.[83] In a general assessment, Stephen Clark has even argued that a sacrifice in which the animal has been treated unjustly counts as unclean and is therefore invalid as a sacrifice.[84] The claim that kosher slaughter practices are rooted in respect for the life of animals and the desire to minimize their suffering has been used by contemporary Jewish scholars to hold slaughter plants to account and to interrupt the logic of commercial meat production.[85] Opposing arguments have, of course, been presented, and will be considered shortly.

An underlying continuity exists between specific ritual requirements such as *shechitah* and full sacrificial rituals like *matal*. *Shechitah* was fundamentally connected with the Temple sacrifice, as evidenced by requirements such as the draining of the blood and checking for any disease or deformity which would constitute a blemish.[86] Two key aspects of continuity show that the rules of ritual and sacrifice have more in common with each other than with modern mass animal slaughter methods. These are the visibility of the slaughter of the animal to its consumers, and the assigning of clear responsibility for the act of killing to an individual person.

The visibility of animal slaughter to eaters of meat is deeply countercultural. Even in Armenia, attempts were made by the patriarchate during the nineteenth century to end the practice following complaints by visitors from the Christian West.[87] In medieval cities in Western Europe, animals were killed for meat in the central areas where their meat was sold – still named 'the Shambles' in some British towns – being led down filthy streets through puddles of congealed blood beneath suspended carcasses ready for sale. Yet in countries like France and Britain, nineteenth-century hygiene legislation forced slaughter off the streets and into abattoirs located far away in the suburbs.[88] Unconsciously echoing Cecil Frances Alexander's description of the location of Christ's crucifixion in her hymn *There is a green hill far away*, Noélie Vialles discusses this new requirement that slaughterhouses, like cemeteries, had to be 'outside the city walls'.[89] The result is that, in the present day, animal slaughter has become an anonymous, invisible and even clandestine activity removed from the general populace. This shielding from view of the killing of animals for meat is mirrored in the domestic sphere of food preparation by a gradual tendency which, in Britain, occurred during the nineteenth century to relocate the carving of whole animals and large joints away from the meal table into another room removed from the gaze of diners.[90] The common attitude that the slaughter and cutting up of animals for meat is acceptable providing that the enclosure, exile and secrecy of these activities are preserved has been confirmed recently in Britain by the widespread outrage expressed after several television food programmes broadcast the killing of animals as the first stage in their preparation, cooking and consumption as meat.

The dehumanization and dismemberment which define the modern slaughterhouse have thus, in the late modern period, been hidden from public view, and with good reason. Yet they point to the second key countercultural principle of sacrificial ritual, following its visibility: the assignment of responsibility for slaughter to a specific person. Inside the slaughterhouse, by contrast, the basic organizational principle is the splitting up of the act of killing into a 'process' for which no-one assumes direct responsibility.[91] This methodology employed in a large modern American slaughterhouse is described as follows:

> At Branding Iron, death is represented in technical terms. The steps are marked out on job descriptions and on factory blueprints, distancing the moment of death from easy capture so that the fatal event is not a moment but a set of stages. This is a calculated death. The transition from live cattle to meat is never marked by a single blow, or even by a single industrial tool in a packing plant. Determining exactly when the killing happens, and identifying which job actually does the deed, is frustrated by the minute divisions of tasks along the way from animal to meat.[92]

In the context of mechanized mass slaughter, the alienation of workers from the product of their activity and the annihilation of their compassion, sensitivity and imagination are essential means of conditioning them to perpetuate slaughter willingly. The compartmentalization of tasks is the principal method of achieving this crucial practical and ethical disengagement of workers from their actions and the consequences of those actions. As Carol Adams puts it, 'they must view the living animal as the meat that everyone outside the slaughterhouse accepts it as, while the animal is still alive'.[93]

It would be worrying enough if the working practices just described were confined to slaughterhouses as a means of arming their battalions of staff to prosecute humankind's war on other animals. In fact, the organizational principles which made the practices possible became, through the twentieth century, an international norm in manufacturing industry. Henry Ford describes forming his concept of the car assembly line from observing the overhead trolley utilized by the Chicago stockyards in the process of making beef carcasses presentable for sale.[94] Perhaps Ford had gained knowledge of the yards from Upton Sinclair's bestselling exposé *The Jungle*. Around the time that Ford was creating his production line, Sinclair had revealed the apocalyptic horror of these establishments to a stunned nation, describing the grim efficiency of the process for dressing beef carcasses in comparatively unemotive terms:

> The beef proceeded on its journey. There were men to cut it, and men to split it; and men to gut it and scrape it clean inside. There were some with hoses which threw jets of boiling water upon it, and others who removed the feet and added the final touches.[95]

The twentieth-century mass-production line which Ford pioneered did not, however, need to maintain this alienation and annihilation for the same reasons as the slaughterhouses on which it was modelled. Many assembly line outputs do not depend directly on the killing and dismemberment of living beings, and the workers staffing them do not, therefore, need to be desensitized to the same degree in order to perform their role in the process. Even so, similar methods of worker organization were preserved in the Fordist production line in order to standardize products, maximize profits through the division of labour, and crucially to establish detailed control over workers' roles. In Sinclair's novel the central character, who is a young Lithuanian immigrant named Jurgis Rudkus, eventually embraces socialism in response to the degradation of humans he has witnessed in the stockyard.[96]

In a provocative assessment, Charles Patterson traces this trajectory further forward through the twentieth century to the methods of mass slaughter deployed in the Holocaust. Patterson compares the systems and principles used to compel animals and humans towards their deaths and the language employed to describe them. Channelling emerges as a common theme, communicated by imagery of the chute, the funnel or the tube and set against a backdrop of extremely efficient mechanistic processing of huge numbers of humans and animals.[97] Indeed, many victims of the Nazi genocide were transported to the death camps in hot, airless cattle trains, just as railroads were essential to the centralization of slaughter in Chicago, the animal killing centre of the United States. Some of the carriages used could be viewed in Paris in an outdoor exhibition in the Jardins des Champs-Elysées during the summer of 2003. Written on the side of each carriage was the number of cattle it was permitted to carry, and a much larger maximum number of human beings. This was in conformity with the elaborate Nazi law concerning the protection of animals during train journeys passed on 8 September 1938, which specified the amount of space to which a range of animals on their way to slaughter were entitled.[98]

Following the national furore sparked by Upton Sinclair's exposé, notable efforts were made in the United States to rehumanize the commercial mass killing of animals. These continue today, inspired in part by new public revelations of abuses of animals perpetrated out of public view.[99] In many American states, they are abetted by legal provisions exempting 'food animals' from the anti-cruelty laws applicable to other animals.[100] Animals in slaughterhouses are thereby placed 'beyond the law' and become bare life. This degradation occurs by a process similar to that by which Christ is dehumanized, passed between different legal authorities and then cast out of the world onto the cross.[101] This provides a Christological perspective on modern animal slaughter which complements the comparison developed in our earlier discussion of the small-scale sacrifice of individual animals.

In light of the shocking violence sometimes perpetrated in slaughterhouses, one might well wonder about the quality of their 'outputs'. An especially notorious description in *The Jungle* concerned the production of sausages, and deserves to be quoted in full:

> There was never the least attention paid to what was cut up for sausage; there would come all the way back from Europe old sausage that had been rejected, and that was moldy and white – it would be dosed with borax and glycerine, and dumped into the hoppers, and made over again for home consumption. There would be meat that had tumbled out on the floor, in the dirt and sawdust, where the workers had tramped and spit uncounted billions of consumption germs. There would be meat stored in great piles in rooms; and the water from leaky roofs would drip over it, and thousands of rats would race about on it. It was too dark in these storage places to see well, but a man could run his hand over these piles of meat and sweep off handfuls of the dried dung of rats. These rats were nuisances, and the packers would put poisoned bread out for them; they would die, and then rats, bread, and meat would go into the hoppers together. This is no fairy story and no joke; the meat would be shoveled into carts, and the man who did the shoveling would not trouble to lift out a rat even when he saw one – there were things that went into the sausage in comparison with which a poisoned rat was a tidbit. There was no place for the men to wash their hands before they ate their dinner, and so they made a practice of washing

them in the water that was to be ladled into the sausage. There were the
butt-ends of smoked meat, and the scraps of corned beef, and all the odds
and ends of the waste of the plants, that would be dumped into old barrels
in the cellar and left there. Under the system of rigid economy which the
packers enforced, there were some jobs that it only paid to do once in a long
time, and among these was the cleaning out of the waste barrels. Every
spring they did it; and in the barrels would be dirt and rust and old nails
and stale water – and cartload after cartload of it would be taken up and
dumped into the hoppers with fresh meat, and sent out to the public's
breakfast. Some of it they would make into 'smoked' sausage – but as the
smoking took time, and was therefore expensive, they would call upon their
chemistry department, and preserve it with borax and color it with gelatine
to make it brown. All of their sausage came out of the same bowl, but when
they came to wrap it they would stamp some of it 'special', and for this they
would charge two cents more a pound.[102]

Do such practices continue today? Consumers of sausages will undoubtedly
hope not, but can do little to verify actual conditions. Slaughterhouses are out
of bounds to most people for a host of regulatory and public-relations reasons.
In such places, the safeguards of animal welfare and meat quality associated
with Christian rituals of animal sacrifice are absent. On a fast-moving conveyor
belt, close attention cannot be given to every animal killed, and spiritual discipline is deemed irrelevant to the task of slaughter. Consumers of this meat are
not involved in its slaughter and have little idea of what has happened to the
meat before it reaches them. Conversely, the slaughterers of the meat are unlikely ever to consume it.

Temple Grandin, a designer and operator of equipment used to kill animals in
slaughter plants, has sought to reorganize some of their processes according to
ritual concepts. As many as one third of all cattle slaughtered in the United States
have been moved through handling facilities which she has designed.[103] Grandin
has described how ritual ideas can promote among workers an understanding of
slaughter as part of a process which places controls on killing, resensitizing
workers and increasing their awareness of death as a sacred moment.[104] She has
introduced measures including the configuration and adornment of factory space,
the naming of pieces of machinery (such as a new cattle ramp and conveyor
restrainer system known as the 'Stairway to Heaven'), rotating workers around
tasks to discourage routinization, and reducing line speed.

But as Grandin herself states: 'The paradox is that it is difficult to care about
animals but be involved in killing them.'[105] The statement is particularly
poignant because underlying her approach is deep personal identification with
the animals to be slaughtered. In her autobiography she describes how, as a
person with autism, she recognizes and understands many of the stimuli to
which cattle are sensitive far more acutely than do most other humans. These
include a sense of living in a world filled with predators, worrying about a
change in routine, and becoming unsettled if objects are moved from their

normal position.[106] Despite this deep empathy, she nevertheless sees animals as unproblematically available to be killed and consumed by humans as meat.

The question of whether classic religious forms of animal slaughter remain less cruel than modern factory methods of killing, which employ the latest technology, is hotly contested. Grandin, for example, argues that the main problem with kosher slaughter is the restraint system – which often involves suspending animals by one leg from a chain – rather than the cut itself, and discusses how this shackling and hoisting system can easily be eliminated.[107] Abuses have been reported in some industrialized kosher slaughter plants, and these plants' originating ritual principles have clearly needed to be re-established through regulation and training.[108] Moreover, it has been argued that comparatively recent new technologies such as electrical stunning provide less painful possibilities. Yet ritual slaughter methods at their best offer principles capable of ameliorating conditions in secular abattoirs, as shown by Grandin's work, and also constitute an important dimension of religious identity.[109]

A complicating factor in legal arguments about religious slaughter practices is that such practices have been seen as more intrinsic to some religions than to others. In Germany in 1995, the Federal Administrative Court ruled Islamic ritual slaughter (*dabh*) illegal on the grounds that it failed to comply with existing animal protection laws and was not a requirement of Islamic law. The ban on *dabh* was overturned by the country's constitutional court in 2002, following a case brought by a Turkish butcher. Jewish religious slaughter (*shechitah*) had, in contrast, been judged part of Jewish law and had therefore been permitted since the 1986 first amendment to the Animal Protection Law.[110] In Britain, recent legislation has sought to balance the possibility that religious slaughter methods cause more animal suffering with the maintenance of religious liberty. Religious slaughter is certainly permitted, but must be carried out in a slaughterhouse with a veterinary surgeon and stunning equipment available if required.[111] In modern multi-faith Western countries, religious slaughter methods raise issues affecting everyone, if only because most meat eaters have probably consumed halal meat. Because far more is produced than required by Muslims, it is frequently served in restaurants run by Muslims and sold in food stores in areas where Muslims live.[112]

What might Christians contribute to debates about methods of animal slaughter? Our discussion suggests that Christians in the modern West have much to learn from Christian traditions of animal sacrifice. The concealment and deliberate forgetting of slaughter, and the lack of respect for nonhuman animal life which this indicates, should be subjected to Christian critique. Attention to rituals of animal slaughter can jolt Christians out of complacent indifference about how they obtain their meat. So, as Stephen Webb reminds us, can the image of the slaughtered carcass on the cross.

For Christians who are meat eaters, sacrifice provides a means of acknowledging the giftedness of all animal life, and that this life is not ultimately human property. Sacrifice also brings meat eaters to face with honesty the reality of animal slaughter, which in the modern world is almost always hidden from view. Some of the principles which sacrifice has promoted, including fellowship between humans and the welfare of animals killed for meat, need to be preserved by modern meat eaters. More radically, Christians who are vegetarians might wish to argue that actual sacrifice and public slaughter should be reinstated, in the hope that large numbers of meat eaters would be repelled by such spectacles and thus motivated to abstain from meat too. The animals killed for meat in the factory-like abattoirs are sacrificed to the idols of profit, instant gratification, and the technological mastery over nature. Christians should consider whether, following Augustine in this if in no other dietary prescription, they should decline this meat as part of their refusal of idolatry.

8 Christian food, heavenly food, worldly food

Throughout this study it has been clear that food is not simply a private matter. All eating affirms and reconfigures human connections with natural and social environments.[1] It is therefore unsurprising that Christian debates about food are often linked to discussions about what attitudes to the wider world Christians should express. In this penultimate chapter we shall examine in greater detail some of the ethical, theological and practical implications of attempts by Christian individuals and groups to use food to negotiate the relationships between forms of life which are world-affirming, world-judging and world-transforming. Our focus will remain on practices and their implications, but we shall also consider possible theological frameworks for their interpretation. These are pressing matters in a present-day context in which the social, economic and political impact of food issues is clear. For this reason, the assumption needs to be challenged that, in choices about food, individual choice is sovereign.

We shall begin by considering how Christian communities have sought not only to regulate eating or allow individuals to exclude some foods from their diet, but to remove particular foods from the menu altogether. We shall then assess a range of accusations brought against vegetarians, including Christian vegetarians, that through their abstinence they disdain creation, fear embodiment, desire unattainable purity or flee from death. The theological concerns motivating these accusations will inform a more nuanced evaluation of dietary abstinence.

Present-day food choices

Underlying the historic Christian disquiet at the heretical implications of dietary restriction, discussed in Chapter Six, was a desire to prevent groups or individuals cutting themselves off from the various networks of worldly connections in which food placed them. To eat with others was not only to express fellowship but to affirm interdependence. Heretics were regarded as using their choices (*hairesis*) about food, as well as about doctrine, to refuse this interdependence by separating themselves from an imperfect world and seeking on earth a false vision of heaven. This desire for separation is evident in the self-presentation of some Christian vegetarian groups. For example, various nineteenth-century groups expressed a desire to eat 'the food that Eden knew'[2] before the Fall, and thereby to found an alternative to a corrupt society with its corrupt diet. By contrast, the monastic community, in which some members ate meat in the same refectory as others who abstained, deliberately maintained a visible context of acknowledged interdependence and solidarity. Asceticism had to be rooted in eating practices deemed ordinary in order not to be regarded as suspect.

Throughout our study, flexible dietary rules have been seen to be a matter of Christian principle, not historical accident. This flexibility has made it possible to localize and adjust food practices to suit individual bodily needs. It has also left space for individual feats of asceticism far exceeding in their rigour any communal requirements. Flexibility makes it possible for high value to be placed on the giving and receiving of hospitality, with normal food choices able to be disrupted temporarily for the sake of wider fellowship and interdependence. Particular foods are restricted but not forbidden, or are forbidden at certain times for certain groups of people, or are confined to particular occasions. All foods nevertheless remain, in principle, available for consumption.

Present-day forms of dietary restriction in the West have many similarities with this Christian tradition of flexibility. Modern food cultures maintain a common table at which anything can be eaten, yet permit individual variation. It is typically assumed that an individual's dietary choices are simply individual, to be catered for if possible but not to be allowed to disrupt anybody else's eating patterns, or wider social assumptions about what is edible or inedible. The category of 'dietary requirements', for example, covers food allergies and intolerances as well as religious and ethical choices. Religious and ethical dietary restrictions are thereby removed from the sphere of public debate, becoming as private and non-negotiable as a congenital digestive problem.

In the modern world, this understanding of diet as an essentially private matter has progressively replaced the shared table which previously permitted individual variations in eating. Reflection on which foods are acceptable or unacceptable on the common menu and which principles of restriction or moderation should be followed has been mostly absent from public discourse, despite its prominence in Christian tradition. The concealment and effective denial of animal slaughter, discussed in Chapter Seven, has contributed to the marginalization of meat abstention. This is despite the enormous impacts of current widespread preferences for meat on natural and social ecology. For example, when Rajendra Pachauri, chair of the United Nations Intergovernmental Panel on Climate Change, suggested that reducing meat production and consumption would be a good way to reduce global carbon emissions, he was careful to say that this should remain a matter of personal choice.[3] Likewise, when a local council in England considered proposals to cut the amount of meat served in canteens, schools and care homes, assurances were issued that 'we are not saying everybody should be vegetarian'.[4] Unfortunately, a lot of writing on 'Christian diet' has embraced this modern privatization uncritically. A recent study of the 'Christian diet' industry draws attention to the absence, in the body of diet literature directed mainly at contemporary evangelical Christian women, of any reference to wider issues of food distribution, justice or sustainability.[5]

The privatization of dietary choice has clear implications for meat abstention. Refusals to eat meat are most likely to be accepted when they do not interfere with the practice of meat eating – but from the perspective of a vegetarian critic this simply allows the death and suffering of animals to continue invisibly and unchallenged. It is easy to add a vegetarian option to the menu, but far more problematic to articulate and discuss the implications of placing meat on the menu. Heated debates among feminist activists in the United States about a proposal not to serve meat at national conferences have shown how calls for public or collective dietary restriction cause disturbance, whereas individual choices do not.[6]

Eating configures humans' relationships with their natural and social environments, and good eating should not cut people off from these relationships. The contemporary situation therefore presents particular challenges. Global climate change and increasing pressure on the world's natural resources make reappraisal of the Western menu more urgent. The most pressing issue for a contemporary Christian theology of food is how to reinstate reflection on diet into public discourse, and inculcate an awareness that responsibility for dietary choice is societal as well as individual. What theological and practical resources might contribute to such public reflection?

Christian cuisines: what is food?

One suggestive source is a small but significant Christian history of changing an entire food culture. Forming new Christian communities and reshaping social life according to Christian principles have sometimes involved not simply accepting all existing foods as clean, but determined efforts to take certain foods off the menu. It has already been seen that Augustine, who helped to establish the Christian pattern of treating all foods as clean, made one important exception to his affirmation of the Christian's liberty of eating. Food sacrificed to idols was to be avoided absolutely, even if the alternative was starvation. Augustine wrote in a context in which avoidance would have been fairly easy. In other situations, however, Christians were surrounded by a single dominant cuisine founded on non-Christian sacrificial rituals. For them, the issues raised were both more pressing and more complex.

The most obvious examples were the first Christian communities in the Roman Empire, in which some of the meat offered for sale originated from sacrifice. This generated uncertainty, with a Christian walking into a butcher's shop unsure of the provenance of any specific piece of meat.[7] Paul's response in 1 Corinthians was to advise Christians to 'eat whatever is sold in the meat market without raising any question on the ground of conscience'.[8] A particular piece of meat should be refused, he stated, only if the Christian is informed that it specifically is a product of sacrifice. This is in order that the conscience of an informer is not judged as a result of passing a negative judgement on the Christian's liberty.[9] A Christian might, by eating idol meat, encourage a 'weak' Christian, or a potential Christian who had not developed sufficient freedom of conscience, to consume such meat too and thereby to lapse into paganism.[10] In general, however, allowing the benefit of the doubt was to be preferred. This probably served to distinguish Christian Jews from other Jews, who in first-century Rome were well known and frequently criticized for declining table fellowship with non-Jews.[11] The alternative of meat abstention was, moreover, also associated with foreign religious practices and beliefs including the transmigration of souls, with the result that loyal citizens like the youthful Seneca soon abandoned it.[12]

In Greece, in contrast, most or all meat was the product of sacrifice. It is there possible to speak of a 'cuisine of sacrifice' – a food culture dependent on sacrifice.[13] This points to a possible reason for the greater prevalence and persistence of Christian sacrificial rituals in the East generally: because sacrifice was so widespread, sacrificing to the Christian God was likely to be the only means, short of complete meat abstention, of avoiding idol meat.

Yet not all Christian communities saw these measures as making meat eating acceptable. Some Christians, especially those living away from urban centres, argued that meat should be excluded from the collective Christian menu. In so doing, they embraced and developed Jewish traditions of vegetable offering.[14] Andrew McGowan presents evidence that many groups of early Christians established what he terms 'ascetic eucharists'.[15] These were meatless meals, taken in order to avoid participating in the cuisine of sacrifice and thereby to establish a different cuisine that corresponded with a different practice of worship and a different form of social existence.

Another important example of Christians changing the menu is found in the history of Christian missions in northern Europe. Historical evidence indicates that horseflesh formed part of the diet of pre-Christian societies in much of this region.[16] In Rome and Greece, however, horses were not generally eaten unless the alternative was starvation.[17] Various missionaries from Rome regarded horse eating as a practice that was incompatible with the Christianization of these societies and should be eliminated. Around 732, Pope Gregory III ordered Boniface, the missionary to the Germans, to forbid horsemeat consumption on the grounds that it was a 'filthy and abominable practice'.[18] This injunction was repeated by Pope Zacharius twenty years later.[19] Yet the recurrence of the issue in penitential codes and letters from missionaries suggests that horsemeat did not disappear completely from the northern European menu until some time after the conversion of these lands to Christianity.[20] When Iceland converted to Christianity in the year 1000 the eating of horseflesh was not outlawed, although was no longer permitted in public.[21]

Scholars disagree about what the ban on horsemeat means. One obvious explanation is that horses were offered in pre-Christian sacrificial rituals, and that their elimination was part of a general effort to extirpate paganism.[22] Yet the particular horror with which hippophagy was regarded cannot be explained satisfactorily purely by its association with pagan ritual. Other interpretations suggest economic or military bases for the ban, noting the relative inefficiency of the horse as a source of meat in comparison with its usefulness as a means of transport or in the military defence of Christian Europe.[23] Although such factors cannot be discounted, they do not explain fully the role which eating or refusing horsemeat performed in the construction of Christian identity.

Neither is it entirely adequate to say that abstention from horsemeat became a positive marker of belonging to the new Christian community. Conscious adoption of different food rules certainly cemented group identity strongly. It provided a clear marker of belonging, and inducted the newly converted Christian into a new identity through re-educating their body and appetite and enacting an everyday physical 'turning away' from past life. But despite persisting in their efforts, Christian missionaries and rulers found it difficult to persuade the converted population to refuse horsemeat. If the need was simply for a marker of communal identity, why not promote one that was less contentious?

In assessing this issue, we should not underestimate the power of deeply held aesthetic perceptions in a clash of menus and of their underlying cosmologies. The disgust expressed in Pope Gregory's letter recalls the horror with which Western commentators are liable even now to describe practices like Chinese consumption of dogs and cats. Missionaries to northern Europe were simply shocked by pagans who treated as food what they regarded not to be food. The place of the horse in the symbolic ordering of the world as an animal which lived and worked closely alongside humans made it seem to them ineligible as food. Missionaries refused food practices that belonged to an unfamiliar and disturbing way of ordering the world and human lives within it. They also condemned food practices which established Christian groups, who claimed the right to define the limits of the Christian community, could not stomach. The letters sent between Rome and northern Europe as Christianity spread constructed an imaginary shared table around which the Christian world was expected to sit.

Is this debate significant today? Readers might well think that the horsemeat episode is best discarded as a historical curiosity. Instead of trying to change a menu, why not place everything on the shared table and learn to eat alongside others who consume particular foods which make us uncomfortable? The most obvious reason for not doing so is that cuisines have social, economic and political implications. There is no fundamental reason why the prophetic Christian call to a just social order should fail to address a society's food practices. If horsemeat consumption really was part of a system of social division or economic oppression, it would make sense to take horsemeat off the menu – just as, in a later age, Christians declined to sell or consume sugar and other slave-grown products as part of their opposition to slavery.[24]

At the very least, Christian freedom to eat any food rests on a prior set of implicit decisions about what counts as 'food'. This is extremely significant in the case of meat, because no animal is food necessarily or automatically.[25] Work is required to turn animals into food, most visibly the physical work of slaughter, dismemberment and cooking.[26] Of equal importance is the symbolic and conceptual labour of converting individual animals into 'meat', and non-human animals as a group into the mass object of human exploitation.[27] Moreover, the ability to turn animals into meat is itself predicated on and supportive of distorted ways of seeing and fashioning the world, in which the status of some humans is maintained by violent subjugation of other animals, including other humans. For proponents of vegetarianism, the various forms of work which turn animals into meat need to be interrupted. The most important way in which this can be done is by refusing to eat meat. Other interruptions to the symbolic production of meat are effected by raising awareness of animal suffering and regarding nonhuman animals as subjects.[28]

Idolatrous consumption

This interruption of meat-producing processes amounts to a stand against idolatry. But what do we mean by idolatry? It might be assumed that identifying a specific act of worship as idol worship simply designates it as the worship of another group, thus serving a polemical agenda of affirming and reinforcing a particular group identity. If idolatry meant only this, then Christian concerns about eating idol food would have few implications for present-day culture, beyond ongoing discussion among some Christians about vegetarianism's possible links with New Age religion and paganism. In fact, idolatry has a deeper theological meaning which yields more fruits for our study.

Idolatry is, fundamentally, misdirected worship, and the resulting mis-orientation of human life. Idolatrous patterns of thought and behaviour can be discerned in a society which claims to be secular, as well as in the lives of people who identify themselves as Christian. To name idolatry is to name the basic misperceptions and distortions of value on which ways of life, including ways of eating, are based. Because God is the 'living and true God', idolatry can be regarded as a pattern of worship leading to death and falsehood.[29]

Animals killed for meat are sacrificed to idols by practices of killing and consuming which reinforce a distorted view of the world and a death-dealing pattern of existence. To refuse to eat what is known to have been sacrificed to idols is to reject the system of idolatry and the opportunity to profit from that system. Carol Adams argues, as a vegetarian, that the presentation of animals as 'meat' is already a sacrifice to the idol of human power over nonhuman nature.[30] Omnivores concerned about the provenance of their meat might also regard factory-farmed meat as a sacrifice to the idol of profit. Vegetarians and omnivores can both see that the sacrifices offered to these idols perpetuate cruelty and suffering along with a distorted way of seeing the world.

What, then, of the injunction to 'eat whatever is sold in the meat market without raising any question on the ground of conscience', because Christians owe no allegiance to idols but receive all their food from God?[31] The problem with taking this command literally today as grounds for opposition to vegetarianism is the power and pervasiveness of idolatry. Today there is no morally neutral meat and no 'secular' meat market. To consume meat is not just to accept the by-products of a cruel and distorted system, but actively to affirm that system. B.R. Myers suggests that the 'idolatry of food ... can be seen in the public's toleration of a level of cruelty in meat production that it would tolerate nowhere else'.[32] This particular form of idolatry is, in other words, not normal but exceptional.

To remove meat completely from the menu would radically alter human understandings of nonhuman animals, because changing the menu changes the ontology of the animal. It would also have the potential to change humans' perception of the nonhuman creation generally and their place in that creation, because meat eating relies on and supports their domination of that creation. The conscientious omnivore, if following this line of reasoning, might agree with the vegetarian that food is not immune from moral critique, even when affirmed as part of God's good creation. Food production systems are just as open to sinful distortion as any other human enterprise, and stand under just as much judgement.

But this, the Christian critic of vegetarianism might argue, surely means that no food is unproblematic and no food production system free from distortion. The vegetarian desire to escape violence, oppression and falsehood in the food system is, on this account, no more than a dream, because humans cannot escape their creaturely connectedness to the natural and social worlds, which are inherently sinful. For instance, in largely vegetarian cultures such as India, animals can also be subjected to sustained neglect, not least because humans have less personal interest in keeping them healthy in order to kill and eat them as meat. Moreover, humans are unable to make perfect choices because, being imperfect, they lack full knowledge of the extent and nature of their misperception and misvaluing of the world. For this reason, contemporary secular critics of vegetarianism often draw attention to the inevitable compromises involved in the consumption of food, and implicitly or explicitly accuse the vegetarian of hypocrisy or self-deception. As Michael Pollan writes provocatively of vegetarianism: 'Dreams of innocence are just that; they usually depend on a denial of reality that can be its own form of hubris.'[33]

The goodness of creation and unnatural foods

Two possible critiques of vegetarianism can easily be elided, but need to be distinguished. It has been argued that vegetarianism, or asceticism more generally, is based on a denial of the goodness of creation and the body. But it has also been suggested that vegetarianism, and asceticism generally, are based on a failure to accept the reality and pervasive effects of the Fall by seeking a pure, trouble-free mode of embodiment. The second line of criticism carries more force, but the first has an interesting history in Christian discourse about dietary change, which we shall first address.

As was shown in the discussion of Augustine's response to Manichaeism and in a range of Christian readings of the Hebrew Bible, the overarching theological context for Christian dietary flexibility has been an affirmation of the goodness of creation. Jewish refusals to eat certain foods were interpreted by Christian critics as irrational and unscriptural denials of the goodness of some parts of creation, as well as evidence of Jewish carnality. Moreover, Christian rejection of Manichaean dualism entailed the rejection of Manichaean dietary restrictions, in order to affirm, against the Manichaeans, the goodness of creation.

Later Christian interpreters of the Hebrew Bible, especially of Genesis 1, saw the affirmation of the whole of creation as 'very good' as evidence of its availability for consumption by humans, who occupied the central position within creation. This reading was supported by Paul's complaint to Timothy about those who

> forbid marriage and demand abstinence from foods, which God created to be received with thanksgiving by those who believe and know the truth. For everything created by God is good, and nothing is to be rejected, provided it is received with thanksgiving.[34]

Thomas Aquinas' account of nonhuman animals, which draws on this text, focuses on the value of animals for humanity and the consequent legitimacy of making use of them.[35] Somewhat differently, John Calvin addresses the tension between Genesis 1.29, where humans are given only plants for food, and Genesis 9.3, where meat eating is legalized. He accounts for this development by arguing that the clear intention of Genesis 1 is to proclaim God's generosity towards humankind, which is realized by the gift of animal food described in Genesis 9. Calvin thus frames refusal of any food as a refusal of divine generosity and due praise to God, in an interpretation which points directly to his critiques of fasting discussed in Chapter Four.[36] For Calvin, the primary issue is not creation's intrinsic goodness for humanity but the call to recognize and accept divine generosity. Nevertheless, the implication remains that all foods may be eaten and should be eaten.

Counter-examples from Christian tradition may, however, be identified in support of efforts to change the menu. Particularly striking is Jerome's defence of ascetic practice in *Against Jovinianus*, in which he refutes the argument that ascetics, by refusing certain foods, deny the goodness of creation, the dignity of humanity within creation and the express instruction of scripture. Jerome first states that he denies neither creation's intrinsic goodness nor its goodness for humanity. But basing arguments about particular foods being permissible on ideas about goodness is, he argues, absurd. This is because animals and other potential foods are useful to humans for a range of reasons, not just for eating. Various animals are good because of their medicinal usefulness, including vipers, the flesh of which counteracts poison, and hyenas, whose gall treats eye problems. Such animals were, Jerome states, 'created not for eating, but for medicine'.[37]

In the following section, he presents an account of differing food practices among different peoples, with an eye to the grotesque and bizarre. Libyans enjoy locusts; in Pontus and Phrygia 'fat white worms with blackish heads, which breed in decayed wood' are eaten, as well as insects; Syrians eat land crocodiles and the Arabians feast on green lizards; the Atticoti, a British tribe, consume human flesh and prize above all else shepherds' buttocks and the breasts of women.[38] Jerome asserts:

> no universal law of nature regulates the food of all nations, and ... each eats those things of which it has abundance ... each race follows its own practice and peculiar usages, and takes that for the law of nature which is most familiar to it.[39]

By demonstrating how contingencies of place and history shape each society's menu, Jerome effectively denaturalizes the range of foods proffered by his opponents. The implication of his argument is that the ascetic's refusal to eat any meat is no less rational than another person's refusal to eat, for example, wolves. In fact, as becomes clear in the argument's next stage, Jerome believes that the ascetic's diet is in fact not less rational but more rational, because it is consistent with the 'love of wisdom'. He asks:

> But suppose all nations alike ate flesh, and let that be everywhere lawful which the place produces. How does it concern us whose conversation is in heaven? Who ... are not bound to the circumstances of our birth, but of our new birth: who by abstinence subjugate our refractory flesh?

At this point, however, the problems with his argument become apparent. By denaturalizing the standard menu, Jerome effectively denaturalizes all decisions about eating. He has raised practical, economic and cultural considerations about the foods which each 'place produces' not in order to affirm or transform those understandings of food, but to transcend them. Christian food is thus delocalized and atemporalized, located 'in heaven' and determined according to 'new birth'. This opens the possibility of a radical critique of all existing food practices: even if 'all nations' eat meat, this does not mean that meat eating is either good or necessary. Yet the critical prophetic argument shifts rapidly towards a denial of the relevance of embodied and historical constraints on dietary choice. Flesh is presented as subjugated and 'refractory'. Moreover, the polemical contrast between 'birth' and 'new birth' hints at anxiety about human embodiment.

We have noted that modern vegetarians have frequently been accused of fearing or denying some aspect of human embodiment. For Pollan, vegetarian diets are a denial of physiology and cultural heritage. In recent feminist debates, they are associated with a refusal to accept embodied human difference and with cultural imperialism.[40] Does the refusal to eat meat, or more generally the removal of any food from the common table, signify a deeper reluctance to accept all the implications of human embodiment in its full particularity and contingency?

Eating towards eden

We should not assume that desiring the 'food that Eden knew', thereby seeking a return to the diet of humanity before the Fall, entails an attempt to escape from embodiment. As intimated above, some careful distinctions need to be made. Eden is, biblically, a place on earth, and the Edenic life is a form of embodied life in continuity with current human life. Vegetarianism that reverts to a supposed Edenic diet is not linked inevitably with bodily denial or punishment. Indeed, the nineteenth-century vegetarians who saw themselves as eating the food of Eden believed, as was seen in Chapter Four, that it would bring the health, vitality and longevity for which humans were originally destined.

Allusions to Eden, far from being denials of embodiment, serve as reminders that different ways of being embodied, and different relationships to nonhuman creation, are possible for human beings. Christopher Southgate, who uses the term 'protological vegetarianism' to describe this discourse, is undoubtedly correct to see its basis as being not a historical claim about the way things once were, but a 'radical critique of the actual world of human experience'.[41] However, it is important to note that this critique is not based on the denial of embodiment. The presence of the Eden narratives in the Bible should bring Christians to reflect on material flourishing, both human and nonhuman, including the material effects of vegetarianism on its practitioners and on nonhuman creation.

But is vegetarianism nevertheless based on a fear of death, especially when allied with efforts to improve bodily health and vitality? Julia Twigg argues that modern vegetarianism is predicated on an inversion of omnivorous eating patterns, identifying meat not with power and energy but with death, decay and excrement. Vegetarian food is presented in sharply contrasting terms as the source of life, and even as 'alive, full of a sort of manna that comes from the life force of nature'.[42] Being a source of purity, vegetarian food offers a this-worldly form of salvation which eschews practices associated with death. After all, in Eden there is no death. Theologically, the claim that vegetarianism is linked to a fear of death could be developed as part of the second Christian critique of vegetarianism noted at the beginning of the previous section – that modern vegetarians seek an illegitimate and premature inauguration of the eschaton through human effort.[43] In this respect, they are similar to the idealistic vegetarian Buthrescae in More's *Utopia*, who 'long only for the future life by means of their watching and sweat' and hope to 'obtain it very soon'.[44] Vegetarian practice is in these terms an instance of human pride, not because it denies creatureliness and materiality but because it provides a means for humanity to claim for itself the capacity to save the created world from its fallenness, and perhaps from death. Similar claims are made empirically or biologically by present-day commentators, who argue that people who refuse meat demand the impossible, both symbolically and practically.[45] By withdrawing from the common table, they seek to remove themselves from the common lot of sinful and mortal humanity.

This analysis is open to challenge. *Any* call for Christians to live in particular ways, in order better to reflect the will of God for humanity, could be interpreted as illegitimate and premature.[46] But as has been seen, Christian communities do in fact adopt countercultural practices and ways of life, including

countercultural food practices.[47] These are interpreted not as efforts to inaugu-
rate the kingdom, but as acts of obedient witness to the transformative power
of God in history.[48] For example, Christian opposition to slavery, including to
foods which were products of slavery, would not now be regarded as an illegitimate overreaching of human limitations. Judging the difference between
premature attempts to initiate the eschaton and obedient witness to God's
transforming power requires careful and possibly extended discernment, which
will be exercised by a community that still has to eat together.

Foods of fear and foods of hope

Forms of hopeful witness can be expressed and established by a range of dietary
practices, against a background of ongoing discernment of the communal menu.
Nevertheless, at least some of the critiques of vegetarianism outlined above, and
some other accounts of dietary restriction discussed in this study, are based on
the assumptions that people who reject a particular item as food do so because
they disparage or fear it, and desire to establish non-negotiable boundaries in
order to avoid what they regard as contamination. Before forms of witness
which are hopeful are considered, this contrary dynamic in the development of
dietary restrictions needs to be evaluated.

The accusation that their refusal of meat is based on fear sounds odd to
many vegetarians. On the contrary, they might argue, vegetarian practice is an
expression of hope for a more just and sustainable way of existing in the world,
and perhaps even for an eschatological peaceable kingdom. Vegetarians might
well argue that it is meat eaters who are afraid – afraid of confronting the
concrete implications of their diet for animal suffering and death, or for global
ecology.

How might these conflicting interpretations of dietary restriction be assessed?
Historically, instances of food practices which appear to arise from fear and
inculcate fear can certainly be identified. In particular, the Cathar approach to
food abstention suggests a governing principle of uncleanness, according to
which meat simply could not be tolerated under any circumstance. Moreover,
the penitential codes of Celtic Ireland, discussed in Chapter Five, reflect fear of
contamination and concern to exclude certain categories of food from the menu
absolutely, especially those which have been in contact with vermin or with
predatory and scavenging animals.

This idea that food avoidances are motivated primarily by a desire to protect
the body from contact with particular impure or abominable items is developed
by Mary Douglas in her classic interpretation of Leviticus.[49] However, as has
already been seen, interpretations of the Hebrew Bible food rules which treat
them as denigrating or rejecting unclean creatures are problematic, as Douglas
herself later realized. Even so, such interpretations have been advanced frequently by Christian anti-Jewish polemicists. It makes more sense to situate
these food rules within a wider context in which the goodness of creation is
acknowledged, including its order and structure, and the many forms of

interrelation between living beings which this structure makes possible. The inedible animals discussed in Chapter Five are not abominable, and uncleanness does not imply moral corruption. Conversely, God is praised for the goodness of creation and creation recognized as gift not only by the consumption of that creation. Indeed, Douglas ultimately accepts that God is also praised when some creatures are deliberately left alone.[50]

Discussions of dietary restrictions in the letters of Paul and in Augustine's anti-Manichaean writings, which draw on those letters, are directed against food practices motivated by fear and which reinforce fear. Paul tells the Corinthians that the idol 'is nothing' and therefore cannot affect those who eat meat sacrificed to it. Only the 'weak' are afraid of the consequences of eating this meat.[51] Idolatry is here both misdirected worship and misdirected fear, being a failure to recognize that only God is to be worshipped and feared.

Can alternative Christian food practices be identified which express and inculcate hope for the renewal and transformation of embodied life and for just and sustainable relationships? The practice of giving thanks to God for food expresses not only the goodness of creation as gift but the hope for a way of living and eating which would properly honour creation. Eating what would now be described as sustainable food, as in the Rule of Basil, and fasting in order to reflect and live out a vision of social and ecological peace, can also be seen as a sign of goodness and hope. In another example, the *matal* sacrifice, emphasizing fellowship and the distribution of food to the poor, offers a practical as well as symbolic challenge to unjust patterns of food distribution and consumption.

The giving and receiving of hospitality, in which the crossing of boundaries is deliberately invited, has recurred frequently in this study. These include boundaries between forbidden and permitted foods. Hospitality destabilizes food avoidances motivated by fear of contamination, creating a space in which communities and individuals are free to interact with each other and even, in a sense, to contaminate each other. More importantly, however, hospitable communities and willing guests both remain aware of the interdependence of creation and its eschatological horizon, which provides the ultimate context for eating. As has been seen, monastic rules left dietary regimes deliberately open to interruption, which was understood in eschatological terms as the guest being welcomed as the returning Christ.

Various Christian dietary practices appear, moreover, to offer the possibility of maintaining around a common table not only different opinions but also different ways of life, in the hope of reconciliation and common transformation. Traditions of dietary flexibility might leave space for processes of discernment to occur as individuals and groups observe different eating patterns and reflect on them. Examining again the Rule of the Master, which expects meat eaters and meat abstainers to eat in the same refectory, we see an unstable relationship which has the potential to shift over time. Commensality guarantees the abstainers' orthodoxy and acceptance of a common lot with their brethren, but their abstention also challenges the meat-eating brethren, reminding them that the menu at the common table is neither unproblematic nor unchangeable. New Testament table fellowship between the 'weak' and the 'strong' might also be seen as a practice which not only acknowledges difference but leaves space for change over time.[52]

How is this diversity within a community different from the contemporary privatization of dietary choice, and the consequent lack of public consideration about which foods the shared menu ought to include? Fear is again relevant. Present-day fear of public discussion about food practices seems to be motivated partly by a fear of passing judgement, being seen to pass judgement, or being judged. The letters of Paul illuminate this predicament, presenting a community in the midst of a process of discerning its entanglement in a range of contemporary food practices which might instantiate or sustain idolatry. Particularly striking are the repeated injunctions to ensure that eating does not become an occasion for mutual hostility or condemnation, a concern which also weighed on rabbinic minds.[53] Although judgements about eating are given based on different interpretations of the Jewish law, these are not permitted to foreclose dialogue. Moreover, Paul offers specific guidance on how to interpret the other's eating: 'Those who eat, eat in honour of the Lord, since they give thanks to God; while those who abstain, abstain in honour of the Lord and give thanks to God.'[54]

What happens when a person's different dietary practice is interpreted as an act of thanksgiving to God? It is noteworthy that the Romans text just quoted does not even allow that a common thanksgiving is possible. A vegetarian might in good conscience be unable to give thanks for a meal of meat if he does not believe that animals are given as food. But neither does the text present a purely relativistic interpretation, with each person's choice being right for her. Eaters and abstainers share, if not a menu, at least their acknowledgement of God and their commitment to honour God, which will have implications for their life and diet which might not yet be clear to any of them. This shared acknowledgement has the potential to create a space for discussion about food choices that is not abstract or theoretical, but begins by recognizing, accepting and attending to each other's everyday ways of honouring God by eating and by abstaining. There is no obligation to agree with, share, or even not be revolted by what the other person does; there is no obligation to desist from one's own critique of idolatry. The only obligation is to take seriously any attempt to eat 'in honour of the Lord', and to refrain from what is often the instinctive first move – a suspicious or condemnatory interpretation motivated by a desire to buttress a sense of personal moral rectitude.

In this final chapter, we have suggested some of the guiding principles which might motivate Christians to change the menu, and some of the concerns which might deter them from doing so. Our attempt to find constructive ways forward in the interpretation and assessment of these different strands of Christian tradition has necessarily drawn on theory. It would be a mistake, however, to see this as making particular concrete dietary practices and choices irrelevant, or as reducing all questions about food to questions about inward attitude. It is simply not that easy, as our preceding discussion has suggested, to separate practices from attitudes, or broad theological claims from the lives in which they are lived out. Any attempt to do so would, moreover, be highly irresponsible at a time when there is an urgent need for attention to the real consequences of actual human food choices.

We have also in this chapter called into question the privatization of food choices and the lack of public reflection on food practices. The question of how to promote such reflection, relating practices to their meanings and configuring a range of practice within a single tradition, has implications beyond the specific issue of food and diet. Our conclusion will examine further some of the implications of beginning with practice when thinking about Christian tradition, theology and ethics.

9   Concluding reflections: practices, everyday life and theological tradition

As suggested in the Preface to this study, there is a developing body of work in Christian theology and ethics which takes practice seriously as a source of theological understanding, not merely as their result or expression. Indeed, 'practice' has become an increasingly popular term in Christian ethics. This is due partly to the widespread appropriation by Christian thinkers of virtue ethics, following its renewal by Alasdair MacIntyre.[1] Christian theologians and ethicists have perceived the need to move beyond an ethics of dilemmas, or of the application of general and abstract principles, towards greater appreciation of the ongoing practices and processes which shape a virtuous character. This approach has a strong basis in Christian tradition, especially in the premodern period.[2] The new focus on practice in Christian ethics can be seen as a reworking and extension of the ancient principle *lex orandi, lex credendi*. Meanwhile, studies of religious practice in non-Christian and non-Western contexts have also raised questions about the modern Western tendency to treat specific 'external' practices as expressions of more fundamental 'internal' commitments or dispositions, rather than as forming or defining those commitments and dispositions.[3]

This reorientation amounts to a widespread acknowledgement that theological and ethical reflection do not work from the top downwards either socially, from the educated elite to the non-educated masses, or individually, from the thinking mind to the acting body. What Christians do, and even what they say about what they do, is not simply the product of an authoritative theological or theoretical blueprint. There have been notable and influential attempts to develop accounts of Christian ethics that begin with what Christians do.[4]

Our approach in this study has differed from many practice-based accounts of Christian theology and ethics. This is because we have mostly discussed not discrete and circumscribed rituals, nor even activities that take place in recognizably religious contexts, but everyday, ubiquitous practices. Where we have focused on practices with a ritual character, such as in Chapter Seven, their association with formal Christian liturgy has frequently been ambiguous. To borrow terms from Daniel Hardy, although we have occasionally described points of 'intensity' in Christian life, we have more often been concerned with 'extensity', the ways in which Christianity is lived out and reflected on in the multiple changing contexts of everyday life.[5] Even in our discussions of monasticism and desert asceticism we have been concerned with how the people who have lived these lives, which were often filled with 'intense' devotion and practice, have related to their wider social contexts. Hardy's terms are useful because they remind us that discussion of Christian life in its 'extensity' does not exclude 'intensity'. We do not suggest that the various accounts of Christianity and food which focus on Eucharistic celebration or other worship are inferior to our own. We do believe, however, that many additional insights can be gained by examining 'extensive' aspects of Christian life.

What are the implications for Christian theology and ethics of this focus on aspects of everyday Christian life? Can practices provide sufficient foundations for constructive theology and ethics, given their enormous variation from place to place and over time, and their frequently contingent nature? The answers to these questions will, as has already been intimated, have implications extending beyond the specific issue of food. The following reflections therefore focus on food practices but identify some of the wider consequences of this study for the shape of theology and ethics.

Explaining embodied practices

When focusing on everyday, 'extensive' practices, it is difficult to separate Christian and non-Christian practices, or religious and secular practices. Examples of this difficulty that we have considered include the links between non-Christian and Christian asceticism in late antiquity, and the political uses of public fasting in post-Reformation England. A similar problem also applies to theories and explanations. It might be legitimate to prefer a theological account of what happens in a liturgy – which is devised and performed as an 'intense' expression of Christian identity – to, for instance, a sociological account. It is less obviously legitimate to prioritize a theological explanation of what Christians eat each day over sociological, economic, cultural or biological explanations.

The meanings of food practices need, like the meanings of other practices, to be understood materially and practically as well as symbolically. Biological, medical and ecological accounts of why people eat what they eat will form an important part of any comprehensive discussion of food practices. Issues like the practical requirements of hygiene or the varying availability of certain foods are by no means marginal to an understanding of which foods are eaten and why. This study has rejected reductive approaches to diet, which treat symbolic or narrative accounts merely as attempts to mask the 'real' reasons for practices. It is not possible to absorb completely the biological into the cultural, the body into its symbolizations, or the flesh into the word.

This point can also be made theologically. Christian theology and ethics, framed by beliefs in the goodness of creation and in the incarnation of the word of God, need to remain attentive to the implications of embodiment and to the given constraints and possibilities of embodied life.[6] This requires theologians and ethicists to attend to a range of ways of understanding embodied life, including a variety of perspectives on why people do what they do and eat what they eat. To say that a given food practice makes sense for hygienic reasons, or is developed in explicit opposition to the practices of a non-Christian group, or serves a particular economic purpose, by no means excludes it as a source of theological reflection.

Cross-cultural and interreligious perspectives, although not primary features of this present study, would need to be incorporated into any broader theology of everyday practice.[7] This becomes obvious when we reflect on the material and biological aspects of practice. It cannot be assumed that an aspect of human bodily experience is the same everywhere, but neither are all differences in the human experience of embodiment functions of religious symbols and narratives. As previously stated, to assume this would be to deny human embodiment and absorb it back into textuality. Our study suggests that a wide range of contingent and embodied factors combine to determine which food practices are followed, how those practices are interpreted and how they affect people's lives. At various points, we have drawn particular attention to the importance of geographical location, wider cultural context, sex and gender, wealth distribution and social class. These are further important dimensions of the 'extensity' of Christian practice. Once they are considered, the reasons for differences between individual Christians and between Christian communities become much more apparent, such that the connections and continuities across time and place, not the differences, seem to require demonstration and explanation. Our reluctance to place all Christians who abstain from meat under a single 'vegetarian' label arises partly from a desire to do justice to this diversity.

Multiple modes of explanation become crucial when the focus of discourse shifts from aetiology onto effects. Practices of the kind we have been describing, which pattern behavioural customs, affect the bodies and worldviews of the people who adopt them. They are not, in other words, simply means of symbolizing, representing or referring to an alternative or transformed reality. Neither are they merely ways of altering some identifiable and delimited part of ordinary life and the ordinary world. Practices have real historical and material effects which extend beyond their immediate environment and the people who participate in them. They are implicated, for good and ill, in ecological relationships, economic systems and power networks. For instance, fasting in Tudor England helped to sustain the naval power of the nascent nation-state, just as decisions about monastic diets impacted on the economy of the surrounding region. Theologically, as was seen in Chapter Eight, Christians' desire to maintain the possibility of prophetic, eschatological action has been accompanied by an awareness of how that action is embedded in a continuing history and affects that history.

A good theological ethics, and an ethical theology, needs to draw on all available evidence about the effects of the practices it describes or advocates. It matters whether Christian food practices lead to starvation, or bodily health; destruction of local and global habitats, or environmental sustainability; wealth concentration, or redistribution; the suffering of nonhuman animals, or their flourishing. On all these issues, non-theological accounts are vital to the formation of good judgements, even when the 'intensities' of Christian life, such as the effects and implications of animal sacrifice, are under scrutiny. These other accounts are even more important to a consideration of everyday life and lifestyles.

Generative puzzles

Many puzzling texts and practices have been encountered in the course of this study. The range of explanatory modes discussed has not made full sense of all of them, such as the worries about Germanic tribes eating horsemeat, or the incorporation into Celtic penitential codes of selected food rules from the Hebrew Bible, or Francis of Assisi's chicken which is reported to have appeared miraculously as fish. This deficiency of explanation points to a striking aspect of many of the food rules and practices which we have studied: their theological and theoretical *generativity*. It is not so much that they prove inexplicable as that they generate a surplus of explanations. Ascetic practices have given rise to a wealth of theological reflection on the nature of the soul, eschatology and the resurrection life. Seasonal fasting was theorized as maintaining social order and promoting peace, or as recalling and participating in foundational narratives of salvation, or as maintaining bodily health. The Armenian *matal* sacrifice has provided the focus for reflection on the nature of community, on Christian identity in relation to Judaism, and on God's gifts. Christian vegetarian groups in Victorian Britain produced a bewildering range of arguments, theological and otherwise, in favour of vegetarianism. The very production of these arguments presumed the existence and importance of vegetarianism as a food practice which did not result from arguments and explanations, but rather gave rise to arguments and explanations.

What is taking place here? Practices prove not only resistant to theorization, but generative of multiple creative theories. Part of what enables this generativity is the sheer persistence of practices over time, embedded in patterns of individual and communal life. The food we eat is incorporated into our physical bodies, but our eating habits become part of us in deeper, longer-term and more complex ways. Individual bodies become habituated to foods. We acquire or lose a taste for certain kinds of food, or for eating at certain times of day. We discover, at different stages of life, that there are foods we cannot swallow or cannot stomach. We find ourselves attracted or repelled by foods. We each have formed in us a set of preferred tastes and sources of nutrition – even from before birth, and certainly from before weaning – and these are re-formed only gradually and often unpredictably. Thus, for example, the 'flexibility' of vegetarians to eat the meat they are offered, or even to abandon vegetarianism if they change their principles, is limited in practice by their bodies' habituation to a meatless diet.

On a larger scale, social 'bodies' are formed in relation to specific cuisines, and habits of food production and consumption. Cuisines are, as we have noted, resistant to change. Changes in cuisine have sometimes been linked to conversion to Christianity, as seen in Chapter Eight. This has frequently provoked struggle, with the desire to maintain an existing cuisine overriding the imperatives for change supposedly related to conversion. Icelanders converted only on the condition that horseflesh could remain on their menu. Descriptions of other cultures by both Christian writers and others evoke a sense of the grotesque by recounting food practices which differ dramatically from those of their readers.

The most obvious, although in some ways most surprising, analogy to draw is with scriptural texts. In such texts, puzzles and opacities stimulate interpretive effort which renders them generative of meaning. Because no interpretation clears up all the puzzles surrounding them, the possibility of new interpretations remains. The texts remain 'useful' for interpretation precisely because of their persistent resistance to being exhausted or reduced to single interpretations. They become transparent to interpreters in particular contexts without their opacity being lost.[8] Something similar can be said about practices sustained through history. These can be repeatedly 'explained' or reflected on in order to uncover previously hidden levels of meaning, without necessarily being 'explained away'. In the case of historically sustained practices, this resistance to being explained away rests in part on the deep-level formation of the bodies, both social and physical, of those who perform them. We might venture a comparison with the liturgical and devotional reading of scriptural texts, which secures their continuing presence in their communities and hence their availability for future reinterpretation.

Which practices matter? Sharing a table

This comparison between historically sustained practices and scriptural texts points to the 'canonical' character of those Christian practices deemed acceptable, to which Chapter Eight alluded. Who decides what is acceptable, and how do they decide? Which habitual practices should be maintained and reflected on, and which should be forgotten? From the wealth and diversity of everyday practices, how does one distinguish between the rightly marginal and the unjustly marginalized, between those which may inform contemporary reflection and those which should remain mere historical curiosity?

The first point to recognize in response is that the theologian's own attitudes to traditions of practice are themselves formed in particular contexts. In our own case, we recognize a complex range of individual and societal factors motivating and shaping our interest in the history of Christian diet, ranging from our own different dietary 'choices' to the urgent calls to rethink Western assumptions about diet in the light of ecological challenges. There is no position outside our own particular, everyday lives from where we can pass judgements about acceptable or valuable forms of living.

Willingness to acknowledge that different practices are part of a tradition, like willingness to sit at table with those eating different foods, arises in a process of historical negotiation. The suggestions raised in Chapter Eight, based on Romans 14, may again be helpful. Contemporary theologians might be asked, in the first instance, to interpret the individual and communal practices of the past as faithful attempts to live out vocations – eating and abstaining 'in honour of the Lord'.[9] Lessons can be learned from encountering and reflecting on these practices without necessarily following them, and even while believing that some of them are bizarre, damaging or dangerous. It is important to recognize, even here, that there will be limits to the capacity of any given interpreter of tradition to share a table by acknowledging others' ways of living and eating as Christian practices.

This is significantly different from another obvious possible approach, which would be to identify and evaluate the principles or theories underlying historical practices. We have already suggested that this would not do justice to the puzzling character of historically sustained practice, which renders it opaque and resistant to interpretation. Mere evaluation would also, by the same token, miss the potential generativity of practices. It might provide a more clear-cut way of 'resolving' disputes or differences, because controversies about practice could then be reduced to theoretical arguments. Yet in so doing, it would tend to exclude from the table of tradition individuals and groups whose ways of life might prove theologically and ethically significant.

In our discussion of the importance of practice, and the ways in which practice exceeds theory, links have become apparent with a strand of reflection in both Jewish and Christian theology on obedience. This has drawn on the critique developed by twentieth-century Jewish philosophers of accounts of theology and ethics which place excessive emphasis on cognition. For Franz Rosenzweig and Emmanuel Levinas, both interpreting the scriptural texts of the commandments, obedience to the divine command precedes those commandments and is the precondition for understanding them. People do not start by considering the rights and wrongs of the commandments, nor even their possibilities and impossibilities. They begin by obeying the commandments, and then undertake further reasoning and analysis from within this context of obedience.[10]

This is a fruitful line of thought for Christian theology and ethics. At the most basic level, it supports our suggestion that persistence in practices, including practices with a strong ethical or religious framework, is not simply a matter of yielding to rational persuasion. More significantly, it points to the importance of vocation as a theological framework for thinking about practice, and thereby to a possible multiplicity of vocations. The key point is that obedience shapes reasoning. Ways of life followed in obedience to God's call shape the ways people reason about God and about the world. One consequence of this emergence of reasoning from obedience is that different practices will give rise to different forms of reasoning. Sharing a table with many others, around which a range of ways of life are acknowledged, will mean encountering different reasonings, negotiating between them and learning from them.

If more attention is given to the diverse forms of everyday life within one particular tradition – to the 'extensities' of Christian existence – valuable insights might be gained on how to negotiate relations between different faiths. In this context we are able only to raise the suggestion, although certain aspects of our study, such as our discussion of Jewish and Muslim ritual slaughter, have pointed to starting points for interfaith engagement. It has certainly been recognized for some time that lived dialogues, in which practical questions of everyday co-existence provide starting points for religious encounters, proceed in different ways and produce rather different results from more theoretical modes of interfaith dialogue.[11] Attention to practice does not imply a lack of interest in religious thought. It does, however, allow us to recognize the complex, ambiguous and shifting relationships between real religious communities.

Recipes for tradition

Our focus on food prompts one further suggestion for how to theorize and use traditions of practice. The development of Christian tradition has been compared to many other forms of 'traditioning', perhaps most notably and successfully to musical and dramatic performance, including improvisation.[12] This approach often leads to a focus on the intensities of Christian practice – central and community-defining performances. For our kind of study, however, an analogy closer to home is more appropriate.

Recipes are an obvious and everyday form of tradition, pertaining to an obvious and everyday practice.[13] We say 'recipes', but the written form of the recipe is clearly secondary to the tradition of practice it represents. Indeed, this is even more true of cooking than of the performing arts. Ways of cooking are learned and transmitted without recipes being written down. A transcription of the recipe, like the record of a set of rules for some aspect of Christian life, or the narrative of a life embodying such rules, enables its survival, geographical transmission and reinterpretation. Locality (what can I buy here?), cultural context (what is acceptable and fits with our cuisine?), individual circumstances (what foods can I stomach?) and practicalities (what cooking techniques do I know and am I equipped for?) will dramatically affect the ways in which culinary tradition is instantiated. Recipes may disappear because they become in practice impossible to follow, or because tastes and assumptions change so radically that particular recipes, such as lark's-tongue pie and roasted dormouse, are no longer tolerated.

In order to understand a cuisine or a single dish we do not only study recipes, even though they are indispensable sources of information. We also consider ingredients, utensils and techniques, aspects which are difficult if not impossible to understand from written records of particular recipes alone. Yet when judging and evaluating practices, in the case of a recipe the proof of the pudding is in the eating. Establishing or adhering to the original intention of whoever recorded the recipe, whether to his or her particular method of cooking the dish or to the reasons for certain instructions, is not fundamental although it may be useful. The end product is the decisive outcome, and its effects will enable others to form a double judgement. First, is this food a genuine example of what it claims to be, standing fully in its particular tradition of practice? Second, is it good food, fit for its present purpose and serving human flourishing here and now?

Decisions about what to eat and what not to eat are likely to be increasingly important for everybody, not least Christians, in a time of rapid environmental and economic change. Against this backdrop, we offer not so much a dietary prescription for healthy food practices as an annotated book of recipes. Determining which of these are consigned to the past for good, and which are adapted for present and future consumption, will be our readers' task just as much as our own.

Notes

Preface

1 Clement of Alexandria, *Instructor* 2.1, in *Ante-Nicene Fathers of the Christian Church* 2 (10 vols; Edinburgh: T&T Clark, 1991) [subsequently *ANF*], p. 237.
2 Peter Singer, 'A vegetarian philosophy', in *Consuming Passions: Food in the Age of Anxiety*, eds Sian Griffiths and Jennifer Wallace (Manchester University Press, 1998), pp. 71–80 (79), highlights a similar situation in philosophical ethics.
3 Melvin Cherno, 'Feuerbach's "Man is What He Eats": A Rectification', *Journal of the History of Ideas* 24 (1963), pp. 397–406.
4 Ludwig Feuerbach, „Das Geheimnis des Opfers, oder, Der Mensch ist, was er isst", in *Gesammelte Werke* (22 vols; Berlin: Akademie, 1969–), vol. 11, pp. 26–52.
5 John Hymers, „Verteidigung von Feuerbachs Moleschott Rezeption: Feuerbachs offene Dialektik", in *Identität und Pluralismus in der globalen Gesellschaft. Ludwig Feuerbach zum 200. Geburtstag*, eds U. Reitemeyer, T. Shibata and F. Tomasoni (Münster: Waxmann, 2006), pp. 111–26.
6 Henning Steinfeld et al., *Livestock's Long Shadow: Environmental Issues and Options* (Rome: Food and Agriculture Organization of the United Nations, 2006), p. 272.
7 *The Rule of St. Benedict* 31, trans. Justin McCann (London: Sheed & Ward, 1989), p. 39, echoing Zech. 14.21.
8 Paul R. Amato and Sonia A. Partridge, *The New Vegetarians* (New York: Plenum, 1989), p. vii.

1 Eating in the Wilderness

1 Samuel Rubenson, *The Letters of St. Anthony: Monasticism and the Making of a Saint* (Minneapolis, MN: Fortress, 1995), pp. 93–94.
2 *The Lives of the Desert Fathers*, trans. Norman Russell, ed. Benedicta Ward (London: Mowbray, 1981), pp. 71–72.
3 Tertullian, *On Fasting* 7–9, in *ANF* 4, pp. 106–8; Jerome, *Against Jovinianus* II.15, in *Nicene and Post-Nicene Fathers of the Christian Church* II.6 (28 vols; Edinburgh: T&T Clark, 1991) [subsequently *NPNF*], pp. 399–400; also Basil of Caesarea, *De Renuntiatione Saeculi* 208, in *The Ascetic Works*, ed. W.K.L. Clarke (London: SPCK, 1925), p. 68.
4 Gen. 3.2–3.
5 Gen. 7.3, 8.17.
6 Ex. 16.3.
7 Ex. 17.3.
8 Ex. 34.28, Deut. 9.9, 9.18.

9   1 Sam. 1.7–8.
10 1 Sam. 7.6.
11 1 Sam. 14.24.
12 1 Sam. 23.14, Ps. 63.1b.
13 1 Kgs 17.6.
14 1 Kgs 21.27–29.
15 2 Kgs 19.1.
16 Dan. 1.12–17.
17 Mt. 4.2, Lk. 4.2.
18 Lk. 2.36–38.
19 Mt. 3.4b, Mk 1.6.
20 2 Cor. 11.27.
21 Tertullian, *On Fasting* 16, pp. 112–13; Gregory the Great, *Morals on the Book of Job* 30.60 (4 vols; Oxford: Parker, 1844–50), vol. 3, pt 2, pp. 405–6; Basil of Caesarea, *De Renuntiatione Saeculi* 208, pp. 67–68. Following Gregory, see David Clines, 'A vegetarian reading', in *Job 1–20*, World Biblical Commentary 17 (Dallas, TX: Word, 1989), pp. l–lii. A similar modern reading encompassing both dietary discipline and indiscipline is Diane M. Sharon, *Patterns of Destiny: Narrative Structures of Foundation and Doom in the Hebrew Bible* (Winona Lake, IN: Eisenbrauns, 2002). For an accessible overview, see Joel R. Soza, *Food and God: A Theological Approach to Eating, Diet, and Weight Control* (Eugene, OR: Wipf & Stock, 2009).
22 Gen. 3.
23 Gen. 25.29–34.
24 Ez. 16.49, 19.27–28.
25 1 Sam. 2.12–17.
26 1 Sam. 14.24–45.
27 1 Kgs 13.7–24.
28 Mt. 14.6–12; Mk 6.21–29.
29 James A. Kelhoffer, *The Diet of John the Baptist: 'Locusts and Wild Honey' in Synoptic and Patristic Interpretation* (Wissenschaftliche Untersuchungen zum Neuen Testament 176; Tübingen: Mohr Siebeck, 2005), pp. 9, 133.
30 Sebastian Brock, 'The Baptist's Diet in Syriac Sources', *Oriens Christianus* 54 (1970), pp. 113–24 (117–21).
31 Brock, 'The Baptist's Diet', p. 119.
32 Lucien Regnault, *La Vie quotidienne des Pères du désert en Égypte au IVe siècle* (Paris: Hachette, 1990), p. 94.
33 Rubenson, *Letters of St. Anthony*, pp. 95–99, 186–87; also Demetrios Katos, 'Origenists in the Desert: Palladius of Helenopolis and the Alexandrian Theological Tradition', *American Benedictine Review* 56 (2005), pp. 167–93; J.A. McGuckin, 'Christian asceticism and the early school of Alexandria', in *Monks, Hermits and the Ascetic Tradition*, ed. W.J. Sheils (Oxford: Blackwell, 1985), pp. 25–39.
34 Samuel Rubenson, 'Origen in the Egyptian monastic tradition of the fourth century', in *Origeniana Septima*, eds W.A. Beinert and U. Kühneweg (Leuven University Press, 1999), pp. 319–37.
35 *The Sayings of the Desert Fathers: The Alphabetical Collection*, trans. Benedicta Ward (London: Mowbray, 1975), pp. 29, 49; *The Lausiac History of Palladius*, trans. W.K. Lowther Clarke (London: SPCK, 1918), pp. 60, 65.
36 Especially Alistair Logan, *The Gnostics: Identifying an Early Christian Cult* (London: T&T Clark, 2006).
37 Evagrius Ponticus, 'The Kephalaia Gnostica', in *Ascetic Behavior in Greco-Roman Antiquity: A Sourcebook*, ed. Vincent L. Wimbush (Minneapolis, MN: Fortress, 1990), pp. 177–85; *Sayings*, pp. 53–55; *Lausiac History*, pp. 132–37.
38 Zech. 8.19; see 2 Kgs 24.10–17, 25.22–26, 2 Chr. 36.17–21. In some Christian accounts these are identified as antecedents to the quarterly ember days, e.g., *The*

Golden Legend: Readings on the Saints, trans. William Granger Ryan (2 vols; Princeton, NJ: Princeton University Press, 1993), vol. 1, p. 139.

39 Eliezer Diamond, *Holy Men and Hunger Artists: Fasting and Asceticism in Rabbinic Culture* (Oxford University Press, 2004), pp. 95–98.

40 *Babylonian Talmud. Seder Nezikin. Baba Bathra* I, 60b (18 vols; London: Soncino, 1961); *Tosefta Sotah. Third Division. Nashim* 15:11–15 (5 vols; New York: KTAV, 1981).

41 Rubenson, *Letters of St. Anthony*, p. 112.

42 Philo of Alexandria, *The Contemplative Life* 73–74, trans. David Winston (New York: Paulist, 1980), p. 54.

43 Philo of Alexandria, *On Providence* 2.69 (Cambridge, MA: Harvard University Press, 1954) pp. 504–5.

44 Roger T. Beckwith, 'The Vegetarianism of the Therapeutae, and the Motives for Vegetarianism in Early Jewish and Christian Circles', *Revue de Qumran* 13 (1988), pp. 407–10.

45 *Lausiac History*, pp. 77–80.

46 *Lausiac History*, p. 49.

47 *Sayings*, p. 53.

48 *Lives*, p. 69.

49 *Lives*, pp. 93–94.

50 *Lives*, p. 63.

51 *Lives*, p. 68.

52 *Lives*, p. 99.

53 *Sayings*, p. 27.

54 Arthur Vööbus, *History of Asceticism in the Syrian Orient: A Contribution to the History of Culture in the Near East* (3 vols; Louvain: Corpus scriptorum Christianorum Orientalium, 1958–88), vol. 2, pp. 24–26, 263; Patrick Olivelle, 'From feast to fast: food and the Indian ascetic', in *Panels of the VIIth World Sanskrit Conference, IX: Rules and Remedies in Classical Indian Law*, ed. Julia Leslie (Leiden: Brill, 1991), pp. 17–36 (24).

55 John Binns, *Ascetics and Ambassadors of Christ: The Monasteries of Palestine, 314–631* (Oxford: Clarendon, 1996), pp. 106–7.

56 Roger S. Bagnall, *Egypt in Late Antiquity* (Princeton, NJ: Princeton University Press, 1996), pp. 23–32; Evelyne Patlagean, « Régimes et nutrition », in *Pauvreté économique et pauvreté sociale à Byzance, 4e–7e siècles* (Paris: Mouton, 1977), pp. 44–53.

57 *Beasts and Saints*, trans. Helen Waddell (London: Constable, 1934), pp. 20–21.

58 *Lausiac History*, p. 155.

59 Athanasius, *The Life of Antony* 7, 89, trans. Robert C. Gregg (Mahwah, NJ: Paulist, 1979), pp. 36, 95.

60 *Lausiac History*, p. 47.

61 *Lives*, p. 54.

62 *Lausiac History*, p. 124.

63 *Lausiac History*, pp. 66–67.

64 *Lausiac History*, pp. 103–4.

65 Eucherius of Lyons, 'In praise of the desert: a letter to Bishop Hilary of Lérins', in *The Lives of the Jura Fathers*, trans. Tim Vivian, Kim Vivian and Jeffrey Burton (Cistercian Studies Series 178; Kalamazoo, MI: Cistercian, 1999), p. 199; see Is. 35.1–2, Ps. 104.13, 65.13.

66 Eucherius of Lyons, 'In praise of the desert', pp. 212–13; see Ps. 104.15, Jn 21.17.

67 Richard Sorabji, *Animal Minds and Human Morals: The Origins of the Western Debate* (London: Duckworth, 1993), p. 173; Porphyry, *On Abstinence from Killing Animals* I.36, trans. Gillian Clark (London: Duckworth, 1999), p. 44.

68 J.A. Philip, *Pythagoras and Early Pythagoreanism* (University of Toronto Press, 1966), p. 139.

69 John Wilkins, '*Hoi polloi*: spiritual choices for the many and the few', in *Eating and Believing: Interdisciplinary Perspectives on Vegetarianism and Theology*, eds Rachel Muers and David Grumett (New York: T&T Clark, 2008), pp. 110–19.

70 Patricia Cox Miller, 'Desert Asceticism and the "Body from Nowhere"', *Journal of Early Christian Studies* 2 (1994), pp. 137–53.

71 James Goehring, 'The dark side of landscape: ideology and power in the Christian myth of the desert', in *The Cultural Turn in Late Ancient Studies: Gender, Asceticism, and Historiography*, eds Dale B. Martin and Patricia Cox Miller (Durham, NC: Duke University Press, 2005), pp. 136–49 (146).

72 Gillian Clark, 'Philosophic lives and the philosophic life: Porphyry and Iamblichus', in *Greek Biography and Panegyric*, eds Tomas Hägg and Philip Rousseau (Berkeley: University of California Press, 2000), pp. 29–51.

73 Anthony Meredith, 'Asceticism—Christian and Greek', *The Journal of Theological Studies* 27 (1976), pp. 313–32 (318–20).

74 Evelyne Patlagean, 'Ancient Byzantine hagiography and social history', in *Saints and their Cults: Studies in Religious Sociology, Folklore and History*, ed. Stephen Wilson (Cambridge University Press, 1983), pp. 101–21 (110).

75 Philip Rousseau, 'The desert fathers and their broader audience', in *Foundations of Power and Conflicts of Authority in Late-Antique Monasticism*, eds A. Camplani and G. Filoramo (Leuven: Peeters, 2007), pp. 89–108.

76 Sigmund Freud, *Civilisation and its Discontents* (New York: Norton, 1961).

77 Ernst Troeltsch, *The Social Teaching of the Christian Churches* (2 vols; London: Allen & Unwin, 1931), vol. 1, p. 106.

78 Aline Rousselle, *Porneia: On Desire and the Body in Antiquity* (Oxford: Blackwell, 1988), pp. 160–64.

79 The sole exception was bread, which some ascetics ate even though heat was required to bake it.

80 Rousselle, *Porneia*, pp. 172–73; idem, « Abstinence et continence dans les monastères de Gaule méridionale à la fin de l'antiquité et au début du Moyen Âge : étude d'un regime alimentaire et de sa function », in *Hommage à André Dupont: etudes médiévales languedociennes*, ed. Guy Barruol (Montpellier: Fédération historique du Languedoc mediterranéen et du Roussillon, 1974), pp. 239–54; Veronika Grimm, *From Feasting to Fasting, the Evolution of a Sin: Attitudes to Food in Late Antiquity* (London: Routledge, 1996), p. 171.

81 Tertullian, *On Fasting* 9, pp. 107–8.

82 *Sayings*, p. 5.

83 Teresa Shaw, *The Burden of the Flesh: Fasting and Sexuality in Early Christianity* (Minneapolis, MN: Fortress, 1998), pp. 125–27; Rousselle, *Porneia*, p. 176; discussing Ancel Keys, Josef Brazek et al., *The Biology of Human Starvation* (2 vols; Minneapolis, MN: University of Minnesota Press, 1950).

84 *Lives*, p. 105.

85 Peter Brown, *The Body and Society: Men, Women and Sexual Renunciation in Early Christianity* (London: Faber & Faber, 1989), p. 217.

86 *Sayings*, pp. 170–71.

87 *Sayings*, p. 135.

88 Brown, *Body and Society*, p. 218.

89 William Ian Miller, 'Gluttony', *Representations* 60 (1997), pp. 92–112.

90 Gen. 3.6.

91 *Evagrius of Pontus: The Greek Ascetic Corpus*, trans. Robert E. Sinkewicz (New York: Oxford University Press, 2006), p. 62.

92 Shaw, *Burden of the Flesh*, p. 144.

93 John Cassian, *Institutes* 5.3, trans. Boniface Ramsey (Mahwah, NJ: Newman, 2000), p. 70.

94 Conrad Leyser, *Authority and Asceticism from Augustine to Gregory the Great* (Oxford: Clarendon, 2000), p. 167.

95 Gregory the Great, *Morals* 31.89, vol. 3, pt 2, p. 491; also Tertullian, *On Fasting* 1, p. 102.
96 Owen Chadwick, *John Cassian* (Cambridge University Press, 1968), p. 94.
97 Shaw, *Burden of the Flesh*, pp. 174–81; Alison Elliott, *Roads to Paradise: Reading the Lives of the Early Saints* (Hanover, NH: University Press of New England, 1987), pp. 140–41; Douglas Burton-Christie, *The Word in the Desert: Scripture and the Quest for Holiness in Early Christian Monasticism* (New York: Oxford University Press, 1993), p. 232.
98 Athanasius, *Life of Anthony* 14, p. 200.
99 Athanasius, *Life of Anthony* 41, p. 207.
100 Rubenson, *Letters of St. Anthony*, p. 119.
101 James E. Goehring, 'The encroaching desert: literary production and ascetic space in Early Christian Egypt', in *Ascetics, Society, and the Desert: Studies in Early Egyptian Monasticism* (Harrisburg, PA: Trinity, 1999), pp. 73–88.
102 David Brakke, *Demons and the Making of the Monk: Spiritual Combat in Early Christianity* (Cambridge, MA: Harvard University Press, 2006); also Jerome Kroll and Bernard S. Bachrach, *The Mystic Mind: The Psychology of Medieval Mystics and Ascetics* (London: Routledge, 2005), pp. 83–87.
103 *Lives*, p. 50, also p. 105.
104 *Lausiac History*, p. 81; *Lives*, p. 65.
105 *Lives*, p. 102.
106 Maria Dembińska, 'Fasting and working monks: regulations of the fifth to eleventh centuries', in *Food in Change: Eating Habits from the Middle Ages to the Present Day*, eds Alexander Fenton and Eszter Kisbán (Edinburgh: Donald, 1986), pp. 152–60.
107 Armand Veilleux, 'Asceticism in Pachomian cenobitism', in *The Continuing Quest for God: Monastic Spirituality in Tradition and Transition* (Collegeville, MN: Liturgical, 1982), pp. 67–79 (73).
108 *Coutumes de Chartreuse* 35 (Paris: Cerf, 1984), pp. 236–37.
109 *Lausiac History*, p. 116.
110 Bagnall, *Egypt*, p. 29.
111 Rules 71–80, in *Pachomian Koinonia*, ed. Armand Veilleux (3 vols; Kalamazoo, MI: Cistercian, 1981), vol. 2, pp. 158–59.
112 Similarly in Cassian, *Institutes* 4.18, p. 80.
113 Jerome, Letter 22.34, in *NPNF* II.6, p. 37; John Cassian, *Conferences* 18.7, trans. Colm Luibheid (Mahwah, NJ: Paulist, 1985), pp. 188–90; *The Rule of St. Benedict* 1, trans. Justin McCann (London: Sheed & Ward, 1989), p. 5.
114 James E. Goehring, 'Monastic diversity and ideological boundaries in fourth-century Christian Egypt', in *Ascetics, Society, and the Desert*, pp. 196–218.
115 *Lives*, p. 65.
116 *The Wisdom of the Desert Fathers: The 'Apophthegmata Patrum' (The Anonymous Series)*, trans. Benedicta Ward (Oxford: SLG, 1975), pp. 33–34.
117 *Wisdom*, pp. 31–32.
118 Basil of Caesarea, *Longer Reponses* 19, in *The Asketikon of St Basil the Great*, ed. Anna Silvas (Oxford University Press, 2005), p. 215.
119 David Amand, *L'Ascèse monastique de Saint Basile: essai historique* (Paris: Maredsous, 1948), pp. 222–23.
120 Susanna Elm, *Virgins of God: The Making of Asceticism in Late Antiquity* (Oxford: Clarendon, 1994), pp. 114–15.
121 Philip Sheldrake, 'The practice of place: monasteries and utopias', in *Spaces for the Sacred: Place, Memory and Identity* (London: SCM, 2001), pp. 90–118.
122 *Life of Brendan of Clonfert* 30, in *Bethada Náem n Érenn. Lives of Irish Saints*, ed. Charles Plummer (2 vols; Oxford: Clarendon, 1922), vol. 2, p. 49.
123 Basil of Caesarea, Homily 331.5; quoted in Phillip Rousseau, *Basil of Caesarea* (Berkeley: University of California Press, 1998), p. 328; summarized in Susan R.

Holman, 'Rich City Burning: Social Welfare and Ecclesial Insecurity in Basil's Mission to Armenia', *Journal of Early Christian Studies* 12 (2004), pp. 195–215 (209).

124 Blake Leyerle, 'Monks and other animals', in *Cultural Turn*, pp. 150–71.

125 *Beasts and Saints*, pp. 14–15.

126 John Moschos, *The Spiritual Meadow* (Kalamazoo, MI: Cistercian, 1992), pp. 86–88.

127 Gen. 9.3, cf. 1.29–30.

2 Food in the Ordered City

1 Max Weber, *The Protestant Ethic and the Spirit of Capitalism* (London: Routledge, 2001), p. 101.

2 *The Rule of St. Benedict* 39, trans. Justin McCann (London: Sheed & Ward, 1989), p. 46.

3 John Coveney, *Food, Morals and Meaning: The Pleasure and Anxiety of Eating* (London: Routledge, 2nd edn, 2006), pp. 25–45.

4 *Rule of St. Benedict* 37, p. 44.

5 In his lost commentaries on Plato's *Phaedo* and *Republic*, preserved in Arabic quotations. See Stephen Gero, 'Galen on the Christians: A Reappraisal of the Arabic Evidence', *Orientalia Christiana Periodica* 56 (1990), pp. 371–411; Richard Walzer, *Galen on Jews and Christians* (London: Oxford University Press, 1949), pp. 15, 91.

6 Guy Sabbah, « Médecine, virginité et ascétisme chez Basile d'Ancyre, *De la véritable intégrité dans la virginité* », in *Hommages à Carl Deroux*, vol. 2: *Prose et linguistique, médecine*, ed. Pol Defosse (Brussels: Latomus, 2002), pp. 561–74. For a similar hot–cold scheme in Hinduism, see Caroline and Filippo Osella, 'Food, Memory, Community: Kerala as both "Indian Ocean" Zone and as Agricultural Homeland', *South Asia: Journal of South Asian Studies* 31 (2008), pp. 170–98 (177, 180).

7 Teresa M. Shaw, 'Creation, Virginity and Diet in Fourth-Century Christianity: Basil of Ancyra's *On the True Purity of Virginity*', *Gender & History* 9 (1997), pp. 579–96 (584–88).

8 John Cassian, *Conferences* 1.7 (trans. Colm Luibheid; Mahwah, NJ: Paulist, 1985), p. 42 (includes *Conferences* 1–3, 9–11, 14, 15, 18).

9 Cassian, *Conferences* 2.5, pp. 64–65.

10 Cassian, *Conferences* 2.17, p. 76.

11 Cassian, *Conferences* 2.19, p. 77.

12 Cassian, *Conferences* 2.21, p. 77.

13 Cassian, *Conferences* 2.24, pp. 78–79.

14 Cassian, *Conferences* 2.26, p. 79.

15 John Cassian, *Conferences* 21.23, in *NPNF* II.11 (trans. Edgar Gibson; Edinburgh: T&T Clark, 1991), p. 513.

16 Cassian, *Institutes* 5.5, pp. 71–72.

17 Cassian, *Institutes* 5.23, pp. 84–85.

18 Cassian, *Institutes* 4.11, p. 46.

19 John Cassian, *Homilies on the Statues* 3.8, in *NPNF* I.9, p. 358.

20 Teresa M. Shaw, *The Burden of the Flesh: Fasting and Sexuality in Early Christianity* (Minneapolis, MN: Fortress, 1998), pp. 131–39.

21 Aline Rousselle, *Porneia: On Desire and the Body in Antiquity* (Oxford: Blackwell, 1988), p. 198.

22 Johanna Maria van Winter, 'Obligatory fasts and voluntary asceticism in the Middle Ages', in *Food in Change: Eating Habits from the Middle Ages to the Present Day*, eds Alexander Fenton and Eszter Kisbán (Edinburgh: Donald, 1986), pp. 161–66.

23 *Seasons for Fasting* 23, trans. Chadwick Hilton (Ann Arbor: UMI, 1985), p. 67.

24 Prosper Guéranger, *The Liturgical Year* (15 vols; Great Falls, MT: Bonaventure, 2000), vol. 1, pp. 22–23; Thomas Talley, *The Origins of the Liturgical Year* (Collegeville, MN: Liturgical, 1992), p. 151.

25 *Seasons for Fasting* 6–13, pp. 62–64.

26 Mt. 9.15, Mk 2.19–20, Lk. 5.34–35.
27 *The Golden Legend: Readings on the Saints*, trans. William Granger Ryan (2 vols; Princeton, NJ: Princeton University Press, 1993), vol. 1, p. 139.
28 Galen, 'On the Humours', in *Galen on Food and Diet*, ed. Mark Grant (London: Routledge, 2000), pp. 14–18 (14).
29 Albertus Magnus, *On Animals: A Medieval Summa Zoologica*, trans. Kenneth Kitchell, Jr and Irven Michael Rennick (2 vols; Baltimore, MD: Johns Hopkins University Press, 1999), vol. 1, pp. 393–432.
30 Bridget Ann Henisch, *Fast and Feast: Food in Medieval Society* (University Park: Pennsylvania State University Press, 1976), pp. 29–31.
31 Robert Mandrou, *Introduction to Modern France 1500–1640: An Essay in Historical Psychology* (London: Arnold, 1975), pp. 24–27; for an earlier period, Michel Rouche, « La faim à l'époque carolingienne : essai sur quelques types de rations alimentaires », *Revue historique* 250 (1973), pp. 295–320.
32 C.J. Bond, 'Monastic fisheries', in *Medieval Fish, Fisheries and Fishponds in England*, ed. Michael Aston (2 vols; Oxford: BAR, 1988), vol. 1, pp. 69–112 (69).
33 In India, where food shortages have been more common and its effects more severe, beef consumption is regarded as taboo through the whole year. See Marvin Harris, 'The riddle of the sacred cow', in *Good to Eat: Riddles of Food and Culture* (New York: Simon and Shuster, 1985), pp. 47–66; idem, 'The origin of the sacred cow', in *Cannibals and Kings: The Origins of Cultures* (New York: Random House, 1977), pp. 209–29.
34 William Langland, *Piers the Ploughman*, trans. Jonathan Frank Goodridge (Harmondsworth: Penguin, 1966), p. 137; also Katherine Dell, 'The Use of Animal Imagery in the Psalms and Wisdom Literature of Ancient Israel', *Scottish Journal of Theology* 53 (2000), pp. 275–91 (286–88).
35 Langland, *Piers the Ploughman*, p. 138; also Stephen T. Newmyer, *Animals, Rights, and Reason in Plutarch and Modern Ethics* (New York: Routledge, 2006), pp. 85–102.
36 Deut. 14.22.
37 Cassian, *Conferences* 21.25 (trans. Gibson), p. 513.
38 David Brakke, *Athanasius and the Politics of Asceticism* (Oxford: Clarendon, 1995), p. 188.
39 Mk 1.12, emphasis added; also Mt. 4.1. Thomas Talley, *The Origins of the Liturgical Year* (Collegeville, MN: Liturgical, 1992), pp. 163–230, provides an excellent discussion of the complex history of the timing and length of Lent.
40 *The Rule of the Master* 28, trans. Luke Eberle (Kalamazoo, MI: Cistercian, 1977), pp. 187–88; Gregory the Great, Sermon 14, in *Forty Gospel Homilies*, trans. Dom David Hurst (Kalamazoo, MI: Cistercian, 1977), pp. 104–5. See Patrick Regan, 'The three days and the forty days', in *Between Memory and Hope: Readings on the Liturgical Year*, ed. Maxwell E. Johnson (Collegeville, MN: Liturgical, 2000), pp. 125–41; Talley, *Origins*, pp. 221–22.
41 E.g., John Henry Newman, *Parochial and Plain Sermons* (8 vols; London: Rivingtons, 1870–79), vol. 6, p. 1.
42 Ronald Hutton, *Stations of the Sun: A History of the Ritual Year in Britain* (Oxford University Press, 1996), p. 151.
43 Hutton, *Stations*, pp. 157–59.
44 Terence Scully, *The Art of Cookery in the Middle Ages* (Woodbridge: Boydell, 1997), pp. 62–64.
45 Venetia Newall, *An Egg at Easter* (London: Routledge & Kegan Paul, 1971), pp. 177–206; Hutton, *Stations*, pp. 198–203.
46 Benjamin J. Kaplan, *Divided by Faith: Religious Conflict and the Practice of Toleration in Early Modern Europe* (Cambridge, MA: Harvard, 2007), pp. 82–84.
47 C. Anne Wilson, 'Preserving food to preserve life: the response to glut and famine from early times to the end of the Middle Ages', in *Waste Not, Want Not: Food*

Preservation in Britain from Early Times to the Present Day (Edinburgh University Press, 1991), pp. 5–31 (24–25).

48 Henisch, *Fast and Feast*, pp. 28–58, especially 44–45.

49 Gerhard Jaritz, 'The standard of living in German and Austrian Cistercian monasteries of the late middle ages', in *Goad and Nail* (Kalamazoo, MI: Cistercian, 1985), pp. 56–70 (58); Henisch, *Fast and Feast*, p. 42.

50 Henisch, *Fast and Feast*, pp. 44, 122.

51 Elizabeth David, *English Bread and Yeast Cookery* (Harmondsworth: Penguin, 1979), pp. 455–56.

52 Ludo Milis, *Angelic Monks and Earthly Men: Monasticism and its Meaning to Medieval Society* (Woodbridge: Boydell, 1992), pp. 146–47.

53 *Heresy Trials in the Diocese of Norwich*, ed. Norman P. Tanner (London: Royal Historical Society, 1977), pp. 11 (table), 23.

54 Ann Hagen, 'Fasting', in *A Handbook of Anglo-Saxon Food: Processing and Consumption* (Pinner: Anglo-Saxon Books, 1992), pp. 127–35 (130–31).

55 *Visitation Articles and Injunctions of the Period of the Reformation*, ed. Walter Howard Frere (3 vols; London: Longmans, 1910), vol. 2, pp. 41–42.

56 *Documentary Annals of the Reformed Church of England*, ed. Edward Cardwell (2 vols; Oxford University Press, new edn, 1844), vol. 1, p. 41.

57 *Statutes at Large*, 2 & 3 Edw. VI, c. 19 (14 vols; London: Eyre and Strahan, 1786–1800).

58 *Visitation Articles*, vol. 1, p. 511.

59 5 Eliz., c. 5, xii, in *Tudor Economic Documents: Being Select Documents Illustrating the Economic and Social History of Tudor England*, eds R.H. Tawney and Eileen Power (3 vols; London: Longmans and Green, 1951), vol. 2, p. 113.

60 *Visitation Articles*, vol. 1, pp. 260–61.

61 Hutton, *Stations*, pp. 192–93; David, *English Bread and Yeast Cookery*, pp. 473–75, who attributes the restrictions to the bread's non-standard size.

62 *Certain Sermons or Homilies Appointed to be Read in Churches in the Time of Queen Elizabeth of Famous Memory* (London: Parker, 1683), pp. 180–81.

63 *Documentary Annals*, vol. 2, p. 55.

64 Richard Hooker, *Of the Laws of Ecclesiastical Polity*, V.72 (3 vols; London: Holdsworth and Ball, 1830), vol. 2, p. 334.

65 Hooker, *Laws*, V.72, vol. 2, p. 348.

66 Hooker, *Laws*, V.72, vol. 2, p. 343.

67 Charlemagne was not himself an exemplar of abstinence. He is said to have consumed a four-course dinner every day accompanied by roast meat carried in by his hunters on a spit, despite being told by his doctors that he should switch to boiled meat for health reasons. His biographer presents this as moderate, at least by royal standards. *The Life of Charlemagne* 22, 24, in *Charlemagne's Courtier: The Complete Einhard*, trans. Paul Edward Dutton (Peterborough, ON: Broadview, 1998), pp. 30–31.

68 Mayke de Jong, 'Charlemagne's Church', in *Charlemagne: Empire and Society*, ed. Joanna Story (Manchester University Press, 2005), pp. 103–35 (128).

69 John Calvin, *Institutes of the Christian Religion* IV.12.17, trans. Henry Beveridge (Grand Rapids, MI: Eerdmans, 1989), p. 463.

70 Calvin, *Institutes* IV.12.20, p. 465.

71 Calvin, *Institutes* IV.12.20, p. 466.

72 Hugh Trevor-Roper, 'The fast sermons of the Long Parliament', in *Religion, the Reformation and Social Change, and Other Essays* (London: Macmillan, 1967), pp. 294–344.

73 Blair Worden, *The Rump Parliament, 1648–53* (London: Cambridge University Press, 1974), pp. 82–83.

74 Charles Latham Cutting, *Fish Saving: A History of Fish Processing from Ancient to Modern Times* (London: Hill, 1955), p. 34; Hutton, *Stations*, p. 170.

75 *Public General Statutes*, 19 & 20 Vict., 1856 (London: HMSO, 1763–), p. 439.

76   Owen Chadwick, *The Victorian Church* (2 vols; London: Black, 1966–70), vol. 1, pp. 37–38.
77   Trevor-Roper, 'Fast sermons', p. 295.
78   Chadwick, *Victorian Church*, vol. 1, pp. 490–91.
79   Rudolph Arbesmann, 'Fasting and Prophecy in Pagan and Christian Antiquity', *Traditio* 7 (1949–51), pp. 1–71.
80   Michel Foucault, *The History of Sexuality* III: *The Care of the Self* (Harmondsworth: Penguin, 1988), pp. 140–41.
81   Jeremy Carrette, *Foucault and Religion: Spiritual Corporality and Political Spirituality* (London: Routledge, 1999), pp. 134–35. See also Richard Valantasis, 'Constructions of Power in Asceticism', *Journal of the American Academy of Religion* 63 (1995), pp. 775–821.
82   Michael Foucault, *Security, Territory, Population: Lectures at the Collège de France, 1977–78* (Basingstoke: Palgrave Macmillan, 2007), esp. pp. 205–8.
83   Foucault, *Security*, p. 207.
84   Maud Ellmann, *The Hunger Artists: Starving, Writing and Imprisonment* (London: Virago, 1993), pp. 12–14.
85   D.A. Binchy, 'Irish History and Irish Law', *Studia Hibernica* 15 (1975), pp. 7–36 (23–24).
86   F.N. Robinson, 'Notes on the Irish practice of fasting as a means of distraint', in *Putnam Anniversary Volume* (New York: Stechert, 1909), pp. 567–83 (583).
87   D.A. Binchy, 'A pre-Christian survival in medieval Irish hagiography', in *Ireland in Early Mediaeval Europe: Studies in Memory of Kathleen Hughes*, eds Dorothy Whitelock, Rosamond McKitterick and David Dumville (Cambridge University Press, 1982), pp. 165–78.
88   *Bethada Náem n Érenn: Lives of Irish Saints*, ed. Charles Plummer (2 vols; Oxford: Clarendon, 1922), vol. 2, pp. 85–87.
89   Gen. 32.22–32.
90   *The Tripartite Life of Patrick, With Other Documents Relating to that Saint*, ed. Whitley Stokes, Rolls Series 89 (London: HMSO, 1887), pp. 112–21.
91   Robinson, 'Notes', p. 571.
92   Veronika Grimm, *From Feasting to Fasting, the Evolution of a Sin: Attitudes to Food in Late Antiquity* (London: Routledge, 1996), p. 195.
93   Grimm, *From Feasting to Fasting*, p. 195.
94   Grimm, *From Feasting to Fasting*, pp. 162–74.
95   Jerome, Letter 54.10, in *NPNF* II.6, p. 105.
96   Jerome, Letter 54.9, p. 105.
97   Galen, 'On the Humours', p. 15.
98   C.J.K. Henry, 'The Biology of Human Starvation: Some New Insights', *Nutritional Bulletin* 26 (2001), pp. 205–11.
99   John Chrysostom, Homily 27 on Acts, in *NPNF* I.11, p. 176.
100 Shaw, *Burden*, pp. 220–54.
101 Caroline Walker Bynum, *Holy Feast and Holy Fast: The Religious Significance of Food to Medieval Women* (Berkeley: University of California Press, 1987), pp. 47–69; also David Brown, *God of Grace and Body: Sacrament in Ordinary* (Oxford University Press, 2007), pp. 204–7.
102 Bynum, *Holy Feast*, p. 220.
103 Bynum, *Holy Feast*, p. 243.

3   Secularizing Diet

1   Gregory the Great, *Dialogues* 2.1, trans. Odo John Zimmerman (Fathers of the Church 39; Washington DC: Catholic University Press of America, 2002), p. 58; Carmen Acevedo Butcher, *Man of Blessing: A Life of St. Benedict* (Brewster, MA: Paraclete, 2006), p. 57.

2 Gregory, *Dialogues* 2.3, p. 66.

3 *The Rule of St. Benedict* 51, trans. Justin McCann (London: Sheed & Ward, 1989), p. 56; Gregory, *Dialogues* 2.12, p. 77.

4 *Rhigyfarch's Life of St. David*, 24, ed. J.W. James (Cardiff: Wales University Press, 1967).

5 David Knowles, *The Monastic Order in England: A History of its Development from the Times of St Dunstan to the Fourth Lateran Council, 940–1216* (Cambridge University Press, 2nd edn, 1976), pp. 461–62; idem, 'The Diet of English Black Monks', *The Downside Review* 52/150 (1934), pp. 275–90 (284–85); Barbara F. Harvey, 'Diet', in *Living and Dying in England, 1100–1540: The Monastic Experience* (Oxford: Clarendon, 1993), pp. 34–71 (41–42); Joseph A. Gribbin, *The Premonstratensian Order in Late Medieval England* (Woodbridge: Boydell, 2001), pp. 78–79.

6 Edmund Bishop, 'The Method and Degree of Fasting and Abstinence of the Black Monks in England before the Reformation', *The Downside Review* 43/123 (1925), pp. 184–237 (206); Harvey, *Living and Dying*, p. 51.

7 *Rule of St. Benedict* 41, p. 47.

8 Harvey, *Living and Dying*, p. 42.

9 Harvey, *Living and Dying*, pp. 40, 51.

10 Harvey, *Living and Dying*, p. 40.

11 Knowles, *Monastic Order*, p. 459.

12 David Sherlock and William Zajac, 'A Fourteenth-Century Monastic Sign List from Bury St Edmunds Abbey', *Proceedings of the Suffolk Institute of Archaeology and History* 36 (1988), pp. 251–73 (258).

13 David Sherlock, *Signs for Silence: The Sign Language of the Monks of Ely in the Middle Ages* (Ely Cathedral Publications, 1992), pp. 11–14.

14 Anselme Davril, « Le langage par signes chez les moines : un catalogue de signes de l'abbaye de Fleury », in *Sous la règle de Saint Benoît: structures monastiques et sociétés en France du Moyen Âge à l'époche moderne* (Geneva: Droz, 1982), pp. 51–74 (57); Kirk Ambrose, 'A Medieval Food List from the Monastery of Cluny', *Gastronomica* 6, 1 (2006), pp. 14–20 (17).

15 C.M. Woolgar, '"Take this penance now, and afterwards the fare will improve": seafood and late medieval diet', in *England's Sea Fisheries: The Commercial Sea Fisheries of England and Wales since 1300*, eds David J. Starkey, Chris Reid and Neil Ashcroft (London: Chatham, 2000), pp. 36–44 (43); Bridget Ann Henisch, *Fast and Feast: Food in Medieval Society* (University Park: Pennsylvania State University Press, 1976), p. 39.

16 Mk 14.36.

17 Mt. 25.35.

18 Mt. 9.15.

19 *Rule of St. Benedict* 53, p. 58.

20 Basil of Caesarea, *Collected Letters*, 14 (4 vols; London: Heinemann, 1926–39), vol. 1, pp. 110–11.

21 John Cassian, *Institutes* 5.24 (trans. Boniface Ramsey; Mahwah, NJ: Newman, 2000), pp. 132–33; also Evagrios the Solitary, 'Outline teaching on asceticism and stillness in the solitary life', in *The Philokalia*, eds G.E.H. Palmer, Philip Sherrard and Kallistos Ware (3 vols; London: Faber and Faber, 1981–84), vol. 1, pp. 31–37 (36).

22 Mt. 9.15, Mk 2.19–20, Lk. 5.34–35.

23 *Rule of St. Benedict* 53, p. 57; Graham Gould, *The Desert Fathers on Monastic Community* (Oxford: Clarendon, 1993), pp. 145–50.

24 *Coutumes de Chartreuse*, 36.1 (Paris: Cerf, 1984), pp. 238–39.

25 Council of Vienne 20, in *Decrees of the Ecumenical Councils*, ed. Norman P. Tanner (2 vols; London: Sheed & Ward, 1990), vol. 2, p. 377.

26 It was also an issue in Dominican houses. William A. Hinnebusch, *The History of the Dominican Order* (2 vols; Staten Island, NY: Alba House, 1966), vol. 1, p. 360.

27   *Rule of St. Benedict* 56, p. 61.

28   Knowles, 'Diet', p. 283; idem, *Monastic Order*, p. 461.

29   *Rule of St. Benedict* 36, p. 43.

30   *The Rule of Saint Augustine* 3, trans. Raymond Canning (London: Darton, Longman and Todd, 1984), pp. 13–15.

31   Knowles, 'Diet', p. 282; idem, *Monastic Order*, p. 461.

32   D.J. Stewart, *On the Architectural History of Ely Cathedral* (London: Van Voorst, 1868), p. 222.

33   *The Chrodegang Rules: The Rules for the Common Life of the Secular Clergy from the Eighth and Ninth Centuries*, rule 20, ed. Jerome Bertram (Aldershot: Ashgate, 2005), pp. 66–67.

34   *The Rule of the Templars* 190–92, ed. J.M. Upton-Ward (Woodbridge: Boydell, 1992), p. 65.

35   *Rule of the Templars* 26–28, p. 26.

36   Origen, 'Homily 27 on Numbers, Concerning the Stages of the Children of Israel (Numbers 33)', in *An Exhortation to Martyrdom, Prayer and Selected Works*, ed. Rowan Greer (New York: Paulist, 1979), pp. 245–69 (245).

37   *Rule of St. Benedict* 37, p. 44.

38   *Rule of St. Benedict* 41, p. 47.

39   Knowles, *Monastic Order*, p. 457.

40   Gregory, *Dialogues* 2.1, pp. 58–59.

41   *Rule of St. Benedict* 41, 49, pp. 47, 55.

42   Harvey, *Living and Dying*, p. 39.

43   G.H. Cook, *English Monasteries in the Middle Ages* (London: Phoenix, 1961), p. 114; Knowles, *Monastic Order*, pp. 463–64.

44   *Coutumes de Chartreuse* 33.5, pp. 234–35.

45   Gerhard Jaritz, 'The standard of living in German and Austrian Cistercian monasteries of the late middle ages', in *Goad and Nail* (Kalamazoo, MI: Cistercian, 1985), pp. 56–70 (57–58).

46   Knowles, 'Diet', pp. 285–86; Bishop, 'Method and Degree', pp. 188–90.

47   C.R. Cheney, *Episcopal Visitation of Monasteries in the Thirteenth Century* (Manchester University Press, 1931), p. 171.

48   Guillaume Mollatt, *The Popes at Avignon, 1305–1378* (London: Nelson, 1963), p. 35.

49   Bernard Guillemain, *La Cour pontificale d'Avignon, 1309–1376: étude d'une société* (Paris: Boccard, 1962), p. 135.

50   Peter McDonald, 'The Papacy and Monastic Observance in the Later Middle Ages: The *Benedictina* in England', *Journal of Religious History* 14 (1986), pp. 117–32 (122).

51   McDonald, 'The Papacy and Monastic Observance', p. 124.

52   Étienne Delcambre, *Servais de Lairuelz et la Réforme des Prémontrés* (Averbode: Praemonstratensia, 1964), p. 62.

53   Alan Hunt, *Governance of the Consuming Passions: A History of Sumptuary Law* (Basingstoke: Macmillan, 1996), pp. 298–301.

54   Thomas Cranmer, *Works* (2 vols; Cambridge University Press, 1844–46), vol. 2, p. 491.

55   *The Autobiography of Gerald of Wales*, trans. H.E. Butler (Woodbridge: Boydell & Brewer, 2005), p. 71.

56   *Autobiography of Gerald of Wales*, p. 72.

57   William Langland, *Piers the Plowman*, book 13, trans. Jonathan Frank Goodridge (Harmondsworth: Penguin, 1966), p. 152.

58   Langland, *Piers the Plowman*, pp. 153–54. See David Moses, 'Soul Food and Eating Habits: What's at Steak in a Medieval Monk's Diet?', *Downside Review* 124 (2006), pp. 213–22 (216).

59   Geoffrey Chaucer, General Prologue 172–76, in *The Canterbury Tales*, ed. Michael Alexander (London: Penguin, 1996), p. 10.

60 Chaucer, General Prologue 223–34, in *The Canterbury Tales*, p. 12.

61 Elizabeth M. Biebel, 'Pilgrims to table: food consumption in Chaucer's *Canterbury Tales*', in *Food and Eating in Medieval Europe*, eds Martha Carlin and Joel T. Rosenthal (London: Hambledon, 1998), pp. 15–26.

62 Bonnie Effros, *Creating Community with Food and Drink in Merovingian Gaul* (Basingstoke: Palgrave Macmillan, 2002), pp. 14, 42.

63 Harvey, *Living and Dying*, pp. 42, 38.

64 Karl A. Gersbach, 'The Historical and Literary Context of Fasting and Abstinence in the Life of St. Nicholas of Tolentino (†1305)', *Augustiniana* 55 (2005), pp. 247–96.

65 Bernard of Besse, in *Francis of Assisi: Early Documents*, eds Regis J. Armstrong, J.A. Wayne Hellmann and William J. Short (4 vols; New York: New City Press, 1999–2002) [subsequently *FA*], vol. 3, p. 50; also Thomas of Celano, in *FA*, vol. 2, pp. 298–99; Anon., in *FA*, vol. 3, pp. 846–47; Jacobus de Voragine, *The Golden Legend: Readings on the Saints*, trans. William Granger Ryan (2 vols; Princeton, NJ: Princeton University Press), vol. 2, p. 228.

66 Lk. 10.8.

67 E.g., Mt. 9.10–11; 26.6–13.

68 The expectation that Francis would abstain from chicken appears to have been based on a particularly rigourist understanding of abstinence. Chicken possessed an ambiguous status in monastic tradition, being meat but not four-footed. Its status was therefore contented by rigourist and permissive interpreters of monastic rules.

69 *Canticle of the Creatures*, in *FA*, vol. 1, pp. 113–14; Thomas of Celano, in *FA*, vol. 1, pp. 234–35, 251; vol. 2, p. 464; Ugolino Boniscambi of Montegiorgio, in *FA*, vol. 3, p. 454; De Voragine, *Golden Legend*, vol. 2, p. 227; Roger Sorrell, *St. Francis of Assisi and Nature: Tradition and Innovation in Western Christian Attitudes toward the Environment* (Oxford University Press, 1988).

70 In *FA*, vol. 1, p. 392; also Thomas of Celano, in *FA*, vol. 1, p. 227.

71 *Earlier Rule*, in *FA*, vol. 1, p. 73; *Later Rule*, in *FA*, vol. 1, p. 102.

72 *Mirror*, in *FA*, vol. 3, p. 359.

73 Rosalind B. Brooke, *Early Franciscan Government: Elias to Bonaventure* (Cambridge University Press, 1959), p. 157.

74 Hinnebusch, *History*, vol. 1, pp. 150–51.

75 G.R. Galbraith, *The Constitution of the Dominican Order, 1216–1360* (Manchester University Press, 1925), pp. 112–13.

76 Hinnebusch, *History*, vol. 1, p. 359.

77 Patrick Olivelle, 'From feast to fast: food and the Indian ascetic', in *Panels of the VIIth World Sanskrit Conference, IX: Rules and Remedies in Classical Indian Law*, ed. Julia Leslie (Leiden: Brill, 1991), pp. 17–36 (30–34).

78 Pierre Bourdieu, *Distinction: A Social Critique of the Judgement of Taste* (London: Routledge & Kegan Paul, 1986), pp. 177–79.

79 G.K. Chesterton, *St. Francis of Assisi* (London: Hodder & Stoughton, 1923), p. 112.

80 Philip Lyndon Reynolds, *Food and the Body: Some Peculiar Questions in High Medieval Theology* (Leiden: Brill, 1999), p. 44.

81 Joan Cadden, 'Albertus Magnus' universal physiology: the example of nutrition', in *Albertus Magnus and the Sciences: Commemorative Essays, 1980*, ed. James A. Weisheipl (Toronto: Pontifical Institute of Mediaeval Studies, 1980), pp. 321–39 (325).

82 Comparisons may be drawn with accounts of non-Christian extreme asceticism. In India, for instance, the highest classes of hermit are believed to subsist on water or air. See Olivelle, 'From feast to fast', p. 28.

83 Reynolds, *Food*, p. 19.

84 Reynolds, *Food*, pp. 383–84.

85 Reynolds, *Food*, pp. 40–41.

86 Caroline Walker Bynum, *The Resurrection of the Body in Western Christianity, 200–1336* (Columbia, NY: Columbia University Press, 1995), esp. pp. 6–17.

87 Macarius Magnes, *Apocrit.* IV.24, in *Porphyry's Against the Christians: The Literary Remains*, ed. R. Joseph Hoffmann (Amherst, NY: Prometheus, 1994), p. 91.
88 Reynolds, *Food*, p. 4.
89 Thomas Aquinas, *Summa Theologiae*, Ia, q. 119, a. 1 (60 vols; London: Blackfriars, 1962–76), vol. 15, pp. 166–67.
90 Reynolds, *Food*, p. 384.
91 Thomas Aquinas, *Summa Theologica*, IIIa suppl., q. 69, a. 1 (22 vols; London: Burns, Oates and Washburn, 1920–24), vol. 20, p. 3.
92 Simon Schaffer, 'Piety, physic and prodigious abstinence', in *Religio Medici: Medicine and Religion in Seventeenth-century England*, eds Ole Peter Grell and Andrew Cunningham (London: Scolar, 1997), pp. 171–203.
93 G.K. Chesterton, *St. Thomas Aquinas* (London: Hodder & Stoughton, 1962), p. 15; James A. Weisheipl, *Friar Thomas d'Aquino: His Life, Thought, and Works* (Oxford: Blackwell, 1975), p. 45. There is no suggestion that Aquinas was unhealthy as a result of his large stature; indeed, various accounts testify to his physical health and beauty. Jean-Pierre Torrell, *Saint Thomas Aquinas* (2 vols; Washington, DC: Catholic University Press of America, 2005), vol. 1, pp. 278–79.
94 Mark D. Jordan, 'The disappearance of Galen in thirteenth-century philosophy and theology', in *Miscellanea mediaevalia* (Berlin: De Gruyter, 1992), pp. 703–17.

4 Fasting by Choice

1 Margaret Aston, *Lollards and Reformers: Images and Literacy in Late Medieval Religion* (London: Hambledon, 1984), p. 93.
2 Anne Hudson, *The Premature Reformation: Wycliffite Texts and Lollard History* (Oxford: Clarendon, 1988), pp. 147–48.
3 Huldrich Zwingli, 'Liberty respecting food in Lent', in *The Latin Works* (3 vols; Philadelphia, PA: Heidelberg Press, 1912–29), vol. 1, pp. 70–112 (70–71).
4 Zwingli, 'Liberty', pp. 73–79.
5 Mk 7.15, Mt. 15.17.
6 Acts 10.15.
7 1 Cor. 6.12.
8 1 Cor. 8.8.
9 1 Cor. 10.25.
10 Col. 2.16.
11 1 Tim. 4.3.
12 Heb. 13.9.
13 Zwingli, 'Liberty', pp. 80–86.
14 Mk 2.23.
15 Lk. 17.20, Gal. 4.9.
16 Zwingli, 'Liberty', pp. 86–87.
17 Zwingli, 'Liberty', pp. 87–89.
18 Zwingli, 'Liberty', pp. 89–109.
19 Mt. 5.29; 18.8.
20 Rom. 14.1.
21 Acts 16.3; cf. Gal. 2.3.
22 Gal. 2.12.
23 Martin Luther, *Treatise on Good Works* 19, in *Luther's Works* (50 vols; Saint Louis, MO: Concordia, 1955–76), vol. 44, p. 74.
24 Martin Luther, *Lectures on Genesis Chapters 6–14*, discussing 9.2–4, in *Works*, vol. 2, pp. 132–38.
25 Luther, *Treatise on Good Works* 21, p. 76.
26 Martin Luther, *To the Christian Nobility of the German Nation Concerning the Reform of the Christian Estate* 19, in *Works*, vol. 44, pp. 115–217 (184).

27 *Food, Cookery, and Dining in Ancient Times: Alexis Soyer's Pantropheon* (Mineola, NY: Dover, 2004), p. 172. Some other sources suggest that the dispensation allowed people to eat butter too.

28 Martin Luther, *Lectures on Genesis Chapters 6–14*, v. 9.2, in *Luther's Works*, vol. 2, pp. 132–34, discussed in David Clough, 'The anxiety of the human animal: Martin Luther on non-human animals and human animality', in *Creaturely Theology: God, Humans and Other Animals*, eds Celia Deane-Drummond and David Clough (London: SCM, 2009), pp. 41–60.

29 Peter Iver Kaufman, 'Fasting in England in the 1560s: "A Thinge of Nought"?', *Archiv für Reformationsgeschichte* 94 (2003), pp. 176–93.

30 John Calvin, *Commentary upon the Acts of the Apostles* (2 vols; Edinburgh: Calvin Translation Society, 1844), vol. 1, pp. 422–23.

31 John Calvin, *Institutes of the Christian Religion* IV.12.20 (Grand Rapids, MI: Eerdmans, 1989), p. 466.

32 Hugh Trevor-Roper, 'The fast sermons of the Long Parliament', in *Religion, the Reformation and Social Change, and Other Essays* (London: Macmillan, 1967), pp. 294–344; Blair Worden, *The Rump Parliament, 1648–53* (London: Cambridge University Press, 1974), pp. 82–83.

33 Jeremy Taylor, *The Rule and Exercises of Holy Living* (London: Longman, Orme, Brown, Green and Longmans, 3rd edn, 1839), p. 207.

34 Rev. 14.1b.

35 John Newton, manuscript CO199, University of Princetown, transcribed by Marylynn Rouse.

36 Diary entry for 30 July 1852, quoted in *John Newton: An Autobiography and Narrative*, ed. Josiah Bull (London: Religious Tract Society, 2nd edn, 1870), pp. 41–42.

37 Richard Cecil, *The Life of John Newton* (ed. Marylynn Rouse; Fearn: Christian Focus, 2000), p. 65, n.

38 Cecil, *Life of John Newton*, p. 70.

39 *John Newton*, ed. Bull, pp. 70, 92–93.

40 Ronald Hutton, *Stations of the Sun: A History of the Ritual Year in Britain* (Oxford University Press, 1996), p. 170; Charles Latham Cutting, *Fish Saving: A History of Fish Processing from Ancient to Modern Times* (London: Hill, 1955), p. 34.

41 Robert Webster, 'The Value of Self-denial: John Wesley's Multidimensional View of Fasting', *Toronto Journal of Theology* 19 (2003), pp. 25–40 (35).

42 J. Brazier Green, *John Wesley and William Law* (London: Epworth, 1945).

43 Webster, 'Value', p. 28.

44 Charles Wallace, 'Eating and Drinking with John Wesley: The Logic of his Practice', *Bulletin of the John Rylands University Library of Manchester* 85 (2003), pp. 137–55 (141–43).

45 John Wesley, letter of 1 November 1724, in *Works* (36 vols; Oxford: Clarendon, 1975–), vol. 25, p. 151.

46 Anita Guerrini, 'Case History as Spiritual Autobiography: George Cheyne's "Case of the Author"', *Eighteenth Century Life* 19 (1995), pp. 18–27 (18).

47 Luigi Cornaro, *A Treatise of Temperance and Sobrietie* (London: Starkey, 1978). See R. Marie Griffith, 'Fasting, dieting and the body in American Christianity', in *Perspectives on American Religion and Culture*, ed. Peter W. Williams (Oxford: Blackwell, 1999), pp. 216–27 (218–19).

48 Alan Rudrum, 'Ethical Vegetarianism in Seventeenth-Century Britain: Its Roots in Sixteenth-Century Theological Debate', *The Seventeenth Century* 18 (2003), pp. 76–92.

49 Christine Hivet, 'A Diet for a Sensitive Soul: Vegetarianism in Eighteenth-Century Britain', *Eighteenth Century Life* 23, 2 (1999), special issue 'The Cultural Topography of Food', pp. 34–42 (36).

50 Guerrini, 'Case History', p. 22.

51 L.A. Clarkson and E. Margaret Crawford, *Feast and Famine: Food and Nutrition in Ireland, 1500–1920* (Oxford University Press, 2001), p. 227.

52 David E. Shuttleton, 'Methodism and Dr George Cheyne's "More Enlightening Principles"', in *Medicine in the Enlightenment*, ed. Roy Porter (Amsterdam: Rodopi, 1995), pp. 316–35.

53 Hivet, 'Diet', pp. 38–39.

54 Guerrini, 'Case History', p. 24.

55 George S. Rousseau, 'Mysticism and millenarianism: "immortal Dr. Cheyne"', in *Millenarianism and Messianism in English Literature and Thought, 1650–1800*, ed. Richard H. Popkin (Leiden: Brill, 1988), pp. 81–126 (98–100).

56 John Coveney, *Food, Morals and Meaning: The Pleasure and Anxiety of Eating* (London: Routledge, 2nd edn, 2006), p. 55.

57 John Wesley, *Primitive Physick; or An Easy and Natural Method of Curing Most Diseases* (London: Strahan, 1747).

58 Wallace, 'Eating', p. 145.

59 John Wesley, journal entry for 30 March 1736, in *Works*, vol. 18, p. 155.

60 Wesley, journal entry for 28 June 1770, in *Works*, vol. 22, pp. 236–37.

61 Susanna Wesley, *The Complete Writings* (Oxford University Press, 1997), p. 280.

62 Wesley, *Complete Writings*, p. 280.

63 John Wesley, 'Upon our Lord's Sermon on the Mount', Sermon 27 (on Mt. 6.16–18) in *Works*, vol. 1, pp. 592–611.

64 Ps. 131.3.

65 Wesley, 'Upon our Lord's Sermon on the Mount', p. 605.

66 Wallace, 'Eating', pp. 150–53.

67 Colin Spencer, *The Heretic's Feast: A History of Vegetarianism* (London: Fourth Estate, 1994), p. 252; Tristram Stuart, *The Bloodless Revolution: Radical Vegetarians and the Discovery of India* (London: HarperPress, 2006), p. 5.

68 Hilda Kean, *Animal Rights: Political and Social Change in Britain since 1800* (London: Reaktion, 1998), pp. 123–24.

69 Julia Twigg, 'The Vegetarian Movement in England, 1847–1981: With Particular Reference to its Ideology', University of London Ph.D. thesis, 1981.

70 Lewis Drummond, *Spurgeon: Prince of Preachers* (Grand Rapids, MI: Kregel, 1992), p. 380.

71 James R.T.E. Gregory, '"A Lutheranism of the Table": religion and the Victorian vegetarians', in *Eating and Believing: Interdisciplinary Perspectives on Vegetarianism and Theology*, eds Rachel Muers and David Grumett (London: T&T Clark, 2008), pp. 135–51, idem, *Of Victorians and Vegetarians: The Vegetarian Movement in Nineteenth Century Britain* (London: Tauris, 2007), pp. 100–3.

72 Samantha Calvert, 'A Taste of Eden: Modern Christianity and Vegetarianism', *Journal of Ecclesiastical History* 58 (2007), pp. 461–81; Derek Antrobus, *A Guiltless Feast: The Salford Bible Christian Church and the Rise of the Modern Vegetarian Movement* (City of Salford Education and Leisure, 1997).

73 Peter J. Lineham, 'Restoring man's creative power: the theosophy of the Bible Christians of Salford', in *Studies in Church History 19: The Church and Healing*, ed. W. J. Sheils (Oxford: Blackwell, 1982), pp. 207–23.

74 Lineham, 'Restoring man's creative power', p. 214.

75 Lineham, 'Restoring man's creative power', p. 217.

76 'Vegetarian Conference and Festival', in *The Truth Tester, Temperance Advocate, and Manx Healthian Journal*, 22 October 1847, p. 2.

77 'Vegetarian Conference and Festival', p. 3.

78 William Booth, *Orders and Regulations for Officers of the Salvation Army* (London: Salvation Army, rev. edn, 1891 [1886]), p. 43.

79 Booth, *Orders and Regulations*, pp. 44–46.

80 *Orders and Regulations for Officers of the Salvation Army* (London: Salvation Army, rev. edn, 1925), pp. 100–4 (101).

81 Booth, *Orders and Regulations*, p. 44.

82 1914 interview quoted in Karen Iacobbo and Michael Iacobbo, *Vegetarian America: A History* (Westport, CN: Praeger, 2004), p. 133.

83 William Booth, *In Darkest England and the Way Out* (London: Salvation Army, 1890), pp. 133–36.

84 Twigg, 'Vegetarian Movement', pp. 190–91.

85 *The Gospel of the Holy Twelve*, ed. G.J. Ouseley (London: Watkins, 1957).

86 Calvert, 'Taste of Eden', pp. 465–66.

87 Gregory, *Of Victorians and Vegetarians*, pp. 104–10; Robert Govett, *Vegetarianism: A Dialogue* (Norwich: Fletcher, 2nd edn, 1883). In this exchange, the protagonists are a 'Vegetarian' and a 'Christian'.

88 Calvert, 'Taste of Eden', pp. 473–79.

89 Samantha Calvert, 'Ours is the food that Eden knew: themes in the theology and practice of modern Christian vegetarians', in *Eating and Believing*, pp. 123–34 (127).

90 Gerald Carson, *Cornflake Crusade* (London: Gollancz, 1959), p. 17.

91 Iacobbo and Iacobbo, *Vegetarian America*, pp. 3–4.

92 Margaret Puskar-Pasewicz, 'Kitchen sisters and disagreeable boys: debates over meatless diets in nineteenth-century Shaker communities', in *Eating in Eden: Food and American Utopias*, eds Etta M. Madden and Martha L. Finch (Lincoln: University of Nebraska Press, 2006), pp. 109–24.

93 Stephen J. Stein, *The Shaker Experience in America: A History of the United Society of Believers* (New Haven, CT: Yale University Press, 1992), pp. 156–58, 305–306.

94 *History of the Philadelphia Bible-Christian Church for the First Century of its Existence from 1817 to 1917* (Philadelphia, PA: Lippincott, 1922), p. 40; Antrobus, *Guiltless Feast*, pp. 85–93. Antrobus also suggests a link with Germany, pp. 93–94.

95 Clement of Alexandria, *Instructor* 2.1, in ANF 2, p. 237.

96 The idea that a vegetarian breakfast expresses Christian virtue was, in historic perspective, contestable. In monasteries, eating would have been postponed until the first meal taken later in the day – a practice commended in the present day by the Benedictine monk and scholar Adalbert de Vogüé, who in his *To Love Fasting: The Monastic Experience* (Petersham, MA: Saint Bede's, 1989) subjects modern constructions of breakfast as an essential meal to sustained critique.

97 Carson, *Cornflake Crusade*, pp. 122–25.

98 Alison Blay-Palmer, *Food Fears: From Industrial to Sustainable Food Systems* (Aldershot: Ashgate, 2008), p. 46.

99 Horace B. Powell, *The Original has this Signature – W.K. Kellogg* (Englewood Cliffs, NJ: Prentice Hall, 1956), pp. 147–50.

100 Andrew R. Heinze, *Adapting to Abundance: Jewish Immigrants, Mass Consumption, and the Search for American Identity* (New York: Columbia University Press, 1990), pp. 175–76. For similar issues currently facing Muslims, see Richard Foltz, *Animals in Islamic Tradition and Muslim Cultures* (Oxford: Oneworld, 2006), pp. 116–19.

101 Carson, *Cornflake Crusade*, pp. 183, 197.

102 Griffith, 'Fasting', p. 220.

103 Carson, *Cornflake Crusade*, pp. 71–72.

104 Carson, *Cornflake Crusade*, pp. 142–44.

105 James C. Whorton, 'Muscular vegetarianism', in *Crusaders for Fitness: The History of American Health Reformers* (Princeton, NJ: Princeton University Press, 1982), pp. 201–38.

106 Eustace Miles, *Better Food for Boys* (London: George Bell and Sons, 2nd edn, 1909).

107 Susan L. Roberson, '"Degenerate effeminacy" and the making of a masculine spirituality in the sermons of Ralph Waldo Emerson', in *Muscular Christianity:*

Embodying the Victorian Age, ed. Donald E. Hall (Cambridge University Press, 1994), pp. 150–72.

108 Clifford Putney, *Muscular Christianity: Manhood and Sports in Protestant America, 1880–1920* (Cambridge, MA: Harvard University Press, 2001), p. 139.

109 Apostolic Constitution of Pope Paul VI, *Paenitemini* (London: Catholic Truth Society, 1973 [1966]); 'Fast and abstinence', eds P.M.J. Clancy, G.T. Kennedy and J.E. Lynch, in *New Catholic Encyclopaedia* (15 vols; Detroit, MI: Gale, 2nd edn, 2003), vol. 5, pp. 632–35; Kallistos Ware, 'The rules of fasting', in introduction to *The Lenten Triodion* (London: Faber & Faber, 1978), pp. 35–37.

110 Tito Colliander, *Way of the Ascetics* (Crestwood, NY: St Vladimir's, 2003), pp. 75–77.

111 Daniel Sack, *Whitebread Protestants: Food and Religion in American Culture* (Basingstoke: Palgrave, 2001), pp. 215–17.

112 Ryan Berry, *Food for the Gods: Vegetarianism and the World's Religions* (New York: Pythagorean, 1998).

113 Carol J. Adams, *The Inner Art of Vegetarianism: Spiritual Practices for Body and Soul* (New York: Lantern, 2000).

114 Donald Altman, *Art of the Inner Meal: Eating as a Spiritual Path* (New York: Harper, 1999).

115 Callum G. Brown, *The Death of Christian Britain* (London: Routledge, 2001), p. 190.

116 Christina Hardyment, *Slice of Life: The British Way of Eating since 1945* (London: Penguin, 1997), p. 148; Teresa Beardsworth and Alan Keil, 'Health-Related Benefits and Dietary Practices Among Vegetarians and Vegans: A Qualitative Study', *Health Education Journal* 50, 1 (1991), pp. 38–42.

117 Iacobbo and Iacobbo, *Vegetarian America*, pp. 222–24.

118 Malcolm Hamilton, 'Eating Ethically: "Spiritual" and "Quasi-religious" Aspects of Vegetarianism', *Journal of Contemporary Religion* 15 (2000), pp. 65–83.

119 'Veggies Fed Up for Lent', *Church Times*, 11 April 2003.

120 'Richard Chartres, Bishop of London', *Church Times*, 24 February 2006.

121 John Wesley, letter to Dr Gibson, 11 June 1747, in *The Letters of the Rev John Wesley, A.M.* (London: Epworth, 1931), pp. 285–86.

122 Tearfund, 'Carbon Fast 2009: Daily Actions', at http://www.tearfund.org/web-docs/Website/campaigning/carbonfast09/A4_Actions_final.pdf, p. 2 [accessed 12 May 2009].

123 For a further example, see Ephraim Isaac, 'The significance of food in Hebraic-African thought and the role of fasting in the Ethiopian church', in *Asceticism*, eds Vincent L. Wimbush and Richard Valantasis (New York: Oxford University Press, 1995), pp. 329–42.

124 Pierre Teilhard de Chardin, 'The awaited word', in *Toward the Future* (San Diego: Harvest, 1975), pp. 92–100 (93).

125 David Grumett, *Teilhard de Chardin: Theology, Humanity and Cosmos* (Leuven: Peeters, 2005), pp. 263–65.

5 Clean and Unclean Animals

1 Nathan Macdonald, *Not Bread Alone: The Uses of Food in the Old Testament* (Oxford University Press, 2008), pp. 17–46, provides an overview and discussion.

2 Mary Douglas, 'The abominations of Leviticus', in *Purity and Danger: An Analysis of Concepts of Pollution and Taboo* (London: Routledge, rev. edn, 2002), pp. 51–71.

3 Roland de Vaux, 'The sacrifice of pigs in Palestine and in the Ancient East', in *The Bible and the Ancient Near East* (London: Darton, Longman and Todd, 1972), pp. 252–69; Frederick J. Simoons, *Eat Not this Flesh: Food Avoidances from Prehistory to the Present* (Madison: University of Wisconsin Press, 2nd edn, 1994), pp. 37–40.

4 Simoons, *Eat Not this Flesh*, pp. 66–71.

5 Douglas, 'Preface to the Routledge Classics Edition', in *Purity and Danger*, pp. x–xxi; see the critique by Walter Houston, *Purity and Monotheism: Clean and Unclean Animals in Biblical Law* (Sheffield: JSOT Press, 1993).

6 Mary Douglas, *Leviticus as Literature* (Oxford University Press, 1999), pp. 166–75; also idem, 'The Forbidden Animals in Leviticus', *Journal for the Study of the Old Testament* 59 (1993), pp. 3–23.

7 Douglas, *Leviticus*, pp. 168, 174.

8 Richard Fardon, *Mary Douglas: An Intellectual Biography* (London: Routledge, 1998), pp. 130, 11–20.

9 Jean Soler, 'The semiotics of food in the Bible', in *Food and Drink in History*, eds Robert Forster and Orest Ranum (Baltimore, MD: Johns Hopkins University Press, 1979), pp. 126–38 (134–35).

10 Lev. 11.19, Dt. 14.18; Oded Borowski, *Every Living Thing: Daily Use of Animals in Ancient Israel* (London: AltaMira, 1998), p. 149.

11 Lev. 11.16, Dt. 14.15; G.R. Driver, 'Birds in the Old Testament', *Palestine Exploration Quarterly* 87 (1955), pp. 5–20, 129–40 (12, 137–38).

12 Lev. 11.17–18, Dt. 14.17–18; Driver, 'Birds', pp. 16–18.

13 Soler, 'Semiotics', p. 135.

14 Lev. 11.21.

15 Lev. 11.9–12, Deut. 14.9–10; cf. Mercedes Salvador, 'The Oyster and the Crab: A Riddle Duo (nos. 77 and 78) in the Exeter Book', *Modern Philology* 101 (2004), pp. 400–19.

16 Noélie Vialles, *Animal to Edible* (Cambridge University Press, 1994), p. 128; also Nick Fiddes, *Meat: A Natural Symbol* (London: Routledge, 1993), pp. 226, 228.

17 Borowski, *Every Living Thing*, p. 45.

18 Douglas, *Leviticus*, pp. 134–7.

19 Ex. 20.10. See Gordon Wenham, 'The Theology of Unclean Food', *Evangelical Quarterly* 53 (1981), pp. 6–15 (10–11), and for later instances of animals subject to the law in Christian Europe, E.P. Evans, *The Criminal Prosecution and Capital Punishment of Animals* (London: Heinemann, 1906); also Claudine Fabre-Vassas, *The Singular Beast: Jews, Christians, and the Pig* (New York: Columbia University Press, 1999), pp. 125–26.

20 Ex. 13.2, 15.

21 Mary Douglas, 'Land animals, pure and impure', in *Leviticus*, pp. 134–51.

22 Corbinian Gindele, „Das Genuss von Fleisch uns Geflügel in der Magister-und Benediktusregel", *Erbe und Auftrag* 40 (1964), pp. 506–7.

23 Ambrose, *Hexameron* 6.4 (16), in *Fathers of the Church* 42 (Washington, DC: Catholic University of America Press, 1977), pp. 235–36.

24 Gerald of Wales, *The History and Topography of Ireland* (Harmondsworth: Penguin, rev. edn, 1982), p. 49.

25 Gerald, *History*, pp. 41–42.

26 Vialles, *Animal to Edible*, p. 4.

27 Josef Semmler, „'Volatilia' zu den benediktinischen Consuetudines des 9. Jahrhunderts", in *Studien und Mitteilungen zur Geschichte des Benediktinerordens* 69 (1958), pp. 163–76.

28 Mt 3.16; see Gabriel Said Reynolds, 'A medieval Islamic polemic against certain practices and doctrines of the East Syrian Church: introduction, excerpts and commentary', in *Christians at the Heart of Islamic Rule: Church Life and Scholarship in Abbasid Iraq*, ed. David Thomas (Leiden: Brill, 2003), pp. 215–30 (222–23).

29 Gen. 9.4; cf. Lev. 1.5, 11, 15; Calum M. Carmichael, 'On Separating Life and Death: An Explanation of Some Biblical Laws', *The Harvard Theological Review* 69 (1976), pp. 1–7. Also Eve Paquette, « La consommation du sang, de l'interdit biblique à l'avidité vampirique », *Religiologiques* 17 (1998), theme 'Nourriture et sacré', pp. 37–52; and for cross-cultural comparison, Anne Luxereau, « Bois le

sang, nous mangerons l'ecorce », *Ethnozootechnie* 48 (1992), theme 'L'homme et la viande', pp. 35–42.

30 1 Sam. 14.32–34; Ramban (Nachmanides), *Commentary on the Torah* (5 vols; New York: Shilo, 1971–76), vol. 3, p. 307; Borowski, *Every Living Thing*, p. 19.

31 Nah. 2.12.

32 Lev. 11.4–7; Dt. 14.7–8.

33 Lev. 11.29.

34 Ramban, *Commentary on the Torah*, vol. 3, pp. 142–43.

35 Lev. 11.27.

36 Lev. 11.13–18; see Ramban, *Commentary on the Torah*, vol. 3, p. 140.

37 Ramban, *Commentary on the Torah*, vol. 3, pp. 140–41.

38 *The Code of Maimonides*, V: *The Book of Holiness* 1.17, trans. L.I. Rabinowitz and P. Grossman (New Haven, CT: Yale University Press, 1965), p. 156.

39 Al-Jāhiz, *Le Cadi et la mouche: anthologie du Livre des animaux*, trans. L. Souami (Paris: Sindbad, 1988), p. 88.

40 Al-Jāhiz, *Le Cadi*, p. 89.

41 Simoons, *Eat Not this Flesh*, pp. 80–82.

42 Robert L. Miller, 'Hogs and Hygiene', *Journal of Egyptian Archaeology* 76 (1990), pp. 135–40 (126–27).

43 Xavier de Planhol, *The World of Islam* (Ithaca, NY: Cornell University Press, 1959), pp. 58–59. In response to the 2009 global 'swine flu' pandemic, the Egyptian government ordered a nationwide pig cull – even though no cases of swine flu had been reported in Egypt and experts advised that such a cull would be ineffective in preventing spread of the disease because it is not passed from pigs to humans. The cull was opposed by Muslim clerics on grounds of animal cruelty, and by Coptic Christians because it undermined their livelihood. Yolande Knell, 'Egypt pigs meet cruel fate in swine flu cull', BBC News Online, 29 May 2009.

44 Soler, 'Semiotics', pp. 130–32.

45 Gen. 9.3.

46 Houston, 'Monotheism without purity', in *Purity and Monotheism*, p. 258 (and 259–82).

47 Hegessipus, *Fragments from Commentaries on Acts*, in *ANF* 8, p. 762.

48 Acts 15.29.

49 Canon 67 of the Quinisext Council (or Council in Trullo), in *The Council in Trullo Revisited*, eds George Nedungatt and Michael Featherstone (Rome: Pontificio Istituto Orientale, 1995), p. 149.

50 'The Canons of Adamnan', in *Medieval Handbooks of Penance: A Translation of the Principal 'Libri Poenitentiales' and Selections from Related Documents*, eds John T. McNeill and Helena M. Gamer (New York: Columbia University Press, 1990), pp. 130–34. This, along with many of the other texts cited, is also available in parallel Latin-English translation in *The Irish Penitentials*, ed. Ludwig Bieler (The Dublin Institute for Advanced Studies, 1975). Neither collection includes the section of the Penitential of Pseudo-Egbert dealing with food, but these canons are listed in Abigail Firey, *A Contrite Heart: Prosecution and Redemption in the Carolingian Empire* (Leiden: Brill, 2009). See David Grumett, 'Mosaic food rules in Celtic spirituality in Ireland', in *Eating and Believing: Interdisciplinary Perspectives on Vegetarianism and Theology*, eds Rachel Muers and David Grumett (London: T&T Clark, 2008), pp. 31–43; Pierre Bonnassie, « Consommation d'aliments immondes et cannibalisme de survie dans l'occident du haut moyen âge », *Annales ESC* (1989), pp. 1035–56.

51 *Medieval Handbooks*, pp. 159, 176.

52 Chs XI.1 and VII.6, in *Medieval Handbooks*, pp. 207, 191.

53 Gratian, *Decretum*, pt. 1, disc. 30, ch. 13, in *Patrologiae Latinae* 187, col. 167. For more on Christian blood prohibitions, see „Blutverbot", in Karl Böckenhoff,

Speisesatzungen mosaischer Art in mittelalterlichen Kirchenrechtsquellen des Morgen-und Abendlandes (Münster: Aschendorffsche, 1907), pp. 37–49.

54 Alastair Hamilton, *The Copts and the West, 1439–1822: The European Discovery of the Egyptian Church* (Oxford University Press, 2006), p. 43.

55 Ch. XI.8, in *Medieval Handbooks*, p. 208.

56 Ann Hagen, 'Tabooed food', in *A Second Handbook of Anglo-Saxon Food and Drink: Production and Distribution* (Hockwold cum Wilton: Anglo-Saxon Books, 1995), pp. 187–94 (191–92).

57 Rob Meens, 'Eating animals in the early Middle Ages: classifying the animal world and building group identities', in *The Animal-Human Boundary: Historical Perspectives*, eds Angela N.H. Creager and William Chester Jordan (Rochester, NY: University of Rochester Press, 2002), pp. 3–28 (11–13).

58 Janet Martin Soskice, 'Blood and defilement', in *Feminism and Theology*, eds Janet Martin Soskice and Diana Lipton (Oxford University Press, 2001), pp. 333–43.

59 Lev. 17.10.

60 Michael J. Cahill, 'Drinking Blood at a Kosher Eucharist? The Sound of Scholarly Silence', *Biblical Theology Bulletin* 32 (2002), pp. 168–82. Markus Bockmuehl, *Jewish Law in Gentile Churches: Halakhah and the Beginning of Christian Public Ethics* (Edinburgh: T&T Clark, 2000), pp. 169–70, notes how Paul and Luke understandably avoid the language of blood-drinking, preferring vaguer associations with the cup.

61 Jn 6.53–56.

62 *Epistle of Barnabas* 10, in *ANF* 1, pp. 143–44.

63 James Carleton Paget, *The Epistle of Barnabas: Outlook and Background* (Tübingen: Mohr, 1994), pp. 149–53.

64 S. Stein, 'The Dietary Laws in Rabbinic and Patristic Literature', *Studia Patristica* 2 (Berlin: Akademie, 1957), pp. 141–53 (146–48); Robert M. Grant, *Early Christians and Animals* (London: Routledge, 1999), pp. 13–14; Katherine Dell, 'The Use of Animal Imagery in the Psalms and Wisdom Literature of Ancient Israel', *Scottish Journal of Theology* 53 (2000), pp. 275–91 (278–85).

65 Philo, *On the Special Laws* 4.97–118 (Cambridge, MA: Harvard University Press, 1939), pp. 66–81.

66 On this medieval shift in Christian attitudes to Judaism, see Jeremy Cohen, *Living Letters of the Law: Ideas of the Jew in Medieval Christianity* (Berkeley: University of California Press, 1999); Anna Sapir Abulafia, *Christians and Jews in Dispute: Disputational Literature and the Rise of Anti-Judaism in the West* (Aldershot: Ashgate, 1998); John Van Engen, 'Introduction: Jews and Christians together in the twelfth century', in *Jews and Christians in Twelfth-century Europe*, eds Michael A. Signer and John Van Engen (Notre Dame, IN: Notre Dame University Press, 2001), pp. 1–8.

67 Abigail Firey, 'The letter of the Law: Carolingian exegetes and the Old Testament', in *With Reverence for the Word: Medieval Scriptural Exegesis in Judaism, Christianity, and Islam*, eds Jane Dammen McAuliffe, Barry D. Walfish and Joseph W. Goering (New York: Oxford University Press, 2003), pp. 204–24.

68 Cohen, *Living Letters*, p. 350.

69 Cohen, *Living Letters*, pp. 351–52.

70 'The Maccabees', in *Aelfric's Lives of the Saints: Being a Set of Sermons on Saints' Days Formerly Observed in the English Church* (4 vols; London: Oxford University Press, 1966), vol. 2, pp. 68–73.

71 Jeremy Cohen, *The Friars and the Jews: The Evolution of Medieval Anti-Judaism* (Ithaca, NY: Cornell University Press, 1982), p. 220.

72 Henri de Lubac, *The Splendor of the Church* (San Francisco, CA: Ignatius, 1986), p. 159; see David Grumett, *Henri de Lubac: A Guide for the Perplexed* (New York: T&T Clark, 2007), pp. 75–94.

73 Henri de Lubac, *Medieval Exegesis*, vol. 2 (Edinburgh: T&T Clark, 2000), p. 52.

74 On recent Jewish interpretations, see Aaron Gross, 'Continuity and Change in Reform Views of *Kashrut* 1883–2002: From the Treifah Banquet to Eco-Kashrut', *CCAR Journal* (Winter 2004), pp. 6–28.

75 Fabre-Vassas, *Singular Beast*, pp. 236–37.

76 Fabre-Vassas, *Singular Beast*, p. 239.

77 W.O.E. Oesterley, 'Why was the Hare Considered "Unclean" Among the Israelites?', *Churchman* 18 (1904), pp. 146–53.

78 *Timotheus of Gaza on Animals* (Paris: Académie internationale d'histoire des sciences, 1949), pp. 28, 19.

79 Clement of Alexandria, *Le Pédagogue* 2.10 (3 vols; Paris: Cerf, 1960–70), vol. 2, pp. 166–67, 172–73. In *ANF* 2 at pp. 259–63, this portion of *The Instructor* is left in Latin rather than translated, lest the uneducated be corrupted.

80 Timothy Insoll, *The Archaeology of Islam* (Oxford: Blackwell, 1999), p. 95.

81 Ad-Damîrî, *Hayât al-hayawân* (*A Zoological Lexicon*), trans. A.S.G. Jayakar (2 vols; London and Bombay: Luzac, 1906–8), vol. 1, p. 42. For critique of this theme, see Melissa Raphael, 'A feminist menstrual taboo', in *Thealogy and Embodiment: The Post-Patriarchal Reconstruction of Female Sacrality* (Sheffield Academic Press, 1996), pp. 167–82.

82 Basil the Great, Homily 7.2, trans. in Grant, *Early Christians and Animals*, p. 81.

83 Augustine, *On the Morals of the Manichaeans* 17.61; *Reply to Faustus the Manichaean* 6.8; in *NPNF* I.4, pp. 85, 172.

84 On early Christians' consumption of fish, see Michael Northcott, 'Eucharistic eating, and why many early Christians preferred fish', in *Eating and Believing*, pp. 232–46, esp. 242–43.

85 Ramban, *Commentary on the Torah*, vol. 1, pp. 118–19.

86 Jn 21.9–14. For more on the social, political, economic and military consequences of the Christian tradition of fish eating, see David Grumett, 'Dining in the kingdom: fish eating and Christian geography', in press.

87 Augustine Thompson, 'The Afterlife of an Error: Hunting in the Decretalists (1190–1348)', *Studia Canonica* 33, 1 (1999), pp. 151–68; idem, 'Misreading and rereading patristic texts: the prohibition of hunting by the Decretalists', in *Proceedings of the Ninth International Congress of Medieval Canon Law, 13–18 July 1992*, eds Peter Landau and Joers Mueller (Vatican City: Biblioteca Apostolica Vaticana, 1997), pp. 135–48.

88 Sg 4.11; Ex. 33.3; Ps 119.103; Rachel Fulton, '"Taste and See That the Lord is Sweet" (Ps. 33:9): The Flavor of God in the Monastic West', *The Journal of Religion* 86, 2 (2006), pp. 169–204.

89 Debra Shostak, 'An appetite for America: Philip Roth's antipastorals', in *Eating in Eden: Food and American Utopias*, eds Etta M. Madden and Martha L. Finch (Lincoln: University of Nebraska Press, 2006), pp. 74–88; Hasia R. Diner, 'Food fights: immigrant Jews and the lure of America', in *Hungering for America: Italian, Irish, and Jewish Foodways in the Age of Migration* (Cambridge, MA: Harvard University Press, 2002), pp. 178–219.

6 Community, Orthodoxy and Heresy

1 Augustine, *Confessions* 4.1 (1) (Oxford University Press, 1998), p. 52.

2 Jason David DeBuhn, *The Manichaean Body in Discipline and Ritual* (Baltimore, MD: Johns Hopkins, 2002), pp. 126–62; J.-E. Ménard, « Les Repas 'sacrés' des gnostiques », *Revue des sciences religieuses* 55 (1981), pp. 43–51.

3 F.C. Burkitt, *The Religion of the Manichees* (Cambridge University Press, 1925), pp. 59–60.

4 Augustine, *Reply to Faustus the Manichean* 5.10; *On the Morals of the Manicheans* 17.53; in *NPNF* I.4, pp. 167, 83.

5 A. von Le Coq, 'Dr. Stein's Turkish *khuastuanift* from Tun-Huang, Being a Confession-Prayer of the Manichaean Auditores', *The Journal of the Royal Asiatic Society* (1911), pp. 277–314 (287).

6 Kurt Rudolph, *Gnosis: The Nature and History of Gnosticism* (New York: HarperSanFrancisco, 1987), p. 341; DeBuhn, *Manichaean Body*, p. 130; Augustine, *Reply to Faustus* 5.10, p. 166.

7 Peter Brown, *Augustine of Hippo: A Biography* (London: Faber & Faber, 1967), pp. 43, 54, 58.

8 Brown, *Augustine*, pp. 203–4.

9 Brown, *Augustine*, pp. 370, 393–95.

10 Richard Lim, 'The *nomen manichaeorum* and its uses in late antiquity', in *Heresy and Identity in Late Antiquity*, eds Eduard Iricinschi and Holger M. Zellentin (Tübingen: Mohr Siebeck, 2008), pp. 143–67 (152–53).

11 Veronika Grimm, 'Augustine and ascetic practice', in *From Feasting to Fasting, the Evolution of a Sin: Attitudes to Food in Late Antiquity* (London: Routledge, 1996), pp. 180–97 (186).

12 François Decret, *L'Afrique manichéenne (IVe–Ve siècles): étude historique et doctrinale* (2 vols; Paris: Études Augustiniennes, 1978), vol. 1, pp. 192–93.

13 Augustine, *On the Morals of the Manichaeans* 17.62, p. 86.

14 Augustine, *On the Morals of the Manichaeans* 17.54, p. 84, discussing Mt. 8.32, 21.19; also *The City of God Against the Pagans* (7 vols; Cambridge, MA: Harvard University Press, 1957–72), vol. 1, pp. 92–93. See Henry Chadwick, 'Humanity in ancient writers, pagan and Christian', in *Studies on Ancient Christianity* (Aldershot: Ashgate, 2006), XXI, p. 3; Issa J. Khalil, 'The Orthodox Fast and the Philosophy of Vegetarianism', *Greek Orthodox Theological Review* 35 (1990), pp. 237–59 (245).

15 Augustine, *On the Morals of the Manichaeans* 17.59, p. 85.

16 Augustine, *Reply to Faustus* 6.4, p. 169.

17 Augustine, *Reply to Faustus* 6.5, p. 170.

18 Augustine, *Reply to Faustus* 6.8, p. 171.

19 Augustine, *On the Morals of the Manichaeans* 17.52, p. 83.

20 Augustine, *On the Morals of the Manichaeans* 14.30, p. 77.

21 Kam-lun Edwin Lee, *Augustine, Manichaeism, and the Good* (New York: Lang, 1999), p. 56.

22 Decret, *L'Afrique manichéenne*, vol. 1, p. 27.

23 Rudolph, *Gnosis*, p. 341; W.B. Henning and S.H. Taqizadeh, 'The Manichean Fasts', *The Journal of the Royal Asiatic Society* (1945), pp. 146–64.

24 *The Kephalaia of the Teacher: The Edited Coptic Manichaean Texts in Translation with Commentary*, 79, 81, ed. Iain Gardner (Leiden: Brill, 1995), pp. 200, 202.

25 Gerald Bonner, *St Augustine of Hippo: Life and Controversies* (London: SCM, 1963), p. 172; *Kephalia* 81, p. 202; Henri-Charles Puech, « Liturgie et pratiques rituelles dans le manichéisme », *Annuaire du Collège de France* 60 (1960), pp. 181–89 (184).

26 Possidius, *Life of St. Augustine* 22, in *The Western Fathers: Being the Lives of SS. Martin of Tours, Ambrose, Augustine of Hippo, Honoratus of Arles, and Germanus of Auxerre* (London: Sheed and Ward, 1954), p. 220.

27 Augustine, *On the Morals of the Catholic Church* 33.72, in *NPNF* I.4, p. 61.

28 Augustine, *Reply to Faustus* 30.5, p. 330.

29 Leo Ferrari, 'The "Food of Truth" in Augustine's Confessions', *Augustinian Studies* 9 (1978), pp. 1–14.

30 Leo Ferrari, 'The Gustatory Augustine', *Augustiniana* 29 (1979), pp. 304–15.

31 Augustine, *On the Good of Marriage* 18, in *NPNF* I.3, p. 407; also Letter 47.6 to Publicola, in *NPNF* I.1, p. 294.

32 David M. Freidenreich, 'Sharing Meals with Non-Christians in Canon Law Commentaries, Circa 1160–1260: A Case Study in Legal Development', *Medieval Encounters* 14 (2008), pp. 41–77.

33   Henricus Institoris and Jacobus Sprenger, *Malleus Maleficarum* 1.14 (2 vols; Cambridge University Press, 2006), vol. 2, p. 184.
34   Grimm, *From Feasting to Fasting*, p. 187.
35   Possidius, *Life* 22, p. 220.
36   Augustine, *Confessions* 10.31 (46), p. 206; Gen. 25.29–34; Mt. 4.3, Lk. 4.3.
37   G. Stroumsa, « Monachisme et Marranisme chez les Manichéens d'Égypte », *Numen* 29 (1982), pp. 184–201 (195).
38   Jerome, Letter 22 to Eustochium 13, in *NPNF* II.6, p. 27.
39   Claire Taylor, *Heresy in Medieval France: Dualism in Aquitaine and the Agenais, 1000–1249* (London: Royal Historical Society, 2005), p. 60.
40   Teresa M. Shaw, 'Ascetic practice in the genealogy of heresy: problems in modern scholarship and ancient textual representation', in *The Cultural Turn in Late Ancient Studies: Gender, Asceticism, and Historiography*, eds Dale B. Martin and Patricia Cox Miller (Durham, NC: Duke University Press, 2005), p. 213–36 (220–21, 226–27).
41   Augustine Casiday, *Tradition and Theology in St John Cassian* (Oxford University Press, 2007), p. 52.
42   Teresa M. Shaw, 'Vegetarianism, heresy, and asceticism in late ancient Christianity', in *Eating and Believing: Interdisciplinary Perspectives on Vegetarianism and Theology*, eds Rachel Muers and David Grumett (London: T&T Clark, 2008), pp. 75–95; Dianne M. Bazell, 'Strife among the Table-Fellows: Conflicting Attitudes of Early and Medieval Christians toward the Eating of Meat', *Journal of the American Academy of Religion* 65 (1997), pp. 73–99 (89–92); M. Alfred Schroll, *Benedictine Monasticism as Reflected in the Warnefrid-Hildemar Commentaries on the Rule* (New York: Columbia University Press, 1941), pp. 176–77.
43   Origen, *Contra Celsum* 8.30, trans. Henry Chadwick (Cambridge University Press, 1953), pp. 473–74.
44   Basil of Caesarea, *The Longer Responses* 18, in *The Asketikon of St Basil the Great*, ed. Anna Silvas (Oxford University Press, 2005), p. 212.
45   Phillip Rousseau, *Basil of Caesarea* (Berkeley: University of California Press, 1998), pp. 191, 195–201.
46   Basil of Caesarea, Letter 2.6 to Gregory, in *NPNF* II.8, p. 112.
47   David Amand, *L'Ascèse monastique de Saint Basile: essai historique* (Paris: Maredsous, 1948), pp. 222–23.
48   Basil of Caesarea, *Letters* 14 (4 vols; London: Heinemann, 1926–39), vol. 1, pp. 110–11.
49   Charges against the Eustathians 8–9, in *Asketikon*, p. 488.
50   Canons of the Council of Gangra 2, 18–19, in *Asketikon*, pp. 490, 492.
51   John Meyendorff, *The Byzantine Legacy in the Orthodox Church* (Crestwood, NY: St Vladimir's, 1982), pp. 199–204.
52   *The Rule of the Master* 53, trans. Luke Eberle (Kalamazoo, MI: Cistercian, 1977), p. 217.
53   *The Book of Pontiffs (Liber Pontificalis): The Ancient Biographies of the First Ninety Roman Bishops to* AD *715*, ed. Raymond Davis (Liverpool University Press, 1989), pp. 42, 44–5, 48; *La Règle du Maître*, ed. Adalbert de Vogüé (3 vols; Paris: Cerf, 1964–65), vol. 2, p. 247, n.
54   Casiday, *Tradition*, p. 52.
55   Henry Chadwick, *Priscillian of Avila: The Occult and the Charismatic in the Early Church* (Oxford: Clarendon, 1976), pp. 79–80, 176, 225.
56   Chadwick, *Priscillian*, pp. 14, 166.
57   Augustine, Letter 36.28 to Casulanus, in *NPNF* I.1, pp. 268–69.
58   John R. Fortin, 'Saint Augustine's *Letter 211* in *The Rule of the Master* and *The Rule of Saint Benedict*', *Journal of Early Christian Studies* 14, 2 (2006), pp. 225–34.
59   *Rule of the Master* 53, p. 217.

60 *The Rule of St. Benedict* 39, trans. Justin McCann (London: Sheed & Ward, 1989), p. 46.

61 Bazell, 'Strife', pp. 81–83; *La Règle du Maître*, vol. 6, p. 1105–8; Marie-Odile Garrigues, 'Honorius Augustodunensis, *De esu volatilium*', *Studia Monastica* 28 (1986), pp. 75–130; Josef Semmler, „'Volatilia': zu den benediktinischen Consuetudines des 9. Jahrhunderts", in *Studien und Mitheilungen zur Geschichte des Benediktinerordens* 69 (1958), pp. 163–76; Schroll, *Benedictine Monasticism*, pp. 176–77.

62 Basil of Caesarea, *The Ascetic Works*, ed. W.K.L. Clarke (London: SPCK, 1925), p. 29; H. Marti, 'Rufinus's Translation of St. Basil's Sermon on Fasting', *Studia Patristica* 16, 2 (Berlin: Akademia, 1985), pp. 418–22 (422); F.X. Murphy, *Rufinus of Aquileia, 345–411: His Life and Works* (Washington, DC: Catholic University of America Press, 1945), p. 50, n. 86.

63 Steven Runciman, *The Medieval Manichee: A Study of the Christian Dualist Heresy* (Cambridge University Press, 1947), pp. 151–52, 159–60; Taylor, *Heresy*, pp. 60, 65, 94, 133.

64 Ylva Hagman, « Le Catharisme, un néo-manichéisme? », *Heresis* 21 (1993), pp. 47–59 (54–55).

65 Anne Brenon, *Les Cathares: vie et mort d'une église chrétienne* (Paris: Grancher, 1996).

66 Runciman, *Medieval Manichee*, p. 160.

67 Bernard of Clairvaux, Sermon 64.5, in *On the Song of Songs* (4 vols; Kalamazoo, MI: Cistercian, 1971–80), vol. 3, p. 172.

68 Dominique Tourault, *Saint Dominique face aux cathares* (Paris: Perrin, 1999).

69 Bazell, 'Strife', pp. 90–91.

70 Tristram Stuart, *The Bloodless Revolution: Radical Vegetarians and the Discovery of India* (London: HarperPress, 2006), p. 7.

71 R.G. [Robert Govett], *The Future Apostacy* (London: Nisbet, 2nd edn, n.d. [c1880]), p. 42.

72 Stuart, *Bloodless Revolution*, pp. 261–63.

73 Stuart, *Bloodless Revolution*, pp. 266–67.

74 Caroline and Filippo Osella, 'Food, Memory, Community: Kerala as both "Indian Ocean" Zone and as Agricultural Homeland', *South Asia: Journal of South Asian Studies* 31, 1 (2008), special issue 'Food: Memory, Pleasure and Politics', pp. 170–98.

75 Jacob A. Klein, 'Afterword: Comparing Vegetarianisms', *South Asia: Journal of South Asian Studies* 31, 1 (2008), pp. 199–212.

76 Pieter Verdam, *Mosaic Law in Practice and Study throughout the Ages* (Kampen: Kok, 1959), p. 19.

77 For an overview of possible reasons for the prohibition, see Marvin Harris, 'The abominable pig', in *Good to Eat: Riddles of Food and Culture* (New York: Simon and Shuster, 1985), pp. 67–87; idem, 'Forbidden flesh', in *Cannibals and Kings: The Origins of Cultures* (New York: Random House, 1977), pp. 193–208.

78 2 Mac. 6.18–7.42. See Peter Schäfer, 'Abstinence from pork', in *Judeophobia: Attitudes Toward the Jews in the Ancient World* (Cambridge, MA: Harvard University Press, 1999), pp. 66–81. For the heightened importance of food rules in the exilic period see Nathan MacDonald, 'Food and drink in Tobit and other "diaspora novellas"', in *Studies in the Book of Tobit: A Multidisciplinary Approach*, ed. M.R.J. Bredin, Library of Second Temple Studies 55 (London: Sheffield Academic Press, 2006), pp. 165–78.

79 Walter Houston, *Purity and Monotheism: Clean and Unclean Animals in Biblical Law* (Sheffield: JSOT Press, 1993), p. 14.

80 Fabre-Vassas, *Singular Beast*, pp. 233–57.

81 Fabre-Vassas, *Singular Beast*, p. 255.

82 Fabre-Vassas, *Singular Beast*, pp. 325–36.

83 Boria Sax, *Animals in the Third Reich: Pets, Scapegoats, and the Holocaust* (London: Continuum, 2000), p. 66.

84 Sax, *Animals*, p. 67.
85 Noël Coulet, « 'Juif intouchable' et interdits alimentaires », in *Exclus et systèmes d'exclusion dans la littérature et la civilisation médiévales* (Aix-en-Provence: CUERMA, 1978), pp. 207–21.
86 Louis Stouff, *Ravitaillement et alimentation en Provence aux XIVe et XVe siècles* (La Haye: Mouton, 1970), pp. 182, 184, 192–93.
87 Solomon Grayzel, *The Church and the Jews in the XIIIth Century, 1254–1314*, ed. Kenneth Stow (2 vols; Detroit, MI: Wayne State University Press, 1989), vol. 2, pp. 247, 251, 255, 270.
88 Michael Alpert, *Crypto-Judaism and the Spanish Inquisition* (Basingstoke: Palgrave, 2001), pp. 196–97.
89 Mary Elizabeth Perry, 'Moriscas and the limits of assimilation', in *Christians, Muslims, and Jews in Medieval and Early Modern Spain: Interaction and Cultural Change*, eds Mark D. Meyerson and Edward D. English (Notre Dame, IN: University of Notre Dame Press, 2000), pp. 274–89 (279); also Deborah Root, 'Speaking Christian: Orthodoxy and Difference in Sixteenth-Century Spain', *Representations* 23 (1988), pp. 118–34.
90 Renée Levine Melammed, 'Crypto-Jewish women facing the Spanish Inquisition: transmitting religious practices, beliefs, and attitudes', in *Christians, Muslims, and Jews*, pp. 197–219 (198).
91 Grayzel, *Church and the Jews*, p. 246; also 39, 267, 270.
92 Marie France Godfroy, « La minorité juive dans le Languedoc hérétique », *Heresis* 13–14 (1990), pp. 393–419.
93 Freidenreich, 'Sharing Meals', p. 47.
94 Jeremy Cohen, *Living Letters of the Law: Ideas of the Jew in Medieval Christianity* (Berkeley: University of California Press, 1999), p. 133.
95 Coulet, « 'Juif intouchable' », pp. 212–13.
96 Kees Wagtendonk, *Fasting in the Koran* (Leiden: Brill, 1968), pp. 41–43, 102–3, 128–29, 137.
97 Muhammad Husayn Haykal, *The Life of Muhammad* (Indianapolis, IN: North American Trust Publications, 1976), pp. 58–61; Marjo Buitelaar, *Fasting and Feasting in Morocco: Women's Participation in Ramadan* (Oxford: Berg, 1993), p. 24.
98 Muhammad Abū Hamīd Al-Ghazālī, *On Disciplining the Soul: Kitāb riyādāat al-nafs and On Breaking the Two Desires: Kitāb kasr al-shahwatayn* (Cambridge: Islamic Texts Society, 1995), pp. 133–34.
99 Kees Wagtendonk, *Fasting in the Koran* (Leiden: Brill, 1968).
100 Buitelaar, *Fasting and Feasting*, pp. 33–34, 112–13; Wagtendonk, *Fasting*, pp. 103–4.
101 Freidenreich, 'Sharing Meals', pp. 58–64; Allan Harris Cutler and Helen Elmquist Cutler, *The Jew as Ally of the Muslim: Medieval Roots of Anti-Semitism* (Notre Dame, IN: University of Notre Dame Press, 1986), p. 411, n. 52.
102 Al-Jāhiz, *Le Cadi*, p. 332; Xavier de Planhol, *The World of Islam* (Ithaca: Cornell University Press, 1959), pp. 57–58.
103 Freidenreich, 'Sharing Meals', pp. 51–58.
104 Ulrich Braukämper, 'On food avoidances in Southern Ethiopia: religious manifestation and socio-economic relevance', in *Proceedings of the Seventh International Conference of Ethiopian Studies 1982, Lund*, ed. Sven Rubenson (Addis Ababa: Institute of Ethiopian Studies, 1984), pp. 429–45.
105 Frederick J. Simoons, *Eat Not this Flesh: Food Avoidances from Prehistory to the Present* (Madison: University of Wisconsin Press, 1994), p. 198.
106 Suliman Bashear, 'Riding Beasts on Divine Missions: An Examination of the Ass and Camel Traditions', *Journal of Semitic Studies* 37 (1991), pp. 37–75.
107 Timothy Insoll, *The Archaeology of Islam* (Oxford: Blackwell, 1999), pp. 98–99, 103–4.
108 Stephen Webb, *Good Eating: The Bible, Diet and the Proper Love of Animals* (Grand Rapids, MI: Brazos, 2001).

109 Nick Fiddes, 'Declining meat: past, present … and future imperfect?', in *Food, Health and Identity*, ed. Pat Caplan (London: Routledge, 1997), pp. 252–67. For the social profile of vegetarians, see Donna Maurer, *Vegetarianism: Movement or Moment?* (Philadelphia, PA: Temple University Press, 2002).
110 Warren Belasco, *Appetite for Change: How the Counterculture took on the Food Industry* (Ithaca, NY: Cornell University Press, 2nd edn, 2007), pp. ix–xi.

7 Sacrifice and Slaughter

1 Jean-Louis Durand, 'Greek animals: towards a topology of edible bodies', in *The Cuisine of Sacrifice among the Greeks*, eds Marcel Detienne and Jean-Pierre Vernant (Chicago, IL: University of Chicago Press, 1989), pp. 87–118 (87).
2 Frances M. Young, *Sacrifice and the Death of Christ* (London: SPCK, 1975), pp. 50–51. For examples, see R.P.C. Hanson, 'The Christian Attitude to Pagan Religions', *Aufsteig und Neidergang der römischen Welt* 23, 2 (1980), pp. 910–73 (915–17); Maria-Zoe Petropoulou, *Animal Sacrifice in Ancient Greek Religion, 100BC–AD200* (Oxford University Press, 2008), pp. 246–51.
3 *The Theodosian Code* 16.9.2 (Princeton, NJ: Princeton University Press, 1952), p. 472.
4 Ingvild Sælid Gilhus, *Animals, Gods and Humans: Changing Attitudes to Animals in Greek, Roman and Early Christian Ideas* (London: Routledge, 2006), pp. 154–57.
5 Prudentius, 'A Reply to the Address of Symmachus', I.449–54, in *Works* (2 vols; Cambridge, MA: Harvard University Press, 1949), vol. 1, pp. 384–85.
6 *Theodosian Code* 16.9, pp. 472–76.
7 Susan Power Bratton, 'Urbanization and the end of animal sacrifice', in *Environmental Values in Christian Art* (State University of New York Press, 2009), pp. 87–106.
8 A. Sharf, 'Animal Sacrifice in the Armenian Church', *Revue des études arméniennes* 16 (1982), pp. 417–49 (418–21).
9 'Epistle of Nerses Shnorhali', in *Rituale Armenorum: Being the Administration of the Sacraments and the Breviary Rites of the Armenian Church together with the Greek Rites of Baptism and Epiphany*, eds F.C. Conybeare and A.J. Maclean (Oxford: Clarendon, 1905), pp. 77–85 (78–79).
10 'Epistle of Nerses Shnorhali', p. 83.
11 'Epistle of Nerses Shnorhali', p. 79.
12 Sharf, 'Animal Sacrifice', pp. 418–21.
13 Canons of St Sahak, in *Rituale Armenorum*, pp. 67–71.
14 'Epistle of Nerses Shnorhali', p. 82.
15 Joseph Tixeront, « Le rite du *matal* », in *Mélanges de patrologie et d'histoire des dogmes* (Paris: Gabalda, 1921), pp. 261–78 (277–78).
16 Tixeront, « Le rite du *matal* », pp. 276–77.
17 Gregory the Great, *Epistle* XI.76, in *NPNF* II.13, p. 85.
18 Tixeront, « Le rite du *matal* », pp. 272, 274.
19 For contemporary German religion, see Ian N. Wood, 'Pagan religions and superstitions east of the Rhine from the fifth to the ninth century', in *After Empire: Towards an Ethnology of Europe's Barbarians*, ed. G. Ausenda (Woodbridge: Boydell, 1995), pp. 253–68 (262–63).
20 Decrees of the Synod of 742, in *The Letters of Saint Boniface*, trans. Ephraim Emerton (New York: Columbia University Press, 1940), p. 92.
21 Letter of Pope Zacharius, 1 May 748, in *Letters of Saint Boniface*, p. 144.
22 William Dalrymple, *From the Holy Mountain: A Journey in the Shadow of Byzantium* (London: Harper, 2005), pp. 169, 340–41; Cérès Wissa-Wassef, *Pratiques rituelles et alimentaires des coptes* (Cairo: Institut français d archéologie orientale du Caire, 1971), p. 332; F.C. Conybeare, 'The Survival of Animal Sacrifice Inside the Christian Church', *American Journal of Theology* 7 (1903), pp. 62–90 (89).

23 Stella Georgoudi, 'Sanctified slaughter in modern Greece: the "kourbánia" of the saints', in *Cuisine of Sacrifice*, pp. 183–203.

24 Mt. 7.6.

25 The presence and key role of clergy is attested in M.D. Girard, « Les 'madag' ou sacrifices arméniens », *Revue de l'orient chrétien* 7 (1902), pp. 410–22.

26 Georgoudi, 'Sanctified slaughter', p. 190.

27 Georgoudi, 'Sanctified slaughter', pp. 195–96.

28 Some Greek prayers are translated in F.C. Conybeare, « Les sacrifices d'animaux dans les anciennes églises chrétiennes », *Revue de l'historie des religions* 44 (1901), pp. 108–14.

29 Georgoudi, 'Sanctified slaughter', p. 199.

30 Georgoudi, 'Sanctified slaughter', p. 190.

31 Michael Findikyan, 'A Sacrifice of Praise: Blessing of the Madagh', *Window Quarterly* 2, 4 (1992), at www.geocities.com/derghazar/MADAGH.DOC [acessed 15 June 2009].

32 Heb. 13.15.

33 Lk. 14.12–14; Heb. 13.16.

34 Georgoudi, 'Sanctified slaughter', p. 185.

35 Bryan S. Turner, *The Body and Society: Explorations in Social Theory* (London: Sage, 2nd edn, 1996), p. xiii, reflecting on the use of Francisco Goya's still life of the head and ribs of a sheep for the cover illustration of the second edition.

36 In classical Greece, most if not all meat was the product of sacrificial ritual, either directly or indirectly, such as from butchers who purchased sacrificial meat. The situation was different in Rome, where a secular meat market also thrived. John Wilkins and Shaun Hill, *Food in the Ancient World* (London: Blackwell, 2006), pp. 143–44; Michael Jameson, 'Sacrifice and animal husbandry in Classical Greece', in *Pastoral Economies in Classical Antiquity*, ed. C.R. Whittaker (Cambridge Philological Society, 1988), pp. 87–119.

37 Walter Burkert, *Homo Necans: The Anthropology of Ancient Greek Sacrificial Ritual and Myth* (Berkeley: University of California Press, 1983), pp. 8–9.

38 Sharf, 'Animal Sacrifice', pp. 427–28.

39 Jone Salomonsen, 'Shielding girls at risk of AIDS by weaving Zulu and Christian ritual heritage', in *Broken Bodies and Healing Communities: Reflections on Church-based Responses to HIV/AIDS in a South African Township*, ed. Neville Richardson (Pietermaritzburg: Cluster, 2009).

40 Harold Walter Turner, *History of an African Independent Church* (2 vols; Oxford: Clarendon, 1967), vol. 2, pp. 349–50, suggests that sacrifice might be an inevitably prominent feature of African Christianity, even when not involving actual sacrifices of animals.

41 Samuel I. Britt, '"Sacrifice Honors God": Ritual Struggle in a Liberian Church', *Journal of the American Academy of Religion* 76 (2008), pp. 1–26 (16).

42 Porphyry, *On Abstinence from Killing Animals*, I.25 (4–9), trans. Gillian Clark (London: Duckworth, 1999), pp. 39–40.

43 Plutarch, *Table-talk* 8, 729F, in *Moralia*, vol. 9 (14 vols; Cambridge, MA: Harvard University Press, 1961), pp. 180–81.

44 Dennis Trout, 'Christianizing the Nolan Countryside: Animal Sacrifice at the Tomb of St. Felix', *Journal of Early Christian Studies* 3 (1995), pp. 281–98 (287, also 291–92).

45 Dalrymple, *From the Holy Mountain*, p. 191.

46 Rebecca West, *Black Lamb and Grey Falcon: The Record of a Journey through Yugoslavia in 1937* (2 vols; London: Macmillan, 1942), vol. 2, pp. 200–10.

47 West, *Black Lamb*, vol. 2, p. 298.

48 West, *Black Lamb*, vol. 2, p. 205.

49 See Michael Beer, '"The question is not, Can they *reason*? nor, Can they *talk*? but, Can they *suffer*?": the ethics of vegetarianism in the writings of Plutarch', in *Eating and Believing: Interdisciplinary Perspectives on Vegetarianism and Theology*, eds

Rachel Muers and David Grumett (London: T&T Clark, 2008), pp. 96–109 (100, 103, 105).

50 Plutarch, 'On the Eating of Flesh' II, 998B, in *Moralia*, vol. 12 (Cambridge, MA: Harvard University Press, 1957), pp. 572–73.

51 Plutarch, 'Whether Land or Sea Animals are Cleverer', 959E, in *Moralia*, vol. 12, pp. 322–23.

52 Carol J. Adams, *The Sexual Politics of Meat: A Feminist-Vegetarian Critical Theory* (New York: Continuum, 1995), pp. 120–41. For a similar current argument, see David Nibert, *Animal Rights/Human Rights: Entanglements of Oppression and Liberation* (Lanham, MD: Rowman & Littlefield, 2002).

53 Tristram Stuart, *The Bloodless Revolution: Radical Vegetarians and the Discovery of India* (London: HarperPress, 2006), p. 38.

54 Clement of Alexandria, *Instructor* 2.1, in *ANF* 2, p. 238.

55 The classic modern statement of this thesis is Frances Moore Lappé, *Diet for a Small Planet* (New York: Ballantine, 1991), pp. 158–82; for its history, see Warren Belasco, *Meals to Come: A History of the Future of Food* (Berkeley: University of California Press, 2006), pp. 4–9; for a recent assessment highlighting the huge stake of arable agribusiness in pastoral farming, Colin Tudge, *So Shall We Reap* (London: Allen Lane, 2003).

56 Plato, *Republic* 373c-e (2 vols; Cambridge, MA: Harvard University Press, 1930–35), vol. 1, pp. 160–65; Daniel Dombrowski, 'Two Vegetarian Puns at *Republic* 372', *Ancient Philosophy* 9 (1990), pp. 167–71.

57 Karen and Michael Iacobbo, *Vegetarian America: A History* (Westport, CT: Praeger, 2004), p. 162.

58 Gen. 4.

59 Ben Rogers, *Beef and Liberty: Roast Beef, John Bull and the English Nation* (London: Chatto & Windus, 2003), pp. 10–18.

60 Jeremy Rifkin, *Beyond Beef: The Rise and Fall of the Cattle Culture* (New York: Dutton, 1993), pp. 52–55.

61 John R. Gillis, *A World of their Own Making: Myth, Ritual and the Quest for Family Values* (Cambridge, MA: Harvard University Press, 1996), p. 92.

62 Georgoudi, 'Sanctified slaughter', p. 185.

63 Gregory of Nyssa, 'On the three-day period of the resurrection of our Lord Jesus Christ', in *The Easter Sermons of Gregory of Nyssa* (Cambridge, MA: Philadelphia Patristic Foundation, 1981), p. 32; see Ex. 22.13.

64 Heb. 10.1–14.

65 René Girard, *Violence and the Sacred* (London: Athlone, 1995).

66 Robert J. Daly, *Christian Sacrifice: The Judaeo-Christian Background before Origen* (Washington, DC: Catholic University of America Press, 1978), p. 493.

67 Lev. 6–7.

68 Stephen H. Webb, *On God and Dogs: A Christian Theology of Compassion for Animals* (New York: Oxford University Press, 1998), p. 166.

69 Num. 28–29.

70 Mal. 1.6–14.

71 Oded Borowski, *Every Living Thing: Daily Use of Animals in Ancient Israel* (London: AltaMira, 1998), pp. 57, 215.

72 Issa J. Khalil, 'The Orthodox Fast and the Philosophy of Vegetarianism', *Greek Orthodox Theological Review* 35 (1990), pp. 237–59 (246).

73 George Galavaris, *Bread and the Liturgy* (Madison: University of Wisconsin Press, 1970), p. 32. Galavaris suggests, less plausibly, that the images point to the influence of pagan sacred animal cults.

74 Karl Barth, *Church Dogmatics* (14 vols; Edinburgh: T&T Clark, 1936–77), III.4, p. 354.

75 Barth, *Church Dogmatics*, III.4, p. 355.

76 Barth, *Church Dogmatics*, III.1, p. 210.
77 James H. Marrow, *Passion Iconography in Northern European Art of the Late Middle Ages and Early Renaissance: A Study of the Transformation of Sacred Metaphor into Descriptive Narrative* (Kortrijk: Van Ghemmert, 1979), pp. 300, n. 480; 301, n. 483.
78 Jn 19.31–34; cf. Ex. 12.7,10,46.
79 Ex. 12.22.
80 Craig S. Keener, *The Gospel of John: A Commentary* (2 vols; Peabody, MA: Hendrickson, 2003), vol. 2, p. 1153.
81 Margaret Barker, *Temple Themes in Christian Worship* (London: T&T Clark, 2008); idem, *The Great High Priest: The Temple Roots of Christian Liturgy* (London: T&T Clark, 2003).
82 Dan Cohn-Sherbok, 'Hope for the animal kingdom: a Jewish vision', in *A Communion of Subjects: Animals in Religion, Science, and Ethics*, eds Paul Waldau and Kimberley Patton (New York: Columbia University Press, 2006), pp. 81–90 (85–86); Ramban (Nachmanides), *Commentary on the Torah* (5 vols; New York: Shilo, 1971–76), vol. 1, p. 58. The claim has a long history in Western thought: Francis Bacon, Isaac Newton and Alexander Pope, among others, argued that the Mosaic sacrificial practices were less cruel than alternatives, especially those more common in the Western Europe of their day such as strangulation or hammer blows to the head. Stuart, *Bloodless Revolution*, pp. 103, 106.
83 Al-Hafiz Basheer Ahmad Masri, *Animal Welfare in Islam* (Markfield: The Islamic Foundation, 2007), pp. 34–35.
84 Stephen R.L. Clark, *Biology and Christian Ethics* (Cambridge University Press, 2000), p. 289.
85 Aaron Gross, 'When Kosher Isn't Kosher', *Tikkun Magazine* 20, 2 (2005).
86 Cohn-Sherbok, 'Hope', p. 86.
87 Girard, « Les 'madag' », p. 417.
88 *Meat, Modernity, and the Rise of the Slaughterhouse*, ed. Paula Young Lee (Lebanon, NH: University Press of New England, 2008).
89 Noélie Vialles, 'A place that is no-place', in *Animal to Edible* (Cambridge University Press, 1994), pp. 15–32 (19).
90 Norbert Elias, *The Civilizing Process: Sociogenetic and Psychogenetic Investigations* (Oxford: Blackwell, rev. edn, 2000), pp. 102–103.
91 Vialles, *Animal to Edible*, pp. 49–52.
92 Ken C. Erickson, 'Beef in a box: killing cattle on the high plains', in *Animals in Human Histories: The Mirror of Nature and Culture*, ed. Mary J. Henninger-Voss (Rochester, NY: University of Rochester Press, 2002), pp. 83–111 (85).
93 Adams, *Sexual Politics*, p. 53.
94 Henry Ford, *My Life and Work* (London: Heinemann, new edn, 1924), p. 81.
95 Upton Sinclair, *The Jungle* (Harmondsworth: Penguin, 1974 [1906]), p. 49.
96 Carol J. Adams and Marjorie Procter-Smith, 'Taking life or "taking on life"? table talk and animals', in *Ecofeminism and the Sacred*, ed. Carol J. Adams (New York: Continuum, 1993), pp. 295–310 (300–301), discusses the continuing interlocking oppressions of workers, who are mostly Hispanic women, and chickens in a North Carolina poultry plant. For a striking painted record of a tour of slaughterhouses, see Sue Coe, *Dead Meat* (New York: Four Walls Eight Windows, 1996).
97 Charles Patterson, *Eternal Treblinka: Our Treatment of Animals and the Holocaust* (New York: Lantern Books, 2002), pp. 109–13; also Mark H. Bernstein, 'The holocaust of factory farming', in *Without a Tear: Our Tragic Relationship with Animals* (Urbana, IL: University of Illinois Press, 2004), pp. 92–115.
98 The 1933 Animal Protection Law of the German Third Reich was probably the strictest in the world, and had been closely preceded by a law that effectively banned kosher slaughter by requiring anaesthetizing or stunning prior to killing.

Boria Sax, *Animals in the Third Reich: Pets, Scapegoats, and the Holocaust* (London: Continuum, 2000), pp. 110–15, 144–48.

99   E.g., Gail A. Eisnitz, *Slaughterhouse: The Shocking Story of Greed, Neglect, and Inhumane Treatment inside the U.S. Meat Industry* (Amherst, NY: Prometheus, 1997).

100   Eisnitz, *Slaughterhouse*, p. 71.

101   For which, see John Milbank, 'Christ the Exception', *New Blackfriars* 82 (2007), pp. 541–56; drawing on Giorgio Agamben, *Homo Sacer: Sovereign Power and Bare Life* (Stanford, CA: Stanford University Press, 1998).

102   Sinclair, *The Jungle*, pp. 163–64. For similar quality-control problems in medieval pie shops, see Martha Carlin, 'Fast food and urban living standards in medieval England', in *Food and Eating in Medieval Europe*, eds Martha Carlin and Joel T. Rosenthal (London: Hambledon, 1998), pp. 27–51 (39–41).

103   Temple Grandin, *Thinking in Pictures, and Other Reports from my Life with Autism* (London: Bloomsbury, 2006), p. 167.

104   Temple Grandin, 'Behavior of slaughter plant and auction employees toward the animals', in *Cruelty to Animals and Interpersonal Violence: Readings in Research and Application*, eds Randall Lockwood and Frank R. Ascione (West Lafayette, IN: Purdue University Press, 1998), pp. 434–42; idem, *Thinking in Pictures*, pp. 238–39.

105   Grandin, 'Behavior', p. 441.

106   Grandin, 'A cow's eye view: connecting with animals', in *Thinking in Pictures*, pp. 167–83.

107   Grandin, *Thinking in Pictures*, pp. 178–79.

108   Gross, 'When Kosher Isn't Kosher'.

109   'German court ends Muslim slaughter ban', BBC News Online, 15 January 2002.

110   R. Jentzsch and J. Schäffer, „Die rechtliche Regelung des rituellen Schlachtens in Deutschland ab 1933", *Deutsche Tierarztliche Wochenschrift* 107, 12 (2000), pp. 516–23.

111   Mike Radford, *Animal Welfare Law in Britain: Regulation and Responsibility* (Oxford University Press, 2001), p. 117, citing the Welfare of Animals (Slaughter or Killing) (Amendment) Regulations 1999, 51 1999/400.

112   Martin Hickman, 'Halal and kosher meat should not be slipped in to food chain, says minister', *The Independent*, 7 April 2008.

8 Christian Food, Heavenly Food, Worldly Food

1   An influential account of eating as connection is Michael Pollan, *The Omnivore's Dilemma: A Natural History of Four Meals* (New York: Penguin, 2006).

2   See Samantha Calvert, '"Ours is the food that Eden knew": themes in the theology and practice of modern Christian vegetarians', in *Eating and Believing: Interdisciplinary Perspectives on Vegetarianism and Theology*, eds Rachel Muers and David Grumett (London: T&T Clark, 2008), pp. 123–34.

3   Richard Black, 'Shun meat, says UN climate chief', BBC News Online, 7 September 2008. The fact that Pachauri is himself Hindu and vegetarian was mentioned in several media reports – emphasizing the personal nature of the issue above the public, scientific basis for his proposals.

4   'Council told to buy less meat', BBC News Online, 19 March 2008.

5   See Lisa Isherwood, *The Fat Jesus: Feminist Explorations in Boundaries and Transgressions* (London: Darton, Longman and Todd, 2008); R. Marie Griffith, 'Fasting, dieting and the body in American Christianity', in *Perspectives on American Religion and Culture*, ed. Peter W. Williams (Oxford: Blackwell, 1999), pp. 216–27 (222–25).

6   See Carol J. Adams, 'The feminist traffic in animals', in *Ecofeminism: Women, Animals, Nature*, ed. Greta Gaard (Philadelphia, PA: Temple University Press,

1993), pp. 195–218; Marti Kheel, 'Toppling patriarchy with a fork: the feminist debate over eating meat', in *Food for Thought: The Debate over Eating Meat*, ed. Steve Sapontzis (Amherst, MA: Prometheus, 2004), pp. 327–43.

7   John Barclay, *Jewish Law from Jesus to the Mishnah: Five Studies* (London: SCM, 1990), pp. 280–81; M. Isenberg, 'The Sale of Sacrificial Meat', *Classical Philology* 70 (1975), pp. 271–73.

8   1 Cor. 10.25.

9   1 Cor. 10.28–29.

10 1 Cor. 8.10–13; David G. Horrell, 'Solidarity, difference and other-regard: the strong and the weak (1 Corinthians 8–10; Romans 14–15)', in *Solidarity and Difference: A Contemporary Reading of Paul's Ethics* (London: T&T Clark, 2005), pp. 166–203.

11 John Barclay, 'Separatism at meals', in *Jews in the Mediterranean Diaspora: from Alexander to Trajan (323 BCE–117 CE)* (Edinburgh: T&T Clark, 1996), pp. 434–37; E.P. Sanders, 'Purity of food', in *Judaism: Practice and Belief, 63 BCE–66 CE* (London: SCM, 1992), pp. 214–17.

12 Mark Reasoner, *The Strong and the Weak: Romans 14:1–15:13 in Context* (Cambridge University Press, 1999), pp. 82–83.

13 Marcel Detienne, 'Culinary practices and the spirit of sacrifice', in *The Cuisine of Sacrifice among the Greeks*, eds Marcel Detienne and Jean Pierre Vernant (University of Chicago Press, 1989), pp. 1–20. For the distinction with Rome, see Ingvild Sælid Gilhus, *Animals, Gods and Humans: Changing Attitudes to Animals in Greek, Roman and Early Christian Ideas* (London: Routledge, 2006), p. 115.

14 Kathryn McClymond, *Beyond Sacred Violence: A Comparative Study of Sacrifice* (Baltimore, MD: Johns Hopkins University Press, 2008), pp. 72–78.

15 Andrew McGowan, *Ascetic Eucharists: Food and Drink in Early Christian Ritual Meals* (Oxford: Clarendon, 1999); and on baptismal Eucharists, Edward Engelbrecht, 'God's Milk: An Orthodox Confession of the Eucharist', *Journal of Early Christian Studies* 7 (1999), pp. 509–26. See the discussion of McGowan's work in Rachel Muers, 'Seeing, choosing and eating: theology and the feminist-vegetarian debate', in *Eating and Believing*, pp. 184–97.

16 Rob Meens, 'Eating animals in the early middle ages: classifying the animal world and building group identities', in *The Animal/Human Boundary: Historical Perspectives*, eds Angela N.H. Craeger and William Chester Jordan (Rochester, NY: University of Rochester Press, 2002), pp. 3–28 (6).

17 Frederick J. Simoons, *Eat Not this Flesh: Food Avoidances from Prehistory to the Present* (Madison: University of Wisconsin Press, 1994), p. 187.

18 Letter to Boniface on sending the pallium, in *The Letters of Saint Boniface*, ed. Ephraim Emerton (New York: Columbia University Press, 1940), p. 58.

19 Letter of 4 November 751, in *Letters of Saint Boniface*, p. 161.

20 François Sigaut, « La viande de cheval a-t-elle été interdite par l'Eglise ? », *Ethnozootechnie* 50 (1992), pp. 85–91; Simoons, *Eat Not This Flesh*, p. 187; Meens, 'Eating animals', p. 6.

21 Orri Vésteinsson, *The Christianization of Iceland: Priests, Power, and Social Change, 1000–1300* (Oxford University Press, 2000), p. 17.

22 Simoons, *Eat Not This Flesh*, p. 86; also Alexandra Sanmark, 'Power and Conversion – A Comparative Study of Christianization in Scandinavia', Ph.D. thesis, University College London, 2003, pp. 218–27.

23 Marvin Harris, 'Hippophagy', in *Good to Eat: Riddles of Food and Culture* (New York: Simon and Shuster, 1985), pp. 88–108.

24 E.g., *The Journal and Major Essays of John Woolman*, ed. Phillips P. Moulton (Richmond, IN: Friends United Press, 1971), pp. 156, 162.

25 Carol J. Adams, *Neither Man nor Beast: Feminism and the Defence of Animals* (New York: Continuum, 1995), esp. pp. 25–38.

26 Claude Lévi-Strauss, *The Raw and the Cooked* (Chicago, IL: University of Chicago Press, 1983).

27 Noélie Vialles, *Animal to Edible* (Cambridge University Press, 1994).

28 Brian Luke, 'Taming ourselves or going feral? Towards a nonpatriarchal metaethic of animal liberation', in *Animals and Women: Feminist Theoretical Explorations*, eds Carol Adams and Josephine Donovan (Durham, NC: Duke University Press, 1995), pp. 290–319, analyses the systems of deception involved in various uses and abuses of nonhuman animals, following Josephine Donovan.

29 1 Thes. 1.9. This account of idolatry is discussed in detail in Rachel Muers, *Living for the Future: Theological Ethics for Coming Generations* (London: T&T Clark, 2008), pp. 58–77; drawing on Alistair McFadyen, *Bound to Sin: Abuse, Holocaust and the Christian Doctrine of Sin* (Cambridge University Press, 2000) and Peter Scott, *Theology, Ideology and Liberation: Towards a Liberative Theology* (Cambridge University Press, 1994).

30 Carol Adams, *The Sexual Politics of Meat: A Feminist-Vegetarian Critical Theory* (New York: Continuum, 1995). For a recent Christian defence of vegetarianism using the language of 'idolatry', see B.R. Myers, 'Hard to Swallow: The Gourmet's Ongoing Failure to Think in Moral Terms', *The Atlantic Monthly*, 28 August 2007, reviewing Pollan, *Omnivore's Dilemma*.

31 1 Cor. 10.25.

32 Myers, 'Hard to Swallow'.

33 Pollan, *Omnivore's Dilemma*, p. 362.

34 1 Tim. 4:3–4.

35 Thomas Aquinas, *Summa Theologiae* IIaIIae, q. 64, a. 1 (60 vols; London: Blackfriars, 1962–76), vol. 37, pp. 18–21.

36 John Calvin, *Genesis* (Edinburgh: Banner of Truth, 1965), pp. 291–93 on verse 9.3, and 99–100 on 1.29.

37 Jerome, *Against Jovinianus* 2.6, in *NPNF* II,6. p. 392.

38 Jerome, *Against Jovinianus* 2.7, pp. 393–94.

39 Jerome, *Against Jovinianus* 2.7, p. 393.

40 See Adams, 'Feminist traffic'; Kathryn Paxton George, *Animal, Vegetable or Woman? A Feminist Critique of Ethical Vegetarianism* (Albany: State University of New York Press, 2000).

41 Southgate, 'Protological and eschatological vegetarianism', p. 251.

42 Julia Twigg, 'The Vegetarian Movement in England, 1847–1981: With Particular Reference to its Ideology', Ph.D. thesis, University of London, 1981, pp. 399–407.

43 See Southgate, 'Protological and eschatological'.

44 Thomas More, *Utopia*, in *Complete Works* (5 vols; New Haven, CT: Yale University Press, 1963–90), vol. 4, p. 227.

45 E.g., Michael P. Leahy, *Against Liberation: Putting Animals in Perspective* (London: Routledge, rev. edn, 1993).

46 See on this Neil Messer, 'Humans, animals, evolution and ends', in *Creaturely Theology: On God, Humans and Other Animals*, eds Celia Deane-Drummond and David Clough (London: SCM, 2008), pp. 211–27.

47 Empirical research by Malcolm Hamilton, 'Eating Death: Vegetarians, Meat and Violence', *Food, Culture and Society* 9 (2006), pp. 155–77, indeed suggests that anti-authoritarianism is a more important motivation that the eschewal of death and violence.

48 As in the work of Mennonite philosopher Matthew Halteman, *Compassionate Eating as Care of Creation* (Washington, DC: The Humane Society of the United States, 2008).

49 Mary Douglas, 'The abominations of Leviticus', in *Purity and Danger: An Analysis of Concepts of Pollution and Taboo* (London: Routledge, rev. edn, 2002), pp. 51–71.

50 Mary Douglas, *Leviticus as Literature* (Oxford University Press, 1999), pp. 166–75.
51 1 Cor. 8.4–7.
52 Neil Elliott, 'Asceticism among the "weak" and the "strong" in Romans 14–15', in *Asceticism and the New Testament*, eds Leif E. Vaage and Vincent L. Wimbush (New York: Routledge, 1999), pp. 231–51, indeed argues that Paul's ultimate objective was to promote asceticism.
53 E.P. Sanders, 'Jewish association with Gentiles and Galatians 2:11–14', in *The Conversation Continues: Studies in Paul and John in Honor of J. Louis Martyn*, eds Robert T. Fortna and Beverly R. Gaventa (Nashville, TN: Abingdon, 1990), pp. 170–88.
54 Rom. 4.6. See David G. Horrell, 'Solidarity and Difference: Pauline Morality in Romans 14:1–15:13', *Studies in Christian Ethics* 15 (2002), pp. 60–78.

9 Concluding Reflections: Practices, Everyday Life and Theological Tradition

1 Alasdair MacIntyre, *After Virtue: A Study in Moral Theory* (London: Duckworth, 3rd edn, 2007).
2 *The Blackwell Companion to Christian Ethics*, eds Stanley Hauerwas and Samuel Wells (Oxford: Blackwell, 2004) is a key example and explication of this approach to Christian ethics, centred on an albeit modern interpretation of the Eucharist. David S. Cunningham, *Christian Ethics: The End of the Law* (London: Routledge, 2008) is shaped by MacIntyre's arguments, focusing on Christian virtues and practices. For Cunningham, food is among the central foci of reflection on Christian practice, particularly common meals and table-fellowship. He also briefly discusses the possibility that contemporary Christians are called to abstain from meat (pp. 362–63).
3 In the realm of clothing, Saba Mahmood, *Politics of Piety: The Islamic Revival and the Feminist Subject* (Princeton, NJ: Princeton University Press, 2005), pp. 22–25, offers a particularly illuminating discussion of different ways of conceptualising the relationship between *hijab* and the 'virtue' of modesty.
4 See *Practicing Theology: Belief and Practice in Christian Life*, eds Miroslav Volf and Dorothy Bass (Grand Rapids, MI: Eerdmans, 2001).
5 Daniel W. Hardy, *Finding the Church* (London: SCM, 2001), especially pp. 109–12.
6 For further discussion of this point, particularly in relation to feminist views of food and eating, see Rachel Muers, 'Afterword', in *Eating and Believing: Interdisciplinary Perspectives on Vegetarianism and Theology*, eds Rachel Muers and David Grumett (London: T&T Clark, 2008), pp. 266–70.
7 David Brown, *God and Grace of Body: Sacrament in Ordinary* (Oxford University Press, 2007), is an important study of the relevance for Christian theology of common, cross-cultural aspects of embodied human life like food, but also sexuality, dance and music. He plausibly argues on theological grounds for a broad account of the mediation of the presence of the grace of God in human society and culture, without assuming that every practice is graced.
8 On the relationship in scriptural interpretation between 'use' and 'resistance to use', and transparency and opacity, see Mike Higton, 'Boldness and Reserve: A Lesson from St Augustine', *Anglican Theological Review* 85 (2003) pp. 445–56.
9 Rom. 14.6.
10 See Randi Rashkover, *Revelation and Theopolitics: Barth, Rosenzweig and the Politics of Praise* (London: T&T Clark, 2005), especially pp. 55–76; Paul D. Janz, *The Command of Grace: A New Theological Apologetics* (London: T&T Clark, 2009), especially pp. 159–83.
11 Michael Barnes, *Theology and the Dialogue of Religions* (Cambridge University Press, 2002).

12 On improvisation, see for example Samuel Wells, *Improvisation: The Drama of Christian Ethics* (London: SPCK, 2004); James Fodor and Stanley Hauerwas, 'Performing faith: the peaceable rhetoric of God's Church', in *Performing the Faith: Bonhoeffer and the Practice of Nonviolence*, ed. Stanley Hauerwas (Grand Rapids, MI: Brazos, 2004), pp. 75–109. On dramatic forms generally, see David F. Ford, *The Future of Christian Theology* (Oxford: Blackwell, 2010).

13 We are grateful to John Paul Bradbury for a conversation that gave rise to this idea.

Select Bibliography

Adams, Carol J., *The Inner Art of Vegetarianism: Spiritual Practices for Body and Soul* (New York: Lantern, 2000).
——, *The Sexual Politics of Meat: A Feminist-Vegetarian Critical Theory* (New York: Continuum, 1995).
——, *Neither Man nor Beast: Feminism and the Defence of Animals* (New York: Continuum, 1995).
——, 'The feminist traffic in animals', in *Ecofeminism: Women, Animals, Nature*, ed. Greta Gaard (Philadelphia, PA: Temple University Press, 1993), pp. 195–218.
Adams, Carol J. and Marjorie Procter-Smith, 'Taking life or taking on life? table talk and animals', in *Ecofeminism and the Sacred*, ed. Carol J. Adams (New York: Continuum, 1993), pp. 295–310.
Ad-Damîrî, *Hayât al-hayawân (A Zoological Lexicon)*, trans. A.S.G. Jayakar (2 vols; London and Bombay: Luzac, 1906–8).
Albertus Magnus, *On Animals: A Medieval Summa Zoologica*, trans. Kenneth Kitchell, Jr and Irven Michael Rennick (2 vols; Baltimore, MD: Johns Hopkins University Press, 1999).
Al-Jāhiz, *Le Cadi et la mouche: anthologie du Livre des animaux*, trans. L. Souami (Paris: Sindbad, 1988).
Altman, Donald, *Art of the Inner Meal: Eating as a Spiritual Path* (New York: Harper, 1999).
Amand, David, *L'Ascèse monastique de Saint Basile: essai historique* (Paris: Maredsous, 1948).
Amato, Paul R. and Sonia A. Partridge, *The New Vegetarians* (New York: Plenum, 1989).
Ambrose, Kirk, 'A Medieval Food List from the Monastery of Cluny', *Gastronomica* 6, 1 (2006), pp. 14–20.
Antrobus, Derek, *A Guiltless Feast: The Salford Bible Christian Church and the Rise of the Modern Vegetarian Movement* (City of Salford Education and Leisure, 1997).
Arbesmann, Rudolph, 'Fasting and Prophecy in Pagan and Christian Antiquity', *Traditio* 7 (1949–51), pp. 1–71.
Ascetic Behavior in Greco-Roman Antiquity: A Sourcebook, ed. Vincent L. Wimbush (Minneapolis, MN: Fortress, 1990).
Asceticism, eds Vincent L. Wimbush and Richard Valantasis (New York: Oxford University Press, 1995).
Asceticism and the New Testament, eds Leif E. Vaage and Vincent L. Wimbush (New York: Routledge, 1999).
The Asketikon of St Basil the Great, ed. Anna Silvas (Oxford University Press, 2005).

Athanasius, *The Life of Antony*, trans. Robert C. Gregg (Mahwah, NJ: Paulist, 1979).

Augustine, *Confessions* (Oxford University Press, 1998).

Barclay, John, *Jews in the Mediterranean Diaspora: from Alexander to Trajan (323 BCE–117 CE)* (Edinburgh: T&T Clark, 1996).

——, *Jewish Law from Jesus to the Mishnah: Five Studies* (London: SCM, 1990).

Bashear, Suliman, 'Riding Beasts on Divine Missions: An Examination of the Ass and Camel Traditions', *Journal of Semitic Studies* 37 (1991), pp. 37–75.

Basil of Caesarea, *The Ascetic Works*, ed. W.K.L. Clarke (London: SPCK, 1925).

Bazell, Dianne M., 'Strife among the Table-Fellows: Conflicting Attitudes of Early and Medieval Christians toward the Eating of Meat', *Journal of the American Academy of Religion* 65 (1997), pp. 73–99.

Beardsworth, Teresa and Alan Keil, 'Health-Related Benefits and Dietary Practices Among Vegetarians and Vegans: A Qualitative Study', *Health Education Journal* 50, 1 (1991), pp. 38–42.

Beasts and Saints, trans. Helen Waddell (London: Constable, 1934).

Beckwith, Roger T., 'The Vegetarianism of the Therapeutae, and the Motives for Vegetarianism in Early Jewish and Christian Circles', *Revue de Qumran* 13 (1988), pp. 407–10.

Belasco, Warren, *Appetite for Change: How the Counterculture took on the Food Industry* (Ithaca, NY: Cornell University Press, 2nd edn, 2007).

——, *Meals to Come: A History of the Future of Food* (Berkeley: University of California Press, 2006).

Bernstein, Mark H., *Without a Tear: Our Tragic Relationship with Animals* (Urbana, IL: University of Illinois Press, 2004).

Berry, Ryan, *Food for the Gods: Vegetarianism and the World's Religions* (New York: Pythagorean, 1998).

Biebel, Elizabeth M., 'Pilgrims to table: food consumption in Chaucer's *Canterbury Tales*', in *Food and Eating in Medieval Europe*, eds Martha Carlin and Joel T. Rosenthal (London: Hambledon, 1998), pp. 15–26.

Binchy, D.A., 'A pre-Christian survival in medieval Irish hagiography', in *Ireland in Early Mediaeval Europe: Studies in Memory of Kathleen Hughes*, eds Dorothy Whitelock, Rosamond McKitterick and David Dumville (Cambridge University Press, 1982), pp. 165–78.

——, 'Irish History and Irish Law', *Studia Hibernica* 15 (1975), pp. 7–36.

Bishop, Edmund, 'The Method and Degree of Fasting and Abstinence of the Black Monks in England before the Reformation', *The Downside Review* 43/123 (1925), pp. 184–237.

Black, Richard, 'Shun meat, says UN climate chief', BBC News Online, 7 September 2008.

Blay-Palmer, Alison, *Food Fears: From Industrial to Sustainable Food Systems* (Aldershot: Ashgate, 2008).

Böckenhoff, Karl, *Speisesatzungen mosaischer Art in mittelalterlichen Kirchenrechtsquellen des Morgen- und Abendlandes* (Münster: Aschendorffsche, 1907).

Bond, C.J., 'Monastic fisheries', in *Medieval Fish, Fisheries and Fishponds in England*, ed. Michael Aston (2 vols; Oxford: BAR, 1988), vol. 1, pp. 69–112.

Bonnassie, Pierre, « Consommation d'aliments immondes et cannibalisme de survie dans l'occident du haut moyen age », *Annales ESC* (1989), pp. 1035–56.

Borowski, Oded, *Every Living Thing: Daily Use of Animals in Ancient Israel* (London: AltaMira, 1998).

Bourdieu, Pierre, *Distinction: A Social Critique of the Judgement of Taste* (London: Routledge & Kegan Paul, 1986).

Bratton, Susan Power, 'Urbanization and the end of animal sacrifice', in *Environmental Values in Christian Art* (State University of New York Press, 2009), pp. 87–106.

Braukämper, Ulrich, 'On food avoidances in Southern Ethiopia: religious manifestation and socio-economic relevance', in *Proceedings of the Seventh International Conference of Ethiopian Studies 1982, Lund*, ed. Sven Rubenson (Addis Ababa: Institute of Ethiopian Studies, 1984), pp. 429–45.

Brenon, Anne, *Les Cathares: vie et mort d'une église chrétienne* (Paris: Grancher, 1996).

Britt, Samuel I., 'Sacrifice Honors God: Ritual Struggle in a Liberian Church', *Journal of the American Academy of Religion* 76 (2008), pp. 1–26.

Brock, Sebastian, 'The Baptist's Diet in Syriac Sources', *Oriens Christianus* 54 (1970), pp. 113–24.

Brown, David, *God of Grace and Body: Sacrament in Ordinary* (Oxford University Press, 2007).

Brown, Peter, *The Body and Society: Men, Women and Sexual Renunciation in Early Christianity* (London: Faber & Faber, 1989).

Buitelaar, Marjo, *Fasting and Feasting in Morocco: Women's Participation in Ramadan* (Oxford: Berg, 1993).

Burkert, Walter, *Homo Necans: The Anthropology of Ancient Greek Sacrificial Ritual and Myth* (Berkeley: University of California Press, 1983).

Butcher, Carmen Acevedo, *Man of Blessing: A Life of St. Benedict* (Brewster, MA: Paraclete, 2006).

Cadden, Joan, 'Albertus Magnus' universal physiology: the example of nutrition', in *Albertus Magnus and the Sciences: Commemorative Essays, 1980*, ed. James A. Weisheipl (Toronto: Pontifical Institute of Mediaeval Studies, 1980), pp. 321–39.

Cahill, Michael J., 'Drinking Blood at a Kosher Eucharist? The Sound of Scholarly Silence', *Biblical Theology Bulletin* 32 (2002), pp. 168–82.

Calvert, Samantha, 'A Taste of Eden: Modern Christianity and Vegetarianism', *Journal of Ecclesiastical History* 58 (2007), pp. 461–81.

Calvin, John, *Institutes of the Christian Religion*, trans. Henry Beveridge (Grand Rapids, MI: Eerdmans, 1989).

Carmichael, Calum M., 'On Separating Life and Death: An Explanation of Some Biblical Laws', *The Harvard Theological Review* 69 (1976), pp. 1–7.

Carrette, Jeremy, *Foucault and Religion: Spiritual Corporality and Political Spirituality* (London: Routledge, 1999).

Carson, Gerald, *Cornflake Crusade* (London: Gollancz, 1959).

Cassian, John, *Institutes*, trans. Boniface Ramsey (Mahwah, NJ: Newman, 2000).

——, *Conferences*, trans. Colm Luibheid (Mahwah, NJ: Paulist, 1985).

Certain Sermons or Homilies Appointed to be Read in Churches in the Time of Queen Elizabeth of Famous Memory (London: Parker, 1683).

Cherno, Melvin, 'Feuerbach's Man is What He Eats: A Rectification', *Journal of the History of Ideas* 24 (1963), pp. 397–406.

Clarkson, L.A. and E. Margaret Crawford, *Feast and Famine: Food and Nutrition in Ireland, 1500–1920* (Oxford University Press, 2001).

Clement of Alexandria, *Le Pédagogue* (3 vols; Paris: Cerf, 1960–70).

Clines, David, *Job 1–20*, World Biblical Commentary 17 (Dallas, TX: Word, 1989).

The Code of Maimonides, V: *The Book of Holiness*, trans. L.I. Rabinowitz and P. Grossman (New Haven, CT: Yale University Press, 1965).

Coe, Sue, *Dead Meat* (New York: Four Walls Eight Windows, 1996).

Cohn-Sherbok, Dan, 'Hope for the animal kingdom: a Jewish vision', in *A Communion of Subjects: Animals in Religion, Science, and Ethics*, eds Paul Waldau and Kimberley Patton (New York: Columbia University Press, 2006), pp. 81–90.

Colliander, Tito, *Way of the Ascetics* (Crestwood, NY: St Vladimir's, 2003).

Conybeare, F.C., 'The Survival of Animal Sacrifice Inside the Christian Church', *American Journal of Theology* 7 (1903), pp. 62–90.

——, « Les sacrifices d'animaux dans les anciennes églises chrétiennes », *Revue de l'historie des religions* 44 (1901), pp. 108–14.

Cornaro, Luigi, *A Treatise of Temperance and Sobrietie* (London: Starkey, 1978).

Coulet, Noël, « 'Juif intouchable' et interdits alimentaires », in *Exclus et systèmes d'exclusion dans la littérature et la civilisation médiévales* (Aix-en-Provence: CUERMA, 1978), pp. 207–21.

'Council told to buy less meat', BBC News Online, 19 March 2008.

Coutumes de Chartreuse (Paris: Cerf, 1984).

Coveney, John, *Food, Morals and Meaning: The Pleasure and Anxiety of Eating* (London: Routledge, 2nd edn, 2006).

Creaturely Theology: God, Humans and Other Animals, eds Celia Deane-Drummond and David Clough (London: SCM, 2009).

The Cuisine of Sacrifice among the Greeks, eds Marcel Detienne and Jean-Pierre Vernant (Chicago, IL: University of Chicago Press, 1989).

The Cultural Turn in Late Ancient Studies: Gender, Asceticism, and Historiography, eds Dale B. Martin and Patricia Cox Miller (Durham, NC: Duke University Press, 2005).

Cunningham, David S., *Christian Ethics: The End of the Law* (London: Routledge, 2008).

Cutting, Charles Latham, *Fish Saving: A History of Fish Processing from Ancient to Modern Times* (London: Hill, 1955).

Daly, Robert J., *Christian Sacrifice: The Judaeo-Christian Background before Origen* (Washington, DC: Catholic University of America Press, 1978).

David, Elizabeth, *English Bread and Yeast Cookery* (Harmondsworth: Penguin, 1979).

Davril, Anselme, « Le langage par signes chez les moines : un catalogue de signes de l'abbaye de Fleury », in *Sous la règle de Saint Benoît: structures monastiques et sociétés en France du Moyen Âge à l'époche moderne* (Geneva: Droz, 1982), pp. 51–74.

DeBuhn, Jason David, *The Manichaean Body in Discipline and Ritual* (Baltimore, MD: Johns Hopkins, 2002).

Dell, Katherine, 'The Use of Animal Imagery in the Psalms and Wisdom Literature of Ancient Israel', *Scottish Journal of Theology* 53 (2000), pp. 275–91.

De Vaux, Roland, 'The sacrifice of pigs in Palestine and in the Ancient East', in *The Bible and the Ancient Near East* (London: Darton, Longman and Todd, 1972), pp. 252–69.

De Vogüé, Adalbert *To Love Fasting: The Monastic Experience* (Petersham, MA: Saint Bede s, 1989).

Diamond, Eliezer, *Holy Men and Hunger Artists: Fasting and Asceticism in Rabbinic Culture* (Oxford University Press, 2004).

Diner, Hasia R., 'Food fights: immigrant Jews and the lure of America', in *Hungering for America: Italian, Irish, and Jewish Foodways in the Age of Migration* (Cambridge, MA: Harvard University Press, 2002), pp. 178–219.

Documentary Annals of the Reformed Church of England, ed. Edward Cardwell (2 vols; Oxford University Press, new edn, 1844).

Dombrowski, Daniel, 'Two Vegetarian Puns at *Republic* 372', *Ancient Philosophy* 9 (1990), pp. 167–71.

Douglas, Mary, *Purity and Danger: An Analysis of Concepts of Pollution and Taboo* (London: Routledge, rev. edn, 2002).

——, *Leviticus as Literature* (Oxford University Press, 1999), pp. 166–75.

——, 'The Forbidden Animals in Leviticus', *Journal for the Study of the Old Testament* 59 (1993), pp. 3–23.

Driver, G.R., 'Birds in the Old Testament', *Palestine Exploration Quarterly* 87 (1955), pp. 5–20, 129–40.

Eating and Believing: Interdisciplinary Perspectives on Vegetarianism and Theology, eds Rachel Muers and David Grumett (New York: T&T Clark, 2008).

Effros, Bonnie, *Creating Community with Food and Drink in Merovingian Gaul* (Basingstoke: Palgrave Macmillan, 2002).

Eisnitz, Gail A., *Slaughterhouse: The Shocking Story of Greed, Neglect, and Inhumane Treatment inside the U.S. Meat Industry* (Amherst, NY: Prometheus, 1997).

Elias, Norbert, *The Civilizing Process: Sociogenetic and Psychogenetic Investigations* (Oxford: Blackwell, rev. edn, 2000).

Ellmann, Maud, *The Hunger Artists: Starving, Writing and Imprisonment* (London: Virago, 1993).

Engelbrecht, Edward, 'God's Milk: An Orthodox Confession of the Eucharist', *Journal of Early Christian Studies* 7 (1999), pp. 509–26.

Erickson, Ken C., 'Beef in a box: killing cattle on the high plains', in *Animals in Human Histories: The Mirror of Nature and Culture*, ed. Mary J. Henninger-Voss (Rochester, NY: University of Rochester Press, 2002), pp. 83–111.

Evans, E.P., *The Criminal Prosecution and Capital Punishment of Animals* (London: Heinemann, 1906).

Fabre-Vassas, Claudine, *The Singular Beast: Jews, Christians, and the Pig* (New York: Columbia University Press, 1999).

'Fast and abstinence', eds P.M.J. Clancy, G.T. Kennedy and J.E. Lynch, in *New Catholic Encyclopaedia* (15 vols; Detroit, MI: Gale, 2nd edn, 2003), vol. 5, pp. 632–35.

Ferrari, Leo, 'The Gustatory Augustine', *Augustiniana* 29 (1979), pp. 304–15.

——, 'The Food of Truth in Augustine's Confessions', *Augustinian Studies* 9 (1978), pp. 1–14.

Feuerbach, Ludwig, „Das Geheimnis des Opfers, oder, Der Mensch ist, was er isst", in *Gesammelte Werke* (22 vols; Berlin: Akademie, 1969), vol. 11, pp. 26–52.

Fiddes, Nick, 'Declining meat: past, present … and future imperfect?', in *Food, Health and Identity*, ed. Pat Caplan (London: Routledge, 1997), pp. 252–67.

——, *Meat: A Natural Symbol* (London: Routledge, 1993).

Findikyan, Michael, 'A Sacrifice of Praise: Blessing of the Madagh', *Window Quarterly* 2, 4 (1992), at www.geocities.com/derghazar/MADAGH.DOC [accessed 15 June 2009].

Firey, Abigail, *A Contrite Heart: Prosecution and Redemption in the Carolingian Empire* (Leiden: Brill, 2009).

——, 'The letter of the Law: Carolingian exegetes and the Old Testament', in *With Reverence for the Word: Medieval Scriptural Exegesis in Judaism, Christianity, and Islam*, eds Jane Dammen McAuliffe, Barry D. Walfish and Joseph W. Goering (New York: Oxford University Press, 2003), pp. 204–24.

Foltz, Richard, *Animals in Islamic Tradition and Muslim Cultures* (Oxford: Oneworld, 2006).

Food in Change: Eating Habits from the Middle Ages to the Present Day, eds Alexander Fenton and Eszter Kisbán (Edinburgh: Donald, 1986).

Foucault, Michael, *Security, Territory, Population: Lectures at the Collège de France, 1977–78* (Basingstoke: Palgrave Macmillan, 2007).

——, *The History of Sexuality* III: *The Care of the Self* (Harmondsworth: Penguin, 1988).

Francis of Assisi: Early Documents, eds Regis J. Armstrong, J.A. Wayne Hellmann and William J. Short (4 vols; New York: New City Press, 1999–2002) [*FA*].

Freidenreich, David M., 'Sharing Meals with Non-Christians in Canon Law Commentaries, Circa 1160–1260: A Case Study in Legal Development', *Medieval Encounters* 14 (2008), pp. 41–77.

Fulton, Rachel, 'Taste and See That the Lord is Sweet (Ps. 33:9): The Flavor of God in the Monastic West', *The Journal of Religion* 86, 2 (2006), pp. 169–204.

Galen on Food and Diet, ed. Mark Grant (London: Routledge, 2000).

Galavaris, George, *Bread and the Liturgy* (Madison: University of Wisconsin Press, 1970).

Garrigues, Marie-Odile, 'Honorius Augustodunensis, *De esu volatilium*', *Studia Monastica* 28 (1986), pp. 75–130.

George, Kathryn Paxton, *Animal, Vegetable or Woman? A Feminist Critique of Ethical Vegetarianism* (Albany: State University of New York Press, 2000).

'German court ends Muslim slaughter ban', BBC News Online, 15 January 2002.

Gersbach, Karl A., 'The Historical and Literary Context of Fasting and Abstinence in the Life of St. Nicholas of Tolentino (1305)', *Augustiniana* 55 (2005), pp. 247–96.

Gilhus, Ingvild Sælid, *Animals, Gods and Humans: Changing Attitudes to Animals in Greek, Roman and Early Christian Ideas* (London: Routledge, 2006).

Gillis, John R., *A World of their Own Making: Myth, Ritual and the Quest for Family Values* (Cambridge, MA: Harvard University Press, 1996).

Gindele, Corbinian, „Das Genuss von Fleisch uns Geflügel in der Magister- und Benediktusregel", *Erbe und Auftrag* 40 (1964), pp. 506–7.

Girard, M.D., «Les 'madag' ou sacrifices arméniens», *Revue de l'orient chrétien* 7 (1902), pp. 410–22.

Girard, René, *Violence and the Sacred* (London: Athlone, 1995).

Goehring, James E., *Ascetics, Society, and the Desert: Studies in Early Egyptian Monasticism* (Harrisburg, PA: Trinity, 1999).

The Gospel of the Holy Twelve, ed. G.J. Ouseley (London: Watkins, 1957).

Govett, Robert, *Vegetarianism: A Dialogue* (Norwich: Fletcher, 2nd edn, 1883).

——[R. G.], *The Future Apostasy* (London: Nisbet, 2nd edn, n.d. [c1880]).

Grandin, Temple, *Thinking in Pictures, and Other Reports from my Life with Autism* (London: Bloomsbury, 2006).

——, 'Behavior of slaughter plant and auction employees toward the animals', in *Cruelty to Animals and Interpersonal Violence: Readings in Research and Application*, eds Randall Lockwood and Frank R. Ascione (West Lafayette, IN: Purdue University Press, 1998), pp. 434–42.

Grant, Robert M., *Early Christians and Animals* (London: Routledge, 1999).

Gregory, James R.T.E., *Of Victorians and Vegetarians: The Vegetarian Movement in Nineteenth Century Britain* (London: Tauris, 2007).

Gregory the Great, *Dialogues*, trans. Odo John Zimmerman (Fathers of the Church 39; Washington DC: Catholic University Press of America, 2002).

——, *Forty Gospel Homilies*, trans. Dom David Hurst (Kalamazoo, MI: Cistercian, 1977).

——, *Morals on the Book of Job* (4 vols; Oxford: Parker, 1844–50).

Griffith, R. Marie, 'Fasting, dieting and the body in American Christianity', in *Perspectives on American Religion and Culture*, ed. Peter W. Williams (Oxford: Blackwell, 1999), pp. 216–27.

Grimm, Veronika, *From Feasting to Fasting, the Evolution of a Sin: Attitudes to Food in Late Antiquity* (London: Routledge, 1996).

Gross, Aaron, 'When Kosher Isn't Kosher', *Tikkun Magazine* 20, 2 (2005).

——, 'Continuity and Change in Reform Views of *Kashrut* 1883–2002: From the Treifah Banquet to Eco-Kashrut', *CCAR Journal* (Winter 2004), pp. 6–28.

Guerrini, Anita, 'Case History as Spiritual Autobiography: George Cheyne's Case of the Author', *Eighteenth Century Life* 19 (1995), pp. 18–27.

Hagen, Ann, *A Second Handbook of Anglo-Saxon Food and Drink: Production and Distribution* (Hockwold cum Wilton: Anglo-Saxon Books, 1995).

——, *A Handbook of Anglo-Saxon Food: Processing and Consumption* (Pinner: Anglo-Saxon Books, 1992).

Hagman, Ylva, « Le Catharisme, un néo-manichéisme? », *Heresis* 21 (1993), pp. 47–59 (54–55).

Halteman, Matthew, *Compassionate Eating as Care of Creation* (Washington, DC: The Humane Society of the United States, 2008).

Hamilton, Malcolm, 'Eating Death: Vegetarians, Meat and Violence', *Food, Culture and Society* 9 (2006), pp. 155–77.

——, 'Eating Ethically: Spiritual and Quasi-religious Aspects of Vegetarianism', *Journal of Contemporary Religion* 15 (2000), pp. 65–83.

Hardy, Daniel W., *Finding the Church* (London: SCM, 2001).

Hardyment, Christina, *Slice of Life: The British Way of Eating since 1945* (London: Penguin, 1997).

Harris, Marvin, *Good to Eat: Riddles of Food and Culture* (New York: Simon and Shuster, 1985).

——, *Cannibals and Kings: The Origins of Cultures* (New York: Random House, 1977).

Harvey, Barbara F., 'Diet', in *Living and Dying in England, 1100–1540: The Monastic Experience* (Oxford: Clarendon, 1993), pp. 34–71.

Heinze, Andrew R., *Adapting to Abundance: Jewish Immigrants, Mass Consumption, and the Search for American Identity* (New York: Columbia University Press, 1990).

Henisch, Bridget Ann, *Fast and Feast: Food in Medieval Society* (University Park: Pennsylvania State University Press, 1976).

Henning, W.B. and S.H. Taqizadeh, 'The Manichean Fasts', *The Journal of the Royal Asiatic Society* (1945), pp. 146–64.

Henry, C.J.K., 'The Biology of Human Starvation: Some New Insights', *Nutritional Bulletin* 26 (2001), pp. 205–11.

Hickman, Martin, 'Halal and kosher meat should not be slipped in to food chain, says minister', *The Independent*, 7 April 2008.

History of the Philadelphia Bible-Christian Church for the First Century of its Existence from 1817 to 1917 (Philadelphia, PA: Lippincott, 1922).

Hivet, Christine, 'A Diet for a Sensitive Soul: Vegetarianism in Eighteenth-Century Britain', *Eighteenth Century Life* 23, 2 (1999), special issue 'The Cultural Topography of Food', pp. 34–42.

Holman, Susan R., 'Rich City Burning: Social Welfare and Ecclesial Insecurity in Basil's Mission to Armenia', *Journal of Early Christian Studies* 12 (2004), pp. 195–215.

Horrell, David G., *Solidarity and Difference: A Contemporary Reading of Paul's Ethics* (London: T&T Clark, 2005).

——, 'Solidarity and Difference: Pauline Morality in Romans 14:1–15:13', *Studies in Christian Ethics* 15 (2002), pp. 60–78.

Hooker, Richard, *Of the Laws of Ecclesiastical Polity* (3 vols; London: Holdsworth and Ball, 1830).

Houston, Walter, *Purity and Monotheism: Clean and Unclean Animals in Biblical Law* (Sheffield: JSOT Press, 1993).

Hunt, Alan, *Governance of the Consuming Passions: A History of Sumptuary Law* (Basingstoke: Macmillan, 1996).

Hutton, Ronald, *Stations of the Sun: A History of the Ritual Year in Britain* (Oxford University Press, 1996).

Hymers, John, „Verteidigung von Feuerbachs Moleschott Rezeption: Feuerbachs offene Dialektik", in *Identität und Pluralismus in der globalen Gesellschaft. Ludwig Feuerbach zum 200. Geburtstag*, eds U. Reitemeyer, T. Shibata and F. Tomasoni (Münster: Waxmann, 2006), pp. 111–26.

Iacobbo, Karen and Michael Iacobbo, *Vegetarian America: A History* (Westport, CN: Praeger, 2004).

Insoll, Timothy, *The Archaeology of Islam* (Oxford: Blackwell, 1999).

The Irish Penitentials, ed. Ludwig Bieler (The Dublin Institute for Advanced Studies, 1975).

Isenberg, M., 'The Sale of Sacrificial Meat', *Classical Philology* 70 (1975), pp. 271–73.

Isherwood, Lisa, *The Fat Jesus: Feminist Explorations in Boundaries and Transgressions* (London: Darton, Longman and Todd, 2008).

Jameson, Michael, 'Sacrifice and animal husbandry in Classical Greece', in *Pastoral Economies in Classical Antiquity*, ed. C.R. Whittaker (Cambridge Philological Society, 1988), pp. 87–119.

Janz, Paul D., *The Command of Grace: A New Theological Apologetics* (London: T&T Clark, 2009).

Jaritz, Gerhard, 'The standard of living in German and Austrian Cistercian monasteries of the late middle ages', in *Goad and Nail* (Kalamazoo, MI: Cistercian, 1985), pp. 56–70.

Jentzsch, R. and J. Schäffer, „Die rechtliche Regelung des rituellen Schlachtens in Deutschland ab 1933", *Deutsche Tierärztliche Wochenschrift* 107, 12 (2000), pp. 516–23.

Kaufman, Peter Iver, 'Fasting in England in the 1560s: A Thinge of Nought?', *Archiv für Reformationsgeschichte* 94 (2003), pp. 176–93.

Kean, Hilda, *Animal Rights: Political and Social Change in Britain since 1800* (London: Reaktion, 1998).

Kelhoffer, James A., *The Diet of John the Baptist: Locusts and Wild Honey in Synoptic and Patristic Interpretation* (Wissenschaftliche Untersuchungen zum Neuen Testament 176; Tübingen: Mohr Siebeck, 2005).

Keys, Ancel, Josef Brazek et al., *The Biology of Human Starvation* (2 vols; Minneapolis, MN: University of Minnesota Press, 1950).

Khalil, Issa J., 'The Orthodox Fast and the Philosophy of Vegetarianism', *Greek Orthodox Theological Review* 35 (1990), pp. 237–59.

Kheel, Marti, 'Toppling patriarchy with a fork: the feminist debate over eating meat', in *Food for Thought: The Debate over Eating Meat*, ed. Steve Sapontzis (Amherst, MA: Prometheus, 2004), pp. 327–43.

Klein, Jacob A., 'Afterword: Comparing Vegetarianisms', *South Asia: Journal of South Asian Studies* 31 (2008), pp. 199–212.

Knell, Yolande, 'Egypt pigs meet cruel fate in swine flu cull', BBC News Online, 29 May 2009.

Knowles, David, *The Monastic Order in England: A History of its Development from the Times of St Dunstan to the Fourth Lateran Council, 940–1216* (Cambridge University Press, 2nd edn, 1976).

——, 'The Diet of English Black Monks', *The Downside Review* 52/150 (1934), pp. 275–90.

Lappé, Frances Moore, *Diet for a Small Planet* (New York: Ballantine, 1991).

The Lausiac History of Palladius, trans. W.K. Lowther Clarke (London: SPCK, 1918).

Leahy, Michael P., *Against Liberation: Putting Animals in Perspective* (London: Routledge, rev. edn, 1993).

The Letters of Saint Boniface, trans. Ephraim Emerton (New York: Columbia University Press, 1940).

Lévi-Strauss, Claude, *The Raw and the Cooked* (Chicago, IL: University of Chicago Press, 1983).

Lineham, Peter J., 'Restoring man's creative power: the theosophy of the Bible Christians of Salford', in *Studies in Church History* 19: *The Church and Healing*, ed. W. J. Sheils (Oxford: Blackwell, 1982), pp. 207–23.

The Lives of the Desert Fathers, trans. Norman Russell, ed. Benedicta Ward (London: Mowbray, 1981).

The Lives of the Jura Fathers, trans. Tim Vivian, Kim Vivian and Jeffrey Burton (Cistercian Studies Series 178; Kalamazoo, MI: Cistercian, 1999).

Luke, Brian, 'Taming ourselves or going feral? Towards a nonpatriarchal metaethic of animal liberation', in *Animals and Women: Feminist Theoretical Explorations*, eds Carol Adams and Josephine Donovan (Durham, NC: Duke University Press, 1995), pp. 290–319.

Luxereau, Anne, « Bois le sang, nous mangerons l'ecorce », *Ethnozootechnie* 48 (1992), theme 'L'homme et la viande', pp. 35–42.

McClymond, Kathryn, *Beyond Sacred Violence: A Comparative Study of Sacrifice* (Baltimore, MD: Johns Hopkins University Press, 2008).

Macdonald, Nathan, *Not Bread Alone: The Uses of Food in the Old Testament* (Oxford University Press, 2008).

——, 'Food and drink in Tobit and other diaspora novellas', in *Studies in the Book of Tobit: A Multidisciplinary Approach*, ed. M.R.J. Bredin, Library of Second Temple Studies 55 (London: Sheffield Academic Press, 2006), pp. 165–78.

McDonald, Peter, 'The Papacy and Monastic Observance in the Later Middle Ages: The *Benedictina* in England', *Journal of Religious History* 14 (1986), pp. 117–32.

McGowan, Andrew, *Ascetic Eucharists: Food and Drink in Early Christian Ritual Meals* (Oxford: Clarendon, 1999).

McGuckin, J.A., 'Christian asceticism and the early school of Alexandria', in *Monks, Hermits and the Ascetic Tradition*, ed. W.J. Sheils (Oxford: Blackwell, 1985), pp. 25–39.

MacIntyre, Alasdair, *After Virtue: A Study in Moral Theory* (London: Duckworth, 3rd edn, 2007).

Mahmood, Saba, *Politics of Piety: The Islamic Revival and the Feminist Subject* (Princeton, NJ: Princeton University Press, 2005).

Marti, H., 'Rufinus's Translation of St. Basil's Sermon on Fasting', *Studia Patristica* 16, 2 (Berlin: Akademia, 1985), pp. 418–22.

Masri, Al-Hafiz Basheer Ahmad, *Animals Welfare in Islam* (Markfield: The Islamic Foundation, 2007).

Maurer, Donna, *Vegetarianism: Movement or Moment?* (Philadelphia, PA: Temple University Press, 2002).

Meat, Modernity, and the Rise of the Slaughterhouse, ed. Paula Young Lee (Lebanon, NH: University Press of New England, 2008).

Medieval Handbooks of Penance: A Translation of the Principal 'Libri' Poenitentiales and Selections from Related Documents, eds John T. McNeill and Helena M. Gamer (New York: Columbia University Press, 1990).

Meens, Rob, 'Eating animals in the early Middle Ages: classifying the animal world and building group identities', in *The Animal-Human Boundary: Historical Perspectives*, eds Angela N.H. Creager and William Chester Jordan (Rochester, NY: University of Rochester Press, 2002), pp. 3–28.

Ménard, J.-E., « Les Repas 'sacrés' des gnostiques », *Revue des sciences religieuses* 55 (1981), pp. 43–51.

Meredith, Anthony, 'Asceticism – Christian and Greek', *The Journal of Theological Studies* 27 (1976), pp. 313–32.

Miles, Eustace, *Better Food for Boys* (London: George Bell and Sons, 2nd edn, 1909).

Miller, Patricia Cox, 'Desert Asceticism and the Body from Nowhere', *Journal of Early Christian Studies* 2 (1994), pp. 137–53.

Miller, Robert L., 'Hogs and Hygiene', *Journal of Egyptian Archaeology* 76 (1990), pp. 135–40.

Miller, William Ian, 'Gluttony', *Representations* 60 (1997), pp. 92–112.

Moses, David, 'Soul Food and Eating Habits: What's at Steak in a Medieval Monk's Diet?', *Downside Review* 124 (2006), pp. 213–22.

Muers, Rachel, *Living for the Future: Theological Ethics for Coming Generations* (London: T&T Clark, 2008).

Myers, B.R., 'Hard to Swallow: The Gourmet's Ongoing Failure to Think in Moral Terms', *The Atlantic Monthly*, 28 August 2007.

Newall, Venetia, *An Egg at Easter* (London: Routledge & Kegan Paul, 1971).

Newmyer, Stephen T., *Animals, Rights, and Reason in Plutarch and Modern Ethics* (New York: Routledge, 2006).

Newton, John, 'manuscript CO199', University of Princetown, transcribed by Marylynn Rouse.

Nibert, David, *Animal Rights/Human Rights: Entanglements of Oppression and Liberation* (Lanham, MD: Rowman & Littlefield, 2002).

Oesterley, W.O.E., 'Why was the Hare Considered Unclean Among the Israelites?', *Churchman* 18 (1904), pp. 146–53.

Olivelle, Patrick, 'From feast to fast: food and the Indian ascetic', in *Panels of the VIIth World Sanskrit Conference, IX: Rules and Remedies in Classical Indian Law*, ed. Julia Leslie (Leiden: Brill, 1991), pp. 17–36.

Osella, Caroline and Filippo Osella, 'Food, Memory, Community: Kerala as both Indian Ocean Zone and as Agricultural Homeland', *South Asia: Journal of South Asian Studies* 31 (2008), pp. 170–98.

Paquette, Eve, « La consommation du sang, de l'interdit biblique à l'avidité vampirique », *Religiologiques* 17 (1998), theme 'Nourriture et sacré', pp. 37–52.

Patlagean, Evelyne, « Régimes et nutrition », in *Pauvreté économique et pauvreté sociale à Byzance, 4e–7e siècles* (Paris: Mouton, 1977), pp. 44–53.

Patterson, Charles, *Eternal Treblinka: Our Treatment of Animals and the Holocaust* (New York: Lantern Books, 2002).

Paul VI, Pope, *Paenitemini* (London: Catholic Truth Society, 1973 [1966]).

Petropoulou, Maria-Zoe, *Animal Sacrifice in Ancient Greek Religion, 100BC–AD200* (Oxford University Press, 2008).

Philo of Alexandria, *On the Special Laws* (Cambridge, MA: Harvard University Press, 1939).

——, *The Contemplative Life*, trans. David Winston (New York: Paulist, 1980).

Pollan, Michael, *The Omnivore's Dilemma: A Natural History of Four Meals* (New York: Penguin, 2006).

Porphyry, *On Abstinence from Killing Animals*, trans. Gillian Clark (London: Duckworth, 1999).

Powell, Horace B., *The Original has this Signature – W.K. Kellogg* (Englewood Cliffs, NJ: Prentice Hall, 1956).

Practicing Theology: Belief and Practice in Christian Life, eds Miroslav Volf and Dorothy Bass (Grand Rapids, MI: Eerdmans, 2001).

Puskar-Pasewicz, Margaret, 'Kitchen sisters and disagreeable boys: debates over meatless diets in nineteenth-century Shaker communities', in *Eating in Eden: Food and American Utopias*, eds Etta M. Madden and Martha L. Finch (Lincoln: University of Nebraska Press, 2006), pp. 109–24.

Radford, Mike, *Animal Welfare Law in Britain: Regulation and Responsibility* (Oxford University Press, 2001).

Raphael, Melissa, *Thealogy and Embodiment: The Post-Patriarchal Reconstruction of Female Sacrality* (Sheffield Academic Press, 1996).

Rashkover, Randi, *Revelation and Theopolitics: Barth, Rosenzweig and the Politics of Praise* (London: T&T Clark, 2005).

Reasoner, Mark, *The Strong and the Weak: Romans 14:1–15:13 in Context* (Cambridge University Press, 1999).

Regan, Patrick, 'The three days and the forty days', in *Between Memory and Hope: Readings on the Liturgical Year*, ed. Maxwell E. Johnson (Collegeville, MN: Liturgical, 2000), pp. 125–41.

Regnault, Lucien, *La Vie quotidienne des Pères du désert en Égypte au IVe siècle* (Paris: Hachette, 1990).

Reynolds, Philip Lyndon, *Food and the Body: Some Peculiar Questions in High Medieval Theology* (Leiden: Brill, 1999).

Rifkin, Jeremy, *Beyond Beef: The Rise and Fall of the Cattle Culture* (New York: Dutton, 1993).

Rituale Armenorum: Being the Administration of the Sacraments and the Breviary Rites of the Armenian Church together with the Greek Rites of Baptism and Epiphany, eds F.C. Conybeare and A.J. Maclean (Oxford: Clarendon, 1905).

Robinson, F.N., 'Notes on the Irish practice of fasting as a means of distraint', in *Putnam Anniversary Volume* (New York: Stechert, 1909), pp. 567–83.

Rogers, Ben, *Beef and Liberty: Roast Beef, John Bull and the English Nation* (London: Chatto & Windus, 2003).

Rouche, Michel, « La faim à l'époque carolingienne : essai sur quelques types de rations alimentaires », *Revue historique* 250 (1973), pp. 295–320.

Rousselle, Aline, *Porneia: On Desire and the Body in Antiquity* (Oxford: Blackwell, 1988).

——, « Abstinence et continence dans les monastères de Gaule méridionale à la fin de l'antiquité et au début du Moyen Âge: étude d'un régime alimentaire et de sa function », in *Hommage à André Dupont: etudes médiévales languedociennes*, ed. Guy Barruol (Montpellier: Fédération historique du Languedoc mediterranéen et du Roussillon, 1974), pp. 239–54.

Rubenson, Samuel, 'Origen in the Egyptian monastic tradition of the fourth century', in *Origeniana Septima*, eds W.A. Beinert and U. Kühneweg (Leuven University Press, 1999), pp. 319–37.

——, *The Letters of St. Anthony: Monasticism and the Making of a Saint* (Minneapolis, MN: Fortress, 1995).

Rudrum, Alan, 'Ethical Vegetarianism in Seventeenth-Century Britain: Its Roots in Sixteenth-Century Theological Debate', *The Seventeenth Century* 18 (2003), pp. 76–92.

The Rule of Saint Augustine, trans. Raymond Canning (London: Darton, Longman and Todd, 1984).

The Rule of St. Benedict, trans. Justin McCann (London: Sheed & Ward, 1989).

The Rule of the Master, trans. Luke Eberle (Kalamazoo, MI: Cistercian, 1977).

The Rule of the Templars, ed. J.M. Upton-Ward (Woodbridge: Boydell, 1992).

Sabbah, Guy, « Médecine, virginité et ascétisme chez Basile d'Ancyre, *De la véritable intégrité dans la virginité* », in *Hommages à Carl Deroux*, vol. 2: *Prose et linguistique, médecine*, ed. Pol Defosse (Brussels: Latomus, 2002), pp. 561–74.

Sack, Daniel, *Whitebread Protestants: Food and Religion in American Culture* (Basingstoke: Palgrave, 2001).

Salomonsen, Jone, 'Shielding girls at risk of AIDS by weaving Zulu and Christian ritual heritage', in *Broken Bodies and Healing Communities: Reflections on Church-based Responses to HIV/AIDS in a South African Township*, ed. Neville Richardson (Pietermaritzburg: Cluster, 2009).

Salvador, Mercedes, 'The Oyster and the Crab: A Riddle Duo (nos. 77 and 78) in the Exeter Book', *Modern Philology* 101 (2004), pp. 400–419.

Sanders, E.P., *Judaism: Practice and Belief, 63 BCE–66 CE* (London: SCM, 1992).

——, 'Jewish association with Gentiles and Galatians 2:11–14', in *The Conversation Continues: Studies in Paul and John in Honor of J. Louis Martyn*, eds Robert T. Fortna and Beverly R. Gaventa (Nashville, TN: Abingdon, 1990), pp. 170–88.

Sax, Boria, *Animals in the Third Reich: Pets, Scapegoats, and the Holocaust* (London: Continuum, 2000).

The Sayings of the Desert Fathers: The Alphabetical Collection, trans. Benedicta Ward (London: Mowbray, 1975).

Schaffer, Simon, 'Piety, physic and prodigious abstinence', in *Religio Medici: Medicine and Religion in Seventeenth-century England*, eds Ole Peter Grell and Andrew Cunningham (London: Scolar, 1997), pp. 171–203.

Scully, Terence, *The Art of Cookery in the Middle Ages* (Woodbridge: Boydell, 1997).

Seasons for Fasting, trans. Chadwick Hilton (Ann Arbor: UMI, 1985).

Semmler, Josef, „'Volatilia' zu den benediktinischen Consuetudines des 9. Jahrhunderts", in *Studien und Mitteilungen zur Geschichte des Benediktinerordens* 69 (1958), pp. 163–76.

Sharf, A., 'Animal Sacrifice in the Armenian Church', *Revue des études arméniennes* 16 (1982), pp. 417–49.

Sharon, Diane M., *Patterns of Destiny: Narrative Structures of Foundation and Doom in the Hebrew Bible* (Winona Lake, IN: Eisenbrauns, 2002).

Shaw, Teresa M., *The Burden of the Flesh: Fasting and Sexuality in Early Christianity* (Minneapolis, MN: Fortress, 1998).

——, 'Creation, Virginity and Diet in Fourth-Century Christianity: Basil of Ancyra's *On the True Purity of Virginity*', *Gender & History* 9 (1997), pp. 579–96.

Sherlock, David and William Zajac, 'A Fourteenth-Century Monastic Sign List from Bury St Edmunds Abbey', *Proceedings of the Suffolk Institute of Archaeology and History* 36 (1988), pp. 251–73.

Shostak, Debra, 'An appetite for America: Philip Roth's antipastorals', in *Eating in Eden: Food and American Utopias*, eds Etta M. Madden and Martha L. Finch (Lincoln: University of Nebraska Press, 2006), pp. 74–88.

Shuttleton, David E., 'Methodism and Dr George Cheyne's More Enlightening Principles', in *Medicine in the Enlightenment*, ed. Roy Porter (Amsterdam: Rodopi, 1995), pp. 316–35.

Sigaut, François, « La viande de cheval a-t-elle été interdite par l'Eglise ? », *Ethnozootechnie* 50 (1992), pp. 85–91.

Simoons, Frederick J., *Eat Not this Flesh: Food Avoidances from Prehistory to the Present* (Madison: University of Wisconsin Press, 1994).

Sinclair, Upton, *The Jungle* (Harmondsworth: Penguin, 1974 [1906]).

Singer, Peter, 'A vegetarian philosophy', in *Consuming Passions: Food in the Age of Anxiety*, eds Sian Griffiths and Jennifer Wallace (Manchester University Press, 1998), pp. 71–80.

Soler, Jean, 'The semiotics of food in the Bible', in *Food and Drink in History*, eds Robert Forster and Orest Ranum (Baltimore, MD: Johns Hopkins University Press, 1979), pp. 126–38.

Sorabji, Richard, *Animal Minds and Human Morals: The Origins of the Western Debate* (London: Duckworth, 1993).

Sorrell, Roger, *St. Francis of Assisi and Nature: Tradition and Innovation in Western Christian Attitudes toward the Environment* (Oxford University Press, 1988).

Soskice, Janet Martin, 'Blood and defilement', in *Feminism and Theology*, eds Janet Martin Soskice and Diana Lipton (Oxford University Press, 2001), pp. 333–43.

Soyer, Alexis, *Food, Cookery, and Dining in Ancient Times: Alexis Soyer's Pantropheon* (Mineola, NY: Dover, 2004).

Soza, Joel R., *Food and God: A Theological Approach to Eating, Diet, and Weight Control* (Eugene, OR: Wipf & Stock, 2009).

Spencer, Colin, *The Heretic's Feast: A History of Vegetarianism* (London: Fourth Estate, 1994).

Stein, S., 'The Dietary Laws in Rabbinic and Patristic Literature', *Studia Patristica* 2 (Berlin: Akademie, 1957), pp. 141–53.

Steinfeld, Henning et al., *Livestock's Long Shadow: Environmental Issues and Options* (Rome: Food and Agriculture Organization of the United Nations, 2006).

Stouff, Louis, *Ravitaillement et alimentation en Provence aux XIVe et XVe siècles* (La Haye: Mouton, 1970).

Stuart, Tristram, *The Bloodless Revolution: Radical Vegetarians and the Discovery of India* (London: HarperPress, 2006).

Taylor, Jeremy, *The Rule and Exercises of Holy Living* (London: Longman, Orme, Brown, Green and Longmans, 3rd edn, 1839).

Tearfund, 'Carbon Fast 2009: Daily Actions', at http://www.tearfund.org/webdocs/ Website/campaigning/carbonfast09/A4_Actions_final.pdf, p. 2 [accessed 12 May 2009].

Thompson, Augustine, 'The Afterlife of an Error: Hunting in the Decretalists (1190–1348)', *Studia Canonica* 33, 1 (1999), pp. 151–68.

——, 'Misreading and rereading patristic texts: the prohibition of hunting by the Decretalists', in *Proceedings of the Ninth International Congress of Medieval Canon Law, 13–18 July 1992*, eds Peter Landau and Joers Mueller (Vatican City: Biblioteca Apostolica Vaticana, 1997), pp. 135–48.

Timotheus of Gaza on Animals (Paris: Académie internationale d'histoire des sciences, 1949).

Tixeront, Joseph, « Le rite du *matal* », in *Mélanges de patrologie et d'histoire des dogmes* (Paris: Gabalda, 1921), pp. 261–78.

Tourault, Dominique, *Saint Dominique face aux cathares* (Paris: Perrin, 1999).

Trevor-Roper, Hugh, 'The fast sermons of the Long Parliament', in *Religion, the Reformation and Social Change, and Other Essays* (London: Macmillan, 1967), pp. 294–344.

The Tripartite Life of Patrick, With Other Documents Relating to that Saint, ed. Whitley Stokes, Rolls Series 89 (London: HMSO, 1887).

Trout, Dennis, 'Christianizing the Nolan Countryside: Animal Sacrifice at the Tomb of St. Felix', *Journal of Early Christian Studies* 3 (1995), pp. 281–98.

Tudge, Colin, *So Shall We Reap* (London: Allen Lane, 2003).

Tudor Economic Documents: Being Select Documents Illustrating the Economic and Social History of Tudor England, eds R.H. Tawney and Eileen Power (3 vols; London: Longmans and Green, 1951).

Turner, Bryan S., *The Body and Society: Explorations in Social Theory* (London: Sage, 2nd edn, 1996).

Twigg, Julia, 'The Vegetarian Movement in England, 1847–1981: With Particular Reference to its Ideology', University of London Ph.D. thesis, 1981.

Valantasis, Richard, 'Constructions of Power in Asceticism', *Journal of the American Academy of Religion* 63 (1995), pp. 775–821.

'Vegetarian Conference and Festival', in *The Truth Tester, Temperance Advocate, and Manx Healthian Journal*, 22 October 1847.

'Veggies Fed Up for Lent', *Church Times*, 11 April 2003.

Veilleux, Armand, 'Asceticism in Pachomian cenobitism', in *The Continuing Quest for God: Monastic Spirituality in Tradition and Transition* (Collegeville, MN: Liturgical, 1982), pp. 67–79.

Vialles, Noélie, *Animal to Edible* (Cambridge University Press, 1994).

Visitation Articles and Injunctions of the Period of the Reformation, ed. Walter Howard Frere (3 vols; London: Longmans, 1910).

Wagtendonk, Kees, *Fasting in the Koran* (Leiden: Brill, 1968).

Walker Bynum, Caroline, *Holy Feast and Holy Fast: The Religious Significance of Food to Medieval Women* (Berkeley: University of California Press, 1987).

Wallace, Charles, 'Eating and Drinking with John Wesley: The Logic of his Practice', *Bulletin of the John Rylands University Library of Manchester* 85 (2003), pp. 137–55.

Ware, Kallistos, 'The rules of fasting', in introduction to *The Lenten Triodion* (London: Faber & Faber, 1978), pp. 35–37.

Webb, Stephen, *Good Eating: The Bible, Diet and the Proper Love of Animals* (Grand Rapids, MI: Brazos, 2001).

——, *On God and Dogs: A Christian Theology of Compassion for Animals* (New York: Oxford University Press, 1998).

Webster, Robert, 'The Value of Self-denial: John Wesley's Multidimensional View of Fasting', *Toronto Journal of Theology* 19 (2003), pp. 25–40.

Wenham, Gordon, 'The Theology of Unclean Food', *Evangelical Quarterly* 53 (1981), pp. 6–15.

Wesley, John, *Primitive Physick; or An Easy and Natural Method of Curing Most Diseases* (London: Strahan, 1747).

West, Rebecca, *Black Lamb and Grey Falcon: The Record of a Journey through Yugoslavia in 1937* (2 vols; London: Macmillan, 1942).

Whorton, James C., *Crusaders for Fitness: The History of American Health Reformers* (Cambridge, MA: Princeton University Press, 1982).

Wilkins, John and Shaun Hill, *Food in the Ancient World* (London: Blackwell, 2006).

Wilson, C. Anne, 'Preserving food to preserve life: the response to glut and famine from early times to the end of the Middle Ages', in *Waste Not, Want Not: Food Preservation in Britain from Early Times to the Present Day* (Edinburgh University Press, 1991), pp. 5–31.

The Wisdom of the Desert Fathers: The 'Apophthegmata Patrum' (The Anonymous Series), trans. Benedicta Ward (Oxford: SLG, 1975).

Wissa-Wassef, Cérès, *Pratiques rituelles et alimentaires des coptes* (Cairo: Institut français d'archéologie orientale du Caire, 1971).

Woolgar, C.M., 'Take this penance now, and afterwards the fare will improve: seafood and late medieval diet', in *England's Sea Fisheries: The Commercial Sea Fisheries of England and Wales since 1300*, eds David J. Starkey, Chris Reid and Neil Ashcroft (London: Chatham, 2000), pp. 36–44.

Woolman, John, *The Journal and Major Essays of John Woolman*, ed. Phillips P. Moulton (Richmond, IN: Friends United Press, 1971).

Worden, Blair, *The Rump Parliament, 1648–53* (London: Cambridge University Press, 1974).

Young, Frances M., *Sacrifice and the Death of Christ* (London: SPCK, 1975).

Zwingli, Huldrich, 'Liberty respecting food in Lent', in *The Latin Works* (3 vols; Philadelphia, PA: Heidelberg Press, 1912–29).

Index

Related titles from Routledge

The Animal Ethics Reader
Second Edition

Edited by Susan Armstrong and Richard G. Botzler

The Animal Ethics Reader is an acclaimed anthology containing both classic and contemporary readings, making it ideal for anyone coming to the subject for the first time. It provides a thorough introduction to the central topics, controversies and ethical dilemmas surrounding the treatment of animals, covering a wide range of contemporary issues, such as animal activism, genetic engineering, and environmental ethics.

The extracts are arranged thematically under the following clear headings, including:

• Theories of Animal Ethics
• Animal Capacities: Pain, Emotion and Consciousness
• Primates and Cetaceans
• Animals for Food

This revised and updated second edition includes new readings on animal consciousness, anthropomorphism, farm animals, vegetarianism, biotechnology and cloning.

Featuring contextualizing introductions by the editors, study questions and further reading suggestions at the end of each chapter, this will be essential reading for any student taking a course in the subject.

With a foreword by Bernard E. Rollin.

Susan J. Armstrong is Professor of Philosophy and Women's Studies at Humboldt State University and has published widely on this and affiliated subjects.

Richard G. Botzler is Professor of Wildlife, also at Humboldt State University and a leading published expert in the field. Together they have edited Environmental Ethics (1998).

ISBN13: 978-0-415-77539-7 (pbk)

Available at all good bookshops
For ordering and further information please visit:
www.routledge.com

New Perspectives for Evangelical Theology
Engaging with God, Scripture, and the World

Edited by Tom Greggs

'Tom Greggs has assembled a group of younger evangelical theologians to compose essays on core theological questions as well some pressing contemporary concerns. The contributors- with courage, resolution, and some heavy artillery from within the great tradition of the Church -break down stereotypes, correct old courses, and build strong, constructive bridges. They are a future generation that is big with promise.'
– The Rev. Dr.theol. Paul F.M. Zahl, Rector,
All Saints Episcopal Church, USA

In this exciting edited collection, Tom Greggs challenges us to think afresh about evangelical theology: where it is today, and where it is headed. Bringing together an outstanding group of young theologians to engage critically and constructively with traditional evangelical theology, the book seeks to open up the field and encourage 'good practice' in its study.

New Perspectives in Evangelical Theology addresses some of the major themes within evangelical theology including election, the Holy Spirit, eschatology, and sanctification. It examines the Bible and the Church, and has chapters on worship and the sacraments. The final section investigates the interaction of evangelicalism and society, considering politics, sex and the body, and other faiths such as Judaism and Islam. Framed by a foreword from David F. Ford and a postscript from Richard B. Hays, the book is an invaluable collection of new thinking.

ISBN13: 978-0-415-47732-1 (hbk)
ISBN13: 978-0-415-47733-8 (pbk)
ISBN13: 978-0-203-86738-9 (ebk)

Doing Contextual Theology

Angie Pears

'Angie Pears offers a wide-ranging and marvelous survey of contextual theologies, particularly those that are committed to liberating thinking and acting. Her interpretations are accurate and generous. She asks the right questions and offers wise answers. Her work does what the best of syntheses do: it takes us to a new place.'
                    – Stephen Bevans, *Catholic Theological Union*, USA

Christian theology, like all forms of knowledge, thinking and practice, arises from and is influenced by the context in which it is done. In *Doing Contextual Theology*, Angie Pears demonstrates the radically contextual nature of Christian theology by focusing on five forms of liberation theology: Latin American Liberation Theologies; Black Theologies; Feminist Informed Theologies; Sexual Theologies; Body Theologies.

Pears analyses how each of these asserts a clear and persistent link to the Christian tradition through The Bible and Christology and discusses the implications of contextual and local theologies for understanding Christianity as a religion. Moreover, she considers whether fears are justified that a radically contextual reading of Christian theologies leads to a relativist understanding of the religion, or whether these theologies share some form of common identity both despite and because of their contextual nature.

Doing Contextual Theology offers students a clear and up-to-date survey of the field of contemporary liberation theology and provides them with a sound understanding of how contextual theology works in practice.

ISBN13: 978-0-415-41704-4 (hbk)
ISBN13: 978-0-415-41705-1 (pbk)
ISBN13: 978-0-203-87782-1 (ebk)

Christian Ethics: The End of the Law
David S. Cunningham

'David Cunningham's enjoyable and highly readable textbook is an excellent introduction to contemporary Christian ethics and is ideally suited for those who have little prior knowledge of Christian belief. His use of literature, film, and music is notably refreshing, as is the imaginative way he draws on the virtues to illuminate practical judgements in different parts of everyday life. This book will deservedly find its way onto the reading lists of many introductory courses on Christian ethics.'
– Robert Song, University of Durham, UK

Christian Ethics provides a biblical, historical, philosophical and theological guide to the field of Christian ethics. Prominent theologian David S. Cunningham explores the tradition of 'virtue ethics' in this creative and lively text, which includes literary and musical references as well as key contemporary theological texts and figures.

   Three parts examine:

• the nature of human action and the people of God as the 'interpretative community' within which ethical discourse arises
• the development of a 'virtue ethics' approach, and places this in its Christian context
• significant issues in contemporary Christian ethics, including the ethics of business and economics, politics, the environment, medicine and sex.

This is the essential text for students of all ethics courses in theology, religious studies and philosophy

ISBN13: 978-0-415-37599-3 (hbk)
ISBN13: 978-0-415-37600-6 (pbk)
ISBN13: 978-0-203-92975-9 (ebk)